The Most Dangerous
Course of Action

Disclaimer: The views presented are those of the author and do not necessarily represent the views of the Department of Defense or its components.

ISBN: 1-4818-5829-7
ISBN-13: 1481858297
Library of Congress Control Number: 2013903413
CreateSpace Independent Publishing Platform,
North Charleston, SC

The Most Dangerous Course of Action

The Next Decade in Transnational Terror and Domestic Extremism

David C. Cox
Introduction by: SMA (R) Julius W. Gates

Dedication

Many individuals and supporting groups deserve heartfelt acknowledgement as they indirectly influenced the decision to produce this book. I would like to thank my beautiful wife and loving daughter, Melissa and Aubrey, for their love and devotion over the years. To my parents, Richard and Kathy for raising me with a strong sense of values and ethical commitment to duty. To Mike who instilled the importance of preparing tomorrow's Army… today. To SMA(R) Julius W. Gates for his support and many years of service to our Country. This book is born of the idea that the responsibility for defense of the Homeland rests with all of us. Every citizen, from the hardworking laborer and housewife to the Serviceman and law enforcement professional have a duty to safeguard our way of life in a manner that does not infringe upon the basic rights guaranteed to us all in the Constitution of the United States.

CONTENTS

Introduction

It is a privilege to write a few words in support of the author and his work on a topic that resonates for all Americans, both at home and abroad. The author, First Sergeant David C. Cox, is a true professional having served in various positions of responsibility for over 14 years in the United States Army. A combat hardened veteran of both Iraq and Afghanistan, he is a leader who places his unit mission and the welfare of his Soldiers in front of his personal needs. He has lived his life by the seven tenets of Army Values (Loyalty, Duty, Respect, Selfless Service, Honor, Integrity, and Personal Courage) in honorable service to our Nation. His keen insights into modern conflicts provide a playbook that empowers every citizen to take actions that may prevent terrorist attacks upon our Homeland. First Sergeant Cox's theory that everyone has an undeniable right to stand up and protect our Constitutional entitlements resonates with great American patriots and supports our founding fathers' vision of our Nation. The lessons and awareness identified need to be shared with our younger generations as they mature into acceptance of their responsibilities as citizens of our Nation.

Since 9-11 and the terrorist attack on our Homeland, hundreds of thousands of our Americans, both male and female have raised their right hand, taken an oath to defend our Homeland and our Constitution against all enemies both foreign and domestic. Many have made the ultimate sacrifice in defense of our country and our way of life. But they have prevailed!

First Sergeant Cox's tome focuses on "now" being the time for us to unite and return to those basic tenets of values that Soldiers are taught to live by, and incorporate them into our collective lives, so that each of us may do his or her utmost to prevent homegrown and foreign terrorist attacks upon our sovereignty and homeland. Relearning that definition of dignity and respect and applying that to our daily way of life, while incorporating "Army Values" as a mantra in our lives can facilitate changes that are so necessary. We must, we can and we will, as a Nation continue to band together to prevent future terrorist attacks and First Sergeant Cox's book provides us with ways to get there.

Julius W. Gates
Sergeant Major of the Army
U.S. Army Retired

1
A Look At The Future Of Terrorism

"Necessity is the mother of invention."
-Plato

No one understands this axiom better than the terrorist or insurgent. He knows that he is outnumbered and outgunned and he uses this to his advantage. He sees angles that the common man does not see, opportunities to be exploited, strengths in his own weakness. In his mind he represents the oppressed, that he will one day be vindicated and that gives him the endurance to carry on. The fear that is his constant companion due to his pursuit has kept him sharp while he remains just one short step ahead of those that hunt him relentlessly. He uses the tools that are at his disposal and is equally comfortable in the use of conventional instruments as well as creatively employing his own wisdom to devise asymmetric threats that the average among us does not see. The never-ending game of cat and mouse has made him artful, scheming and deceptive.

Those individuals that have already answered the call to battle against the West and survived have now gained valuable combat experience. As the war in Afghanistan draws to a close, the jihadist veterans will return to their homeland and begin to teach the next generation the hard fought lessons learned just as they did after Iraq. Retribution in the wake of defeat will be sought against the lands of the West and attempts will be made to recapture a modicum of their former glory. But terrorism is not limited to foreign threats. There are enemies at home as well. Domestic-based threats, particularly those involving "home-grown" terrorists are worrisome due to decreased likelihood for detection. Individuals that already hold American citizenship are shielded by Constitutionally protected rights and have already accomplished the most difficult task of many terrorist groups attempting to strike on American soil- getting into the country undetected.

A combination of bloodshed and economic pain would be felt, as terrorism will strike at our most vulnerable innocents and national infrastructure. Soft targets, those without an existing security apparatus, will be chosen for their perceived sanctity and remoteness from existing government affiliations. The determination by these groups to exact pressure on legitimate nations through the use of large-scale, indiscriminate violence has already begun to have an effect on our law enforcement apparatus steering them away from their traditional investigative role and toward preventative involvement.

The world as we know it is changing at a pace greater than it has since the Industrial Revolution. Technological developments will change the nature of terrorism as well, creating new vulnerabilities to be exploited along with every added comfort. The Internet has become an important tool for recruitment, encouragement, education, and misinformation. The most charismatic of extremist organizations have exploited this tool and are as capable as law enforcement in its manipulation. Like the governments they seek to overthrow, terrorist organizations and disenfranchised individuals will seek to develop new technologies for their own purposes while staying a step ahead of their pursuers. Some will cling to the old ways for their simplistic and effective shock value. Guns and explosives have withstood the test of time and have become known as the great equalizer among men. Others will seek the holy grail of terrorism, the weapon of mass destruction that puts them on equal footing with the most powerful nations of the world. Finally, a few will look to the future and enlist our own technological Achilles' heel against us for their own political, economic, and ideological purposes.

Before 9/11 terrorism was viewed as becoming obsolete. The world demonstrated their impatience with nation-state sponsored terrorism and despot regimes as evidenced following Iraq's invasion of Kuwait. Iran, long suspected for its indirect endorsement of terrorism has been economically isolated for decades by way of international sanctions and trade embargoes. The Lockerbie bombing subjected Libya to crippling economic sanctions far outweighing more than any political benefit that could have been gained. Why then, has terrorism persisted in the face of international condemnation and public rejection? The answer is a matter of perception based upon social class, regional upbringing and religious conservatism. It is a viewpoint and a learned behavior. The tactics of terrorism will exist as long as they are successful in influencing the political behaviors of nation-states. Globalization and urbanization means that our world is getting a bit smaller and our enemies a bit closer.

The following chapters will identify and distinguish the terrorists' most likely course of action from his most dangerous. These are doctrinal terms that allow military planners to anticipate and prepare for the activities of an enemy. The hope is that attention is drawn to these concerns and that the law enforcement and disaster management teams that will one day respond to these crises are better prepared. Parallel planning and equal contemplation must accompany these trains of thought while we weigh the outcomes of each against the consequences of our own inaction. This forecasting is based upon historical case studies, known technological capabilities, and the creative ingenuity that is present within us all, including the terrorist. But, before that it is important to look back and consider a key moment in our history that has come to characterize the present approach to combating terrorism.

An argument exists that in the period between the fall of the Berlin Wall and 9/11 the United States experienced a time of foreign policy aimlessness driven by a euphoric high after winning the Cold War. Certain transgressions went unanswered and a blind eye was turned toward the actions of the comparatively minor hostile regimes as the West enjoyed this period of relative tranquility. Meanwhile, enemies that had been deemed impotent continued to plot... and sharpen their swords. 9/11 was a stark reminder of realities of the world and served to remove some of the comfortable naïveté that had been allowed to creep in during a decade of peace.

It was the fourth year of the war in Afghanistan and the second year of the war in Iraq when, addressing the graduating class of the United States Military Academy at West Point, President George W. Bush delivered a rousing speech to the newly commissioned officers as they prepared for deployment to military units engaged in the war on terror. The President channeled former President Harry S. Truman by saying that America was at war with an enemy "animated by a new fanatic faith".[1] He equivocated the past nation-state enemies to the current small-cell terrorist groups seeking political and ideological gain albeit through much more extreme acts of mass murder designed to degrade the legitimacy and perceived strength of lawful government. He acknowledged the differences of the two eras in that the U.S. and the Soviet Union maintained an uneasy peace through the concept of "mutually assured destruction" and the resulting collateral damage if the world's two superpowers went to war. He recognized that in the war on terror the United States was once again in a dead heat with her opposition. Although terrorist organizations had the desire, they lacked the capability to initiate an attack on such a catastrophic scale as the nuclear holocaust fears of the Cold War and that the U.S., despite all of its technological advantages was having a difficult time decisively defeating an enemy without a state sponsor. By evoking President Truman's stance toward the Communist Party in China and the U.S.S.R. following World War II, President Bush likened the impasse faced by the United States during the Cold War to the modern terrorist threat. In a sense, we were stalemated.

Bruce Hoffman, of the RAND Corporation was quoted by Russ Howard in the article "Homeland Security and the New Terrorism" and claimed that when compared to the risks faced today, intelligence agencies yearn for the days of predictable and measured use of force to accomplish an objective by means of conventional warfare."[2] As recently as 2010, rings of Russian spies were exposed as living in the United States after a prolonged intelligence sting operation. This revelation was considered a respite from the horrors of the global war on terrorism in the eyes of the media and the public while many of the repatriated agents were offered jobs in the Russian government, big business, and enjoyed worldwide celebrity status in the period immediately following their deportation. The collective response from the American public was almost a sigh of relief that the latest threat to the homeland was not bearded militant Islamists but attractive Russian spies quietly gathering data under the streetlights of New York City. The incident was resolved quickly, neatly, and without any real hazards to be overcome by the public. The appeal of the Cold War was that, in comparison to today's risks, the threat was real, yet somehow intangible. There were no televised images of national landmarks crumbling in flames or Sarin gas attacks in subway tunnels. For the most part, airline hijackings and political rebellion rarely culminated in the loss of life on a scale proportionate to their capability for destruction. The men that held "the button" during that period could be reasoned with as their respective countries had far too much to lose in an all-out conflict.

The international allies and intelligence partnerships cultivated during the Cold War are still relevant during the current conflict. Countries, such as the members of the North Atlantic Treaty Organization, that have proven themselves staunch allies throughout that era and are still critical to the United States due to their geographical locations and shared interest in world stability. Their continued cooperation is essential as is the intelligence gained from those countries concerning the planning, financing and logistics of potential threats to the U.S. Additionally, America must continue to develop new allies both overseas and domestically. The Arab, African and Asian regions as well as members of those cultural communities already in the United States must now become full partners in the war on terror. America's greatest strength is it's ethnic and religious diversity and the ability to learn from and adapt to an ever-changing state of affairs.

The race for military supremacy has been going on since the first sharpened spear that was able to attain further reach and accuracy than the handheld club, to the use of folded steel over copper in swords and now, advanced weaponry that is able to nullify the technological achievements of the last hundred years. It could be argued that America possesses the most sophisticated and effective fighting force that the world has ever seen. But, a scenario where one side is technologically superior to the capabilities of the other does not necessarily guarantee an immediate victory; consider the recent conflicts in Afghanistan, and Libya, or further back- Vietnam. In Afghanistan the Taliban, outnumbered and without the significant resources of NATO have resorted to archaic tactics such as couriers to prevent signal intercept of messages. The tactics that they are currently using are so primitive when compared to the technology of the Coalition Forces yet still, there is a strategic gap that the Allies are having a difficult time closing.

The idea that a combatant with inferior technology is more willing to sacrifice himself in the face of overwhelming superiority has some merit but is not entirely true by itself. One tactic of the insurgency has been the use of suicide bombings to strike targets that would be extremely difficult to destroy by conventional means. The use of suicide bombers is far more dramatic and likely to gain the media attention that it is intended to produce, more than the conventional attacks that are so common around the world. Repeated news broadcasts of the same suicide attack are misleading and create the impression that they are much more common and prevalent than what they really are. In reality an extremely small number of these events occur when compared with the number of conventional engagements. A technologically inferior combatant is simply more likely to resort to the use of an insurgency with extremist methods in the face of an overwhelmingly advanced military

By comparison, it is easy to strategize a conflict involving technologically equivalent nations as they attempt to outmaneuver the other in a conflict involving conventional strategy on air, land, and sea. It is far more difficult to manage the consequences of such an engagement that devolves into an insurgency or employs the asymmetrical tactics of the Internet. The idea of mutual deterrence is a throwback to the Cold War between the U.S., USSR and their respective allies as they played a decades-long chess game that slowly siphoned the resources of both economies until one eventually collapsed. From a sociological perspective, the functionalist would argue that conflicts such as the Cold War and Afghanistan are good for a nation, in that, they allow for a challenge and opportunity to reassess and refine it's military capabilities. Such challenges are necessary and force the established structure to evolve.

The goal of President Reagan's "Star Wars" program was intended as the first step toward ridding the world of nuclear weapons. By creating a defensive measure capable of destroying intercontinental ballistic nuclear missiles it would render these weapons obsolete over a period of time. The many technologies that were necessary to create a functional defensive network in effect set off another 'space race' intended for the military domination of the immediate space around the globe. Henslin refers to the emerging technologies such as the various Future Combat Systems projects in development as examples of President Reagan's goals realized.[3] However, there will never come a point when any country or terrorist group announces that they have achieved the pinnacle of technological advancement. This holds true for the conventional strategy employed by most nation states and unconventional tactics employed by most insurgencies. All sides will continue to compete for military superiority in a never-ending arms race. This also holds true for terrorism, as each group will attempt to surpass the acts of those who came before them with devastating consequences. We cannot go back to the stalemate that was the Cold War or our own naiveté in the days before September 11th. There will be no negotiated surrender or reduction in arms by either side. We are now in the era of ultra-terrorism, facing the prospect of the radicalized use of violence and we cannot go back.

Emerging technologies that were considered the stuff of science fiction just a few short years ago are a reality today and will mold the landscape of future terrorism. Three-dimensional printing technologies are now capable of molding individual weapon components that can be assembled and fired in minutes. This increasingly popular advanced printing system utilizes plastics and other substances to construct 3-D objects with moving sections. A project operating out of the University of Texas has already printed, assembled, and test fired a semiautomatic replica of an AR-15 rifle, an assault weapon similar to the one used in the Connecticut school massacre, all with components imaged and produced on a 3-D printer.[4] This has enormous implications as weapons, or other devices, can be constructed by messages sent over existing telecommunications networks. Worse yet, the printers primarily use plastics in the molding process making anything produced undetectable by X-ray or metallic scanners. Physical barriers can now be bypassed as long as a signal can be received by the machine, giving anyone the capability to produce such components using blueprints available on the Internet.

Drone technology, once the sole domain of the U.S. government, is now the source of a new technological escalation among nation-states and non-state actors. The high-end aircraft used by developed countries employ stealth technology, high-resolution camera equipment, GPS guided missiles, and are able to remain airborne for extended periods. Battlefield losses, leaked schematics, as well as the second and third-tier proliferation of these technologies have now placed them in the hands of at least 70 countries and terror groups. Libyan opposition forces were known to have purchased a sophisticated surveillance drone from a Canadian aerotech company in their bid to overthrow Moammar Gadhafi. Some of the wealthier cartels in Mexico and South America have displayed interest in the purchase of unmanned aircraft in an effort to stay ahead of drug enforcement agencies. It is the next logical progression to see a surveillance UAV outfitted with weapons or an explosive device-making it a guided missile in the hands of low-end bidders. This technology is already within the reach of terror and criminal organizations and advanced versions will continue to be sought by these groups.

So-called "third world" countries known for unstable governance, poor economies, and porous borders will continue to produce the majority of foot soldiers for terror collectives. These organizations will seek to usurp fledgling governments as well as provide shelter to transnational terrorists. States that currently sponsor terror groups will distance themselves from those policies as world bodies turn against them as the support of these organizations becomes increasingly costly in economic and political capital. Disavowed groups will attempt to seek the support of weaker states in the Horn of Africa, the Middle East and Southwest Asia.

Due to the United States expected military dominance throughout the globe, hostile nation-states will continue to seek out asymmetric capabilities to be used against conventional U.S. military forces, overseas interests, and the homeland. State and non-state actors will employ tactics designed to influence the political spectrum and enduring will of the American public rather than face a conventional military force. Perceived American weakness will be exploited by applying political and paramilitary strategies in an effort to curb conventional American dominance both abroad and on U.S. soil.

The national infrastructure capabilities of the United States will be targeted using increasingly sophisticated techniques designed to produce utility gridlock, reduce public confidence, and achieve greater casualties than previous attacks. Civilians will suffer by way disruptions in transportation, communications, financial hubs, and logistical centers in the hopes that they will supply the necessary political pressure to influence national policy. The infrastructure has already demonstrated that it is vulnerable to naturally occurring events during disastrous storms and energy drain due to increased demand. The trend will continue to encourage attacks on the interconnected computer networks that are vulnerable to interruption through cyber terrorism as a low-cost, high profile, and high-payoff alternative to attacks with conventional munitions or attempts at acquiring weapons of mass destruction.

It may be that the threats posed by the terrorist actors of today will recede over time to be replaced by new dangers. A wider range of terrorist organizations, offshoots of existing groups, domestic terrorism, lone-wolves, and criminal elements will all expand their operations and present new challenges for the Department of Homeland Security in the years to come. These threats may manifest themselves in a multitude of forms ranging from the most sophisticated, and catastrophic use of weapons of mass destruction to the comparatively low-tech use of small arms, improvised explosive devices or the virtual worlds of cyber terrorism. As technology and extremist related information is proliferated we are likely to see an increase in the terrorist modification of successful tactics. Mass shootings, improvised explosive devices, cyber-terrorism, drone technology and the race to acquire a weapon of mass destruction will mark the timeline of terrorism in the years to come.

2
The Evolving Doctrine Of Terror

Consider the recent media reports of extreme violence occurring throughout the world. A gunman opens fire on a crowded movie theater in Colorado (technically a mass murder), an explosive is detonated targeting a busload of Israeli tourists, a team directs a running gunfight that goes on for days through the hotels and streets of Mumbai. What do they have in common? They were all directed at civilians in a recreational environment and they were all highly successful from the perspective of the perpetrators. If anything, the terrorist recognizes a winning strategy and only modifies technique when absolutely necessary. These attacks against "soft targets" will become the norm in the circles of political influence dominated through terrorism. Groups will attempt to capitalize on the successes of their predecessors by upstaging previous attacks in body count and destruction. The lone wolf, the grassroots radical, and the transnational terrorist organizations are limited in their ability to effectively strike against "hard targets" as they have become reinforced significantly over the last three decades.

At the dawn of the modern age of terrorism, say the last thirty years or so, most targets were considered "soft" from the terrorist viewpoint. Many of us remember images of airline hijackers waving guns from cockpit windows in the '80s or the Munich massacre at the 1972 Olympic Games. Embassies were stormed with overwhelming force and overtook staffers possessed of a relaxed security posture and the false sense of security provided by one's nationality. Even the leftist terrorist organization, the Weather Underground, was able to successfully carry out bombings in the heart of our nation's capitol, right under the noses of the Secret Service and Capitol Police. As the success of these attacks were increasingly publicized and mimicked by other organizations, improvements to security were proposed and then adopted at many locations. However, despite all our wealth and influence, our resources are finite. Security cannot be impenetrable at all areas. So then a threat matrix must be drawn up and resources diverted to areas assessed as being the most likely target. Those that are under a greater likelihood of threat receive more resources than those that are not. For the most part, this is a prudent and successful strategy from the point of view of the state. However, the terrorist shifts his tactics to targets that are more suitable in an effort to identify weakness. These are known as the "soft targets" and include anything that one would not expect such an attack to occur, the terrorist is limited by only his own imagination in this respect. In the international realm, this may involve targeting foreign embassies in Western-backed emerging democracies; in Western nations this will involve targeting the citizens of these nations. This shifting tactic has proven successful in the Benghazi consulate attack in Libya and reinforced by international calls to kidnap Westerners made by Ayman Al-Zawahiri, both in late 2012.

This alteration of tactics has been used against airline security as protocols have changed in light of the 9/11 attacks. Increasingly sophisticated methods involving nearly undetectable liquid components and explosives concealed within mail in cargo holds have been adopted in response to improved security measures at most international airports. As detection technology has advanced enabling officials to search for nonmetallic items, terrorists have now considered other means to circumvent security. One startling tactic thought to be in consideration has been the use of surgery to implant explosives within the bodies of animals and people traveling aboard flights. It is then a natural progression that as the flight itself becomes too difficult a target passengers will be attacked before the plane ever arrives at the terminal. In fact, any place that large numbers of people congregate becomes a target.

For years after 9/11 there were fears of mass shootings in malls during holiday Christmas shopping, targeting not only the people but also the open celebration of religion. Think back to the Norway massacre committed by Anders Breivik in 2011 against a youth camp or the Fort Hood shootings committed by U.S. Army Major Nidal Hassan. Although, it could easily be argued that both of these acts were committed by deranged individuals and are likely to remain anomalies in the annals of criminal lore, the fact that they were carried out to completion draws attention to itself. This is exactly the sort of act that is likely to be repeated where so many other attempts at terrorism have failed. Extremist groups have sought to demonstrate their proficiency by attempting to repeat the spectacular, and media drawing, attacks of 9/11 but many have become known more for their failures than successes. As such, transnational terror groups have begun to set their sights on more achievable goals. The targeting of vacation locales by transnational terrorists, likely to be attended by wealthy Westerners overseas has been identified as a noticeable trend in jihadist circles. This is partially due to the individuals who frequent these areas often include the idle wealthy, business elite, media representatives, and government officials-all high profile.

Unfortunately, if the dedication toward a cause is great enough and there is no concern about capture, these sorts of attacks against soft targets are relatively easy to carry out. In fact, anyone with the predisposition toward this sort of cold, calculated violence can carry out mass murder under the auspices of a cause using easily accessible weapons. Simply put, it is impossible for the government to protect everything or shore up every possible contingency. Indeed, when you distribute your limited security resources to protect every potential target, you are ultimately unable to effectively protect any of them. Inevitably, some terrorist attacks will succeed and their effectiveness will be gauged in the media and public opinion. The government and public response to such events will determine whether the attacks were successful and likely to be repeated. The acknowledgement that it is impossible to prevent every act of terrorism will lead to a more effective dialogue geared toward identifying threats and allocating those resources

While it is unfortunate that attacks against soft targets will continue, society isn't powerless to deter them. Terrorism can be understood and steps taken to prevent such attacks while mitigating their effects. In some ways patterns begin to form, borne from the successful employment of terror tactics. These patterns tend to come in waves; suicide bombings and insider threats have been two popular methods in recent years. The late 60's, 70's, and 80's saw the heavy use of airline hijackings as a political weapon. Even if the original perpetrators are killed or captured, successful methodology lives on and is evolved by new generations. In a contemporary age of extremist terror the trend seems to indicate a propensity toward sensational violence that pushes the boundaries of what has come before. There appears to be few discriminatory factors separating what might be considered a legitimate target from innocents as all are increasingly accepted as collateral damage.

The methodology employed by terror groups appears to be derived from the group itself, at least initially. Those that have the technical skills and resources employ tactics that are likely to be successful given those constraints leading to regional trends. Terror groups operating in Pakistan's lawless northwestern tribal areas employ similar tactics as terrorists operating in eastern Afghanistan just across the border. Emerging groups operating in Somalia and the Horn of Africa improvise and improve upon tactics that have shown promise in their respective region. Militants will be successful operating in environments where they have access to weapons, recruits, a marginally supportive populace and targets- never straying far from their prey. Whereas an entirely different skill set is required for the aspiring terrorist operating in the Western culture, a comparatively more hostile environment.

Humans are creatures of habit and, despite our desire to believe otherwise, very few of us display any real creativity or ingenuity. Those that are able to bring innovative ideas to fruition tend to rise to the top of their field and are often imitated by others. This applies to the terrorist as well as the layperson. As long as a tactic is successful it will continue to be employed in much the same manner as it has before creating opportunities for the counterterrorist to exploit this natural human weakness. The focus on the methodology used in attacks will allow observers to identify current trends as well as anticipate future evolutions of a tactic.

As terrorists evolve their doctrine, so too does the counterterrorism practitioner. The evolvement of Western counterterrorism doctrine can be measured in the billions of dollars spent on improvements to security, intelligence improvements and the complete overhaul of the national security apparatus. This effort has resulted in the noticeable decline in the number of successful terror attacks in the West and the increase number of attacks focused on Western interests based in the region from which the attackers originate. International travel has become markedly more difficult for the transnational terrorist due to improved international and interagency coordination. Aspiring terrorists with Western citizenship and passport credentials are now more highly prized than their better-trained counterparts hailing from 'red flagged' countries such as Yemen or Pakistan. The failure to successfully carry out attacks in the United States and Europe has raised calls from inside jihadist circles to focus on straightforward operations within their own region where resources and operatives are already in place. This begs a tradeoff in that operatives are less susceptible to detection at an international border increasing the opportunity for success while resulting in only a marginal victory against a less desirable target.

One such evolvement of the counterterrorism strategy has been the blending of intelligence products and communication among domestic law enforcement agencies regarding data exploited during observation and analyzed after collection. This synthesis requires a closer union between these law enforcement and intelligence assets similar to the concept of 'fusion centers' already seeing some early success by the Department of Homeland Security. While there have been many efforts made to improve communications between the intelligence and law enforcement efforts of the United States, several key agencies were not an integrated part of this process until the introduction of the fusion centers. If you could imagine an agency representative from each of the intelligence gathering hubs working alongside law enforcement, criminal analysts, and military personnel all under the same roof toward a common objective then you have imagined the goal of the fusion center. This cooperation and sharing of information, this fusion, is the key to effective data analysis that ultimately produces actionable intelligence.

Fusion centers serve as an information hub and conduit between federal, state, and local agencies that facilitate collection, analysis, and sharing of threat-related intelligence among partnered organizations.[5] These agencies are operated at the local level but have the unique advantage of access to information-sharing capabilities between state and federal support services. This horizontal and vertical communication greatly increases the quality, quantity, and speed with which information is processed and disseminated to field units regardless of their parent organization. One example of this collaborative process occurred immediately following the attempted Times Square bombing in 2010 by Faisal Shahzad, another plot involving an individual working nearly alone. Analysts at an integrated fusion center in Florida discovered that Shahzad had an association with two individuals in their state and passed this information on to the FBI's Joint Terrorism Task Force to further the investigation.[6]

The next evolution in terror trends is coming in response to counter-terrorism improvements by the West. While the champion trophy of terror attacks would involve the employment of a weapon of mass destruction against an American metropolis most groups would settle for a reasonable success against a Western interest in any accessible country. The attack against the American embassy in Libya, which coincided with a planned demonstration, is an act likely to be emulated at embassies in the Middle East and Africa. The large amounts of chemical weapons that are being clung to by an unstable Syrian regime are a highly sought after prize that could be employed against nearby Israel or NATO forces conducting observation or humanitarian operations. There is an added uncertainty that comes in to play when considering the possibility of these weapon systems falling into the hands of an extremist militant organization during a political coup or fledgling successors to a fallen political party seeking to prove their emerging authority and military might in the region. The encouragement of lone wolf operatives to mirror the successes of the active shooter scenarios in the United States and Norway along with indications of Al Qaeda experimentation with the surgical implantation of explosives inside humans and animals to avoid detection are all likely trajectories in the next wave of terror technique.

3
Active Shooters And Lone Wolves

So many terror groups seek to emulate the "success" of 9/11 in an effort to gain worldwide recognition for their particular cause, respect from other groups, and the support of like-minded individuals. This support comes in many forms, usually economic or resource-based, and is critical to the long-term success of these ideologies. However, Western governments have worked diligently to shore up the security loopholes that were exploited by Al Qaeda in the months leading up to that disaster. The establishment of the Department of Homeland Security in the United States and the cooperation of many international intelligence services have begun to have an effect on the freedom of movement that these groups once enjoyed. International commerce is more carefully monitored and assets that were once shared between these groups, shell organizations, and supporting governments have been isolated, frozen, or even awarded to the relatives of victims in landmark lawsuits. Much of this activity has begun to have an effect on international terrorism driving them back to the most basic modus operandi of their trade- terror by any available means.

Resourcefulness and creativity have been the hallmark of most successful terrorists since the first use of fear as an influencing factor in human behavior. In an open society such as Western culture particularly the United States, with their protected freedoms, the terrorist simply has more room to maneuver than in a 'closed' society. The many failures of terror outfits attempting to gather and construct the necessary components for explosive devices has merely resulted in a number of arrests leading to intelligence, which leads to further arrests. There almost seems to a preoccupation or dogged fascination with the employment of spectacular, technically complex attacks that have been the downfall of many a would-be domestic terrorist. Consider the 'active shooter', these individuals are typically unknown until after the fact. From the moment that Charles Whitman opened fire from the University of Texas clock tower in 1966, killing 16 and wounding 31 to Adam Lanza who killed 20 schoolchildren and six adults in Connecticut in 2012 these events have been called unspeakable for the fact that they target the innocent. Names such as William Spengler, responsible for the murder of two firefighters in New York, or James Holmes, best known for the murder and attempted murder of almost 100 people at a Colorado movie showing in 2012 come to mind. Mall and school shootings have come to be regarded as appalling events for which there are no defense. Regardless of the fact that they do not fit the federal definition of terrorism, events such as these have become more prominent in our society and with each successful employment of these tactics they are more likely to be used again- possibly as a tactic of a politically motivated terrorist.

Active shooters are individuals who are actively engaged in the killing or attempt to kill people in a confined or populated area. Firearms are the primary weapons of choice and there is usually no pattern or method of victim selection. These scenarios are unpredictable and tend to evolve rather quickly. Over half of these scenarios run their course in under 12 minutes, which corresponds to the national average police response time. Locations are usually identified as soft targets meaning that they have minimal or no security presence and there are few preventative measures to deter such an attack. Still, because they have primarily been committed by the mentally unstable, most of these scenarios result in the shooters death. According to statistics gathered by the New York Police Department, 46% of these incidents are ended by the application of police force, 40% end in the shooters suicide, 14% of the time the shooter will surrender, and in less than 1% of cases does the attacker flee.[7]

The significance of terror as a weapon is multiplied in the form of copy-cat activities as other like-minded individuals are emboldened by powerful successes broadcast through the media. These events are nearly impossible to predict from the perspective of the security manager or victim. Almost all of these individuals display an extreme commitment to their task and tend to share a strong identity and kinship with extremist ideology. Extremist religion and right-wing dogma continue to be the most malleable, open to interpretation, and suitable for the lone wolf terrorist. Many have experience with social isolation, exclusion, and have displayed suicidal tendencies. The criminal profile of the typical active shooter is a white male, socially isolated, possible behavioral health issues and without a criminal record. This individual's life has been marked by failure, or perceived social inadequacies, and takes it upon himself to exact retribution and power over others through the act of mass murder. Killers who commit mass murder tend to target those who they believe would torment them or are somewhat responsible for their distress. There are hundreds of thousands who fit this profile and do not act on homicidal impulses. It could be said that many display the symptoms but do not actually contract the disease.

Detection and interception of these individuals is of particular concern to government agencies at all levels, from local to federal, as they are capable of significant damage that is out of proportion to their available resources. Questions of how to prevent such attacks and how to identify these individuals before they implement their plan continue to trouble these organizations. While active shooters act primarily because of behavioral or psychological issues, lone wolves act out of an extreme commitment to cause. The concern now becomes, 'how long before lone wolves apply the tactics of the active shooter?' Lone wolves have turned what should, by most accounts, be their greatest weakness into their greatest strength. They are isolated from others and that deficit of human interaction lessens the opportunities for them to be discovered. This avoidance of contact makes their intentions incredibly difficult to discern and gives them a singular, all-important advantage over conventional terrorist organizations. Militants who operate in minimally manned cells have an almost 100 percent increase in the likelihood of detection when compared to the lone wolf. Without others to communicate their intentions, message interception becomes impossible for law enforcement. Anders Breivik was keenly aware of this weakness in other terrorist and criminal groups as he wrote in his manifesto, *European Declaration of Independence*, "Do absolutely everything by yourself".[8]

The fluid and openly interpretive nature of religion and extremist ideology makes it difficult to positively identify these individuals within their already segregated political, religious or activist circles. Law enforcement might be able to gain insight into the motivations of these individual actors by examining the motivations of the alienated or disenfranchised movements with which they typically identify. The motivations for their behavior are so varied in that the actors themselves span the full spectrum in defiance of categorization from religious extremity to social placement to behavioral patterns. Consistency is difficult to discern given all of the other 'white noise' obscuring identifiable patterns or methods employed by these individuals.

For the few who do reach out and attempt to make their extremist views known in an effort to have their them reaffirmed, if only in their own mind, it is difficult for them to be confirmed as terrorists as opposed to radicals. It is important to note that most terrorists espouse an extremist ideology but the reverse cannot be said of most extremists. Those who make bold, radical claims will not always act upon them and in a society, such as the United States where the freedom of speech is a constitutionally protected right; law enforcement is limited in their ability to investigate these elements unless violence is identified as a potential and likely act.

Government and law enforcement bureaucracies are especially futile in the face of the ambiguous nature of the lone wolf threat. With so little initial information to develop a criminal or terror profile, and without the mechanisms of communication or leadership hierarchy to be detected, the possibility of detection or preemption by law enforcement dwindles. This places local and federal law enforcement in a precarious and unenviable position of being held responsible for perceived intelligence and structural failures as politicos, the media, and citizens alike begin to lay blame in an effort to shore up these 'failures'. The reality is that there is no such thing as complete security. There is no form of law enforcement or intelligence that could possibly identify every hopeful terrorist. The challenge of detection becomes even more exacerbated in a society where the value of civil liberties and the protections afforded by the law are held in such high esteem.

Individuals who have previously displayed no proclivity toward breaking the law or otherwise made themselves known to the law enforcement or intelligence radar are especially challenging in that there is no initial thread to chase or legal justification for further surveillance. Without a traceable link between a suspect and a known criminal or terrorist organization these suspects are often prioritized on a much lower category receiving far less investigative attention. This is not to say that the undertaking set before intelligence and law enforcement is ineffectual and should be abandoned. Absolute protection is impossible so the task becomes one of synchronizing parallel resources focused toward prevention while acknowledging that some of these acts will still occur and their effects will require mitigation.

It would appear that the benefits of lone wolf terrorism have not gone unnoticed in the circles of right wing and religious extremism. In fact, the idea of individuals acting largely unilaterally as a means of maintaining operational secrecy has been around for some time. The concept of 'leaderless resistance' was popularized by the white supremacist Louis Beam in the early 1980's and encouraged a resistance against the U.S. government in which individuals or small groups would work toward a common strategic goal while remaining independent and without ever reporting to a single leader or command hierarchy. This idea has taken hold in Islamist circles as well in light of the advanced worldwide intelligence network employed by the West since 9/11.

Terrorist acts perpetrated by such 'lone wolves' are considered to be the most unpredictable and difficult to prevent by counterterrorism units, law enforcement, and the intelligence community. The threat of these scenarios coupled with the freedoms guaranteed in open societies requires a difficult balancing act for security services. However, it is a known fact that most lone wolves identify with extremist movements, and it is the identification and awareness of the members of these organizations that intelligence agencies should concern themselves with. However, the fact that these individuals operate alone lends to some weaknesses in their schemes. They do not participate in terror networks or training camps that can be infiltrated or traced. They do not enjoy the benefits of rehearsals or additional skill sets practiced by other members who could potentially be turned them against them as witnesses in legal proceedings. Because they are alone it is more difficult for them to conduct large-scale, technical attacks. Without the reinforcement of a close-knit social support network they cannot rely on others for assistance in complicated plots. Nonetheless, for all these weaknesses lone wolves are still cunning and lethal, as such attacks have been attributed to the deaths of 42 law enforcement officers between 1990 and 2009.[9]

Law enforcement has begun to adapt their methods in response to these scenarios. It is common knowledge in these circles that most active shooter scenarios result in the death of the perpetrator, usually by their own hand. The commitment of these shooters is so great that they realize that they will die in the end and will attempt to cause as much death as possible in the minutes before they go. There is usually no specific target selection of victims; rather targets are usually selected for convenience. Visible, cowering, and stationary targets are easier to hit with a weapon and often fit the mental image of the shooters own self-projection of his power over the victim. Police forces have now adopted the technique of organizing into small teams and moving to clear a location rather than waiting for more heavily armed SWAT teams to arrive. The focus of police in such scenarios is the elimination, rather than the arrest, of the shooter. Police will bypass the innocent, injured, or dead in an effort to quickly identify and eliminate the threat. Unarmed potential victims are most likely to survive by locking themselves down or evacuating to the nearest exit. As a last resort, when the shooter is at close range and there is no available exit the odds of survival are greater if an attempt is made to incapacitate the shooter. The quick mobilization of civilian employees and law enforcement reflects the reality that authorities have begun to rehearse for these scenarios as they increasingly become commonplace.

There is a certain effective simplicity in the "Run, Hide, Fight" campaign prepared by the city of Houston to combat active shooters. In the way that "Stop, Drop, and Roll" are taught to most of us at a young age and can be easily remembered during a stressful situation this campaign provides a course of action for potential victims that, if rehearsed, can reduce the chances of becoming a target. One must first take a moment to determine where the gunfire is coming from, this is not as easy as it sounds. Many civilians have been taught by television and movies that the sound of a discharged weapon is thunderous and accompanied by flames out of the end of a barrel. In fact, gunfire is actually much quieter than portrayed in the media and often mistaken for fireworks or described as a "popping" sound. Reverberations from nearby structures and hallways can echo the noise and provide misleading information as to its point of origin. If there is more than a single gunman, as occurred in the Columbine scenario, exact determination of the threat location can be confusing. In the initial seconds of an attack it is worthwhile to take a moment and determine where the threat is located so that an escape plan may be formulated.

Most active shooters so far have been poor marksman with minimal training in the use of their chosen weapons. James Holmes of the Colorado movie massacre was able to kill 12 people despite the obvious tactical advantage of surprise and over 200 stationary targets at close range. Active shooters build up the courage to carry out the attack spending an inordinate amount of time fantasizing over their projection of power and in these fantasies they rarely leave room for the possibility of their own failures. Failures to maintain the weapon or clear malfunctions have led to casualties far below what would have been otherwise expected. Active shooters tend to carry out their attacks at close range for two reasons: 1.) The satisfaction of seeing their targets perish in intimate detail fulfills their fantasy of power 2.) Lack of confidence in their own weapon proficiency. There are exceptions to every rule, such as Charles Whitman who had received advanced military marksmanship training.

Obviously, it is much harder to hit a moving target than a stationary one. At distances exceeding 25 yards the accuracy of a pistol is reduced dramatically. Most potential victims can cover this distance in just a few seconds as they move away from the attacker. The act of movement while increasing distance will increase the odds of survival for would-be targets. The use of angles and barriers between the shooter and the target decrease the likelihood of a successful strike on a target. Angles such as up/down in the case of stairs or vertical floors or left/right as targets move away from the threat all increase the difficulty of making the shot. These movements should be unpredictable for the shooter and quickly mapped out by the target. Moving cover to cover in quick succession and without an obvious pattern away from the shooter should be the goal.

Many shooters have attempted to issue law enforcement-style commands to their victims in an effort to achieve compliance and a greater casualty count. Commands such as "Stop!" or "Get Down!" have been used with varying degrees of success in several shootings. The compliant response by victims is due to a combination of fear, uncertainty, and a willingness to appease the attacker in the hopes of surviving the engagement. None of these commands should be followed in an active shooter scenario. The single focus of potential targets should be to create distance, apply physical barriers for cover or concealment and when cornered, be prepared to fight. This last is a survival instinct that is within us all but has been buried to some degree depending upon life experiences. Those with the knowledge and training of law enforcement, first responders, and the military are more accustomed to running toward the sound of the guns when everyone else is running away.

Almost always, there are far more wounded than killed in attacks such as these. The instinct to survive is capable of carrying many of us through grievous wounds until proper medical care can be applied. Most wounds are survivable, as long as medical care is forthcoming, and rarely do they immediately incapacitate the victim. However, many civilians will experience the symptoms of shock as they realize that they are wounded and will immediately immobilize themselves by falling to the ground. This provides the shooter another opportunity to approach the victim, now stationary, and re-engage. Training programs developed by law enforcement, the military, and even professional athletes teach that the body can, and should, continue to function toward a goal in spite of severe pain and beyond the perceived limitations of the mind.

For those that are able to safely contact emergency personnel the most important information for responding officers is the location of the shooter. Officers will organize into small teams and move to the last known location in an attempt to neutralize the suspect. A 'second wave' of emergency responders will arrive comprised of a mixture of law enforcement and medical personnel to assist in securing the scene, interviewing witnesses, and facilitating medical treatment.

The de-legitimization of such acts of terror through the distribution of counter narratives in the popular media is one tactic that may be employed by law enforcement agencies so that the actors do not become revered or idolized by potential followers. The media did an excellent job of this following the Connecticut school shootings in 2012. Media focus was primarily on the victims and heroic actions of the adults who tried to save as many children as possible. Portrayals of the shooter, Adam Lanza, primarily characterized him as a troubled man with a psychosocial disorder in a model likely to be emulated in the media reaction to future active shooter scenarios. This counter-tactic, coupled by an awareness by the public of potential warning signs including the fact that most active shooters share similar features in that they are young, male, often exhibit disturbing psychological behaviors, and may have expressed an intense interest in extremist ideologies and weapons. As stated before, there are exceptions to every rule including the identifying sex of the perpetrator. There have been two cases of female active shooters in U.S. history, Brenda Spencer, who in 1975 opened fire on a San Diego elementary school killing two and wounding nine and Heather Smith who in 1985 killed an ex-boyfriend and another man at school before committing suicide. A heightened scrutiny of individuals possessing these characteristics would contribute to their early identification before mobilization.

Like crime, it is impossible to achieve a complete success rate in detection and prevention of terrorism. In comparison to other forms of terrorism, lone wolves are relatively few, granting law enforcement fewer opportunities to develop a profile of such perpetrators. Lone wolf terrorists have repeatedly displayed affection for the use of explosives in their plots while generally ignoring the many active shooter scenarios that have played out in recent years. The concern is that after so many repeated failures at attempting to acquire the necessary materials, assemble a functional explosive device, select a target without detection, and employ the device that the terrorist cell, or lone wolf extremist, will turn to the comparatively simpler active shooter situation as an option. The shared experiences of intelligence, law enforcement, and analysts regarding data and strategy are critical to the development of future responses to such unique forms of terrorism. The unlikely alternative is to attempt to physically secure all would-be targets against probable threats, a suggestion that is even more implausible than the notion of predicting all lone wolf incidents.

4
The Rebirth Of Right-Wing Domestic Terrorism

Radicalized Islam is the usual suspect in stateside discussions about terrorism, however so called "homegrown terrorists" pose a credible and growing menace to domestic security and more needs to be done to recognize and safeguard against this threat. The extreme right, the extreme left, the sovereign citizen movement, and those who have taken up with radicalized interpretations of religion of all faiths comprise the ranks of domestic terrorists. Long before jihadism became the villain in U.S. national security narratives there were men like Timothy McVeigh and Terry Nichols, responsible for the bombing of the Alfred P. Murrah building and killing 168 people. In the wake of that bombing, government at all levels took steps to combat the threat from within. The realization that domestic terrorism could only be effectively countered by multi-level interagency cooperation and intelligence sharing among local, state, and federal services redefined the relationship among these organizations. But there is still more to be done. In the wake of 9/11, priorities have shifted to external threats and have allowed extremist groups already operating within U.S. borders to promulgate their own message, recruit new members, adapt their tactics and quietly prepare for resurgence. The federal government must take concrete steps to reassess the reach of right-wing extremism, revisit the argument over civil liberties as they apply to law enforcement collection efforts, and clarify the federal governments' conflicting views on foreign and domestic terrorism.

Several themes highlight the dangers posed by the resurgence of such groups. Domestic terrorists appear to be responsible for up to two dozen events since 9/11 as several watchdog organizations have reported a sharp increase in the growth of these movements over the last few years. They include those who encourage and act upon extremist ideologies in the name of white supremacy, anarchism, sovereignty, black separatism, animal and environmental rights. These groups appear to have shifted tactics away from the conventional in favor of activities that are less overt and are much more likely to make use of the Internet for communications and recruitment. Domestic extremism has come to embrace the leaderless resistance model by forming decentralized groups comprised of cells or individuals making detection and infiltration very difficult for law enforcement. The rise of these groups appears to be driven by antipathy over the transformation of racial demographics within the U.S., frustration over weakened national economic conditions, and the mainstream propagation of conspiratorial theories regarding domestic and foreign government intervention in the freedoms of American citizens. Some of these groups are driven more by the success of criminal enterprises, including the sale of arms and drug trafficking, more so than their extremist ideologies.

A handful of recent events including horrific shooting rampages in New York, a Sikh temple in Wisconsin, and the Fort Hood military installation has forced Americans to reexamine their definition of terror. In times of crisis and in the face of such extreme acts it would be easy to lump all of these events under the generalized category of "domestic terror". In fact, they are all terrible acts that cause fear and serve to intimidate law-abiding citizens who wonder what would drive anyone to commit such crimes. But to compile all acts of mass murder into a single class is reckless and serves only to further obscure an already complicated issue. It is important to differentiate between anomalistic mass murder, hate crimes, and true domestic terrorism if for no other reason than to establish a common vernacular among the federal and state law enforcement agencies that must investigate these matters. The Federal Bureau of Investigation is the primary investigative agency charged with purview over the realm of domestic terrorism and they define it as such, "Domestic terrorism is the unlawful use, or threatened use, of force or violence by a group or individual based and operating entirely within the United States or Puerto Rico without foreign direction committed against persons or property to intimidate or coerce a government, the civilian population, or any segment thereof in furtherance of political or social objectives".[10] While similar in the end result, the means by which law enforcement investigates and the tools used to predict and prevent such acts are quite different. That is where the difference lies, in the motivation for the act- "in furtherance of political or social objectives."

The ideologies behind domestic terrorism vary and encompass a broad spectrum of factions. On the extreme left exist anarchic and Communist groups seeking to overturn the current political and social order, to the extreme right which espouses the philosophies of hate groups such as the white supremacists or acolytes of the sovereign citizen movement. Then there are the groups that believe there is justification in the use of terror for causes such as environmental, anti-abortion or animal rights. Currently, the right-wing groups display a greater willingness to resort to extreme acts of violence in the name of their cause. Right-wing extremists are responsible for committing far more violent attacks with the intent to commit murder than jihadist organizations in the United States. In the last twenty years these groups have been linked to 145 attacks, which have resulted in the deaths of 348 people.[11] Yet, counterterrorism efforts continue to be shaped with a focus on jihadist threats despite the fact that 25 of the 35 terrorist incidents recorded in the U.S. between 2004 and 2011 were linked to domestic terrorism.[12]

The white supremacist movement encompasses those who commit criminal acts in support of an ideology that purports that the white race is above all others. They number among the Ku Klux Klan (KKK), racist skinheads, and others whose perception of the world is divided between whites and all others who are viewed as the enemy. In fact these groups believe that the white race is the victim, having lost common ground due to the behind-the-scenes manipulations of other races and religions, and now suffers due to the machinations of these groups. David Lane, active in white-power circles in the mid-80's, coined the "Fourteen Words", considered an extremely popular white-power sentiment and slogan around the world: "We must secure the existence of our race and a future for white children".[13] In the United States white-power groups display an obsession with Nazi Germany and the reign of Adolph Hitler as a political figure and advocate of world dominated by the Aryan race. In an effort to broaden the ranks, George Rockwell, considered the father of neo Nazism in the 1950's, amended the description of "Aryan" to include those of Southern and Eastern European ancestry. Rockwell also linked concepts of neo-Nazism to religion leading to the Christian Identity movement.[14]

Racist skinheads are known as the most violent segment of the white supremacy movement.[15] These groups date back to the 1980's in the United States but were originally established in Britain in the 60's, today there are elements in many countries around the world. Low-level members can be identified through physical appearance- shaved heads, bomber jackets, suspenders, and steeled-toe boots comprise the uniform of the foot soldiers while members of organizational leadership or the political wing maintain a more conservative appearance in order to remain accessible to the mainstream. However violence has been integrated deeply into the subculture of this group, known for involvement in 36 of 53 violent incidents recorded by the FBI between 2007 and 2009.[16]

Many of the right-wing collectives are fueled by racial and religious intolerance and have experienced an explosion in growth in the last decade. Since 2000 the number of these groups has grown by 65 percent reaching a height of 1,018 hate groups active in the U.S. in 2011.[17] 148 of these groups considered themselves to be "patriot groups" much like the one that formerly recruited Timothy McVeigh. Membership has also increased in armed militias with goals and values resembling the anti-government sovereign movement and now number almost 1,300 chapters.[18] These numbers are a dramatic increase from the previous decade reflecting a deep mistrust of foreign influences and the U.S. government fueled by conspiratorial rhetoric.

In 2009 the Extremism and Radicalization Branch of the DHS issued a threat analysis of right wing extremism that blamed the economic and political climate of the time for fueling the radicalization and recruitment of the far right.[19] This report highlighted a dismal economic climate as well as the election of the nations' first African American president for the drive in radicalization and recruitment. Fears of illegal immigration, increased restrictions on gun laws and concerns over the inviolability of Second Amendment rights were also cited as reasons for the uptick in activity. National, political, and financial troubles were compared to a similar period in the mid-1990's when rightwing extremism experienced a resurgence "fueled largely by an economic recession, criticism about the outsourcing of jobs, and the perceived threat to U.S. power and the sovereignty by other foreign powers".[20] It was during this period in U.S. history that Timothy McVeigh, himself a former member of a right wing fringe group, bombed the Murrah building.

Militia groups began to materialize in the 1990's as armed, paramilitary organizations established to defend against what they perceived as the excesses of an intrusive government. It was during this period that the original Brady Bill was enacted, leading to fears that the government, using the full extent of local police forces and the National Guard would confiscate personally owned firearms. Groups tend to form around a central, charismatic leader and have been known to establish training compounds used to rehearse military tactical battle drills and weapons training. These compounds are also typically the central location for lessons in movement ideology, fundraising, and recruitment. Most extremists in these organizations tend to come to the attention of law enforcement in their efforts to acquire illegal, high-powered assault weaponry or explosive materials not typically accessible to the public. Some of them are encouraged through extremist conspiratorial idiom that speaks of a "New World Order" in which the United

States is subordinate to a shadowy world body controlling the government and media.

Since the 1970's there has also been a growing sovereign citizen movement derived from the Posse Comitatus sect who operate under the belief that even though they physically reside inside the U.S. they are separate or 'sovereign' from it. Current membership is estimated at 300,000 although this is difficult to confirm, as the group tends to subscribe to the leaderless resistance model choosing to operate as individuals and only gather in large groups to train, plan, socialize, and spread their ideology. The most common axiom of this ideology holds that a ruse government designed to take away the rights of ordinary citizens has replaced the legitimate federal government. A common tactic is to sidestep the U.S. judicial system by ignoring laws, evading taxes, destroying government-issued documentation and identification in an effort to cut ties with what they perceive as an illegal administration. In some cases these groups have created and attempted to circulate their own fake currency, identification, license plates, and driver licenses. These activities have been dubbed "paper terrorism" and include non-violent retaliatory activities designed to flood the judicial system with frivolous lawsuits and court filings designed to intimidate or defraud targeted individuals, institutions, and government entities. Some believe that by creating fictitious entities that are autonomous from the federal government that they will enjoy diplomatic immunity and are no longer required to pay taxes or subject to federal, state, or local law.

Law enforcement elements struggle to define and accurately track the crimes of these groups when compared to the more thoroughly investigated foreign threats. Acts of jihadist terrorism can be tried under anti-terrorism laws that pertain to the material support to foreign terror groups. Domestic terror is often tied to criminal law in that these acts are usually tried under laws designed to prosecute weapons or explosive violations, property destruction, or seditious conspiracy.[21] This is partly due to laws that are meant to protect the rights of American citizens, particularly the right to free speech, and limit investigation conducted by government law enforcement agencies. Laws that protect civil liberties also prevent law enforcement from tracking the activities of those engaged in hateful or provocative discourse unless a crime is suspected. The free expression of viewpoints, no matter how offensive, is a constitutionally protected right that cannot be exploited by law enforcement without a specific and legitimate just cause. The efforts of counterterrorist agents should be focused on proactive measures however, these agencies must often straddle a perilously thin line between investigative technique and the violation of civil liberties.

In the last decade, right-wing extremists have been linked to plots to assassinate judges and law enforcement personnel, carried out attacks on abortion clinics and synagogues, and have compiled the materials necessary to build rudimentary chemical weapons.[22] But, in response to law enforcement efforts the extreme right has also had to undergo an evolution in order to maintain relevance while avoiding criminal prosecution. They are more disorganized than they were ten years ago and have suffered several blows due to deaths and the imprisonment of key leadership and inspirational figures. These disruptions have further encouraged decentralized operations and forced members to embrace the leaderless resistance concepts once preached by Louis Beam. Groups are now smaller, and more conscious of the potential risk of law enforcement infiltration by new members. The risks associated with large, public gatherings have driven members toward the Internet for the purposes of recruitment, fundraising, organization, and mobilization.

Technology has contributed to the audience of these groups by providing a forum to send and receive extremist messages. In previous decades, members had to physically travel in order to attend meetings and run the risk of exposure and condemnation. Now, the Internet provides a somewhat secure and anonymous radicalization experience that can be absorbed in the comfort of one's own home and convenience of schedule. Some extremists are unwilling to affirm their controversial views in the public spotlight and, to them, the exploitation of "free space" in the virtual world where conflict with skeptics can be minimized are important to these adherents. This anonymity also contributes to an increasingly violent message that can be composed from the other end of the information superhighway. Following the deadly shooting rampage at the Sikh temple in Wisconsin, which killed six and wounded four, support for the act erupted on hate group websites including the neo-Nazi Vanguard News Network which posted this message from the site operator, Alex Linder, "Take your dead and go back to India and dump their ashes in the Ganges, Sikhs".[23] One count of such hate websites indicated that there were as many as 657 similar extremist forums in operation and based inside the U.S..[24] Psychologist John Suler, Ph.D. has coined a term for this behavior, the "online disinhibition effect", in which factors such as dissociative anonymity, asynchronicity, and personality variables combine with the minimization of authority to become factors that allow the most vitriolic statements to propagate on social mediums, especially the Internet.

The federal government lends its own inconsistencies to the subject by its refusal to categorize domestic extremist groups as terrorist organizations. Groups such as the various factions of Al-Qaeda and Abu Sayyaf are foreign terror organizations that have been designated by the Secretary of State as enemies of the United States. By identifying them as such their means of utilizing the support or resources that are subject to U.S. government influence are effectively curtailed. The legal criteria for this designation currently only apply to *foreign* terror groups that retain the capability and intent to engage in terrorism. As of December 2012 there are 51 groups that have been designated as foreign terrorist organizations without any such official categorization for domestic groups. Without such a classification, it is difficult for law enforcement to track these groups' activities over a range of time and assess the progress of efforts against them. It also contributes to a persistent, and incorrect, perception that terrorism is strictly a foreign-borne venture.

Advocacy groups, such as the American Civil Liberties Union have countered with the argument that the categorization of domestic groups as terror organizations due to their charged oratory and encouragement of violence would only serve to stifle free speech freedoms and would have the potential to be abused by aggressive law enforcement tactics. Mike German, a 16-year veteran of the FBI and current policy counsel for the ACLU is concerned with the government and law enforcement need for "obsessive" data collection and the use of fusion centers for intelligence gathering. "We've moved away from surveillance based on individual suspicion, the Fourth Amendment standard of probable cause and a warrant has basically evaporated," said German. "Because there are non-law enforcement agencies working in these [fusion] centers- military, private companies- their authority to conduct domestic law enforcement intelligence gathering is quite questionable".[25] German recommends the targeting of individuals over organizations with respect to domestic terrorism due to the potential civil liberty implications associated with the labeling of groups.

In light of this information and the threat that these groups will pose to government officials, ethnic and religious groups in the future there are several recommendations that law enforcement bodies should begin to consider in order to defend against domestic terrorism. The designation of domestic terror groups or individuals in a manner similar to the designation of foreign terror organizations by the State Department should be given some thought. While First Amendment concerns will complicate this discussion, the end result of a decision in favor of this revision to policy would make it easier to prosecute material support litigation and serve to de-legitimize the goals and methods of these groups in the eyes of all but the most ardent supporters. Also due to concerns of citizen privacy, the collection of intelligence across law enforcement agencies at all levels is inconsistent and without established standards for integration and analysis. The formal identification and designation of these groups would lead to federal standardization that would lead to a more consistent quality of data assessment and sharing among agencies. Violent jihadism has been the primary focus of federal efforts since 9/11 while allowing law enforcement to struggle with the growing problem of domestic terrorism within the United States. Federal agencies and legislative bodies must take the lead and address recommendations designed to shore up contradictions in the foreign versus domestic counter-terrorism strategy.

5
Securing Our Borders

In the years since the findings of the 9/11 Commission and subsequent establishment of the Department of Homeland Security, the face of American border security has changed dramatically. The stated goal of the Department mission is to "prevent terrorist attacks within the United States, reduce the vulnerability of the United States to terrorism, and minimize the damage, and assist in the recovery from terrorist attacks that do occur in the United States." Currently, the United States shares a 6,400 mile-long border with Canada, a key economic partner with shared interests in national security. To our South lies the border of Mexico, a 1,969-mile stretch of largely unregulated no-man's land with a history of porous crossing areas susceptible to penetration. To our East and West are the Atlantic and Pacific oceans and even within our own borders are hundreds of airports servicing nearly two million travelers on a daily basis. From a homeland security standpoint, how can all of the many agencies involved be effectively coordinated and supported with accurate intelligence, enhanced coordination, and improved technology? From a larger strategic outlook the many challenges presented with protecting such a large physical area while still maintaining financially viable trade practices with our international associates and providing for the security of our citizens even as we respect the freedoms afforded to each of our own is a daunting task. Yet every day, a relatively small number of American citizens accomplish just that by seeking close coordination with partnering agencies, improving the flow of accurate and timely information, and remaining adaptable to the evolving threat posed by individual extremists and terrorist organizations.

Of primary importance is the assurance of safe, free, and economical conduct of business across our borders. Along with the contributions that business, which directly corresponds to our national security, is the need to ensure security by preventing weapons, dangerous materials, criminals, and terrorists from entering. Border security is more than just ports, air terminals, and checkpoints. It means stopping these elements at the furthest point away from the United States, preferably outside the country. This means cooperation with other nations as stakeholders and the sharing of intelligence. The U.S. Customs and Border Protection (CBP) agency is now the largest administrator of information outside of the intelligence services. Cooperation on an international level is beneficial to the national security of all involved countries and establishes the United States on solid ground with respect to border security.

The United States recognizes that securing our borders must be given precedence. Many changes have been implemented to that end, including the unification of the CBP to allow for more standardized inspections to be conducted regarding commercial and immigration issues. Prior to the creation of the CBP, Customs was able to inspect less than one-quarter of rail containers, 15% of vehicles, and 5% of sea containers entering the United States.[26] As a result of the bills implemented by the results of the 9/11 Commission a necessary reorganization and modernization of procedures at the borders has developed a more streamlined and efficient customs process. This process has resulted in the detention of almost two million illegal immigrants, increased radiation-detection capabilities by deploying personal radiation detectors and portal monitors, established the National Targeting Center to coordinate anti-terrorism efforts among its agencies, and established the Customs Trade Partnership Against Terrorism to work with the commercial industry and emphasize sound security methods throughout the trading process. Since 2004, the Border Patrol has increased the number of intelligence analysts working along the U.S.-Mexico border, doubled the number of border agents from 10,000 to 20,700, and increased the number of officers assigned to land-sea-air ports of entry to 20,600.[27] The CBP has incorporated new technologies along our borders and entry control points such as aerial and ground surveillance equipped with thermal imaging cameras, non-intrusive detection capabilities designed to identify weapons, and radioactive isotope isolators that could identify the presence of radiological materials.

In December of 2010 the U.S. Government Accountability Office (GAO) completed its' Quadrennial Homeland Security Review (QHSR) as mandated in the 9/11 Commission Act of 2007. The five mission goals examined in the QHSR were identified as terrorism prevention, border security, enforcing immigration law, cyber-security, and ensuring resilience to disasters. The GAO found that the DHS had made significant strides in each of these areas when compared to the state of affairs after 9/11 although it still had several strategic recommendations based upon common themes across the spectrum of the DHS mission. These strategic goals included establishing a comprehensive threat awareness system accessible to the public, strengthening the capabilities of local communities in order to be better prepared to contend with a crisis, encouraging a national culture of cooperation across all of the agencies affiliated with DHS, and developing and implementing new technologies that would contribute to the overall security posture of the country.[28]

While DHS, along with the many cooperating agencies have upgraded their operations, many challenges remain that demand attention. Less than two percent of our northern and southern borders are actively patrolled and several hundred thousand persons continue to enter this country illegally each year. Budgetary conflicts hinder the development of new technologies preventing their swift employment. Joint operations with Canadian and Mexican authorities have improved cooperative efforts and created a sense of shared understanding regarding potential threats but gaps in information sharing and compatible communications networks hamper full collaboration. The question now remains, "Are the current security procedures that are already in place at our southern border enough to also have the additional effect of preventing terrorist operatives attempting that avenue of infiltration?"

Recently, the government of the United States has announced a renewed intensification of border security practices along its borders and immigration checkpoints. President Obama, alongside Canadian Prime Minister Stephen Harper, publicly stated that this renewed commitment would emphasize inter-agency information sharing and improving screening procedures along the U.S.-Canada border.[29] This reinvigoration of the priority afforded to border security should include the increased use of advanced and proven technologies such as biometric identification and database sharing across the many law enforcement and intelligence services responsible for securing the borders. Reduced tax-initiatives and preferential status could be granted by the government when dealing with private companies that have played an active role in bettering their own security procedures or develop new technologies that have a significant impact on homeland security. Finally, our neighbors to the north and south must be given the full cooperation as would be afforded an agency within the United States as they also hold a large stake in our national security. Joint operations must continue with an importance placed on shared intelligence, economic prosperity to all concerned countries, and mutual goals of national security.

The United States has a fixed amount of resources to allocate across many supporting agencies, departments and bureaus that provide for the defense of our government. These organizations are extremely competitive with one another, vying for their share of limited funding each fiscal year making it imperative that each agency be prepared with a sound budget plan that is effective and monetarily responsible. The division of these limited resources must be able to maintain the existing organizational framework as well as adapt to the constantly evolving needs that are inherent in a fluid security environment. New technologies, training, and the implementation of new ideas must be given special consideration when allocating funds to the department.

The defense of the homeland, like the tactics used by terrorists, should be a constantly evolving organism. The worst possible course of action would be for the agencies responsible for securing this nation to rest on their past successes and become stagnant, assured of their relative safety. Stagnancy allows defenders to get comfortable behind their walls of protection, preventing efficient simplification and often resulting in the growth of a complicated conventional bureaucracy. Just as the enemy seeks weaknesses to exploit within our professional organization and society we must also strive to identify our Achilles' heel. Tactics in use by the enemy are similar to water building against a dam in that eventually, given enough time and pressure, they will find a crack and a way through the system.

The United States must take advantage of its position as a world leader in industry and technology and direct these strengths toward providing for its own security. The 9/11 Commission Report recommended the implementation of a biometric entry-exit screening system at all U.S. border crossing points.[30] This program was in its infancy immediately following the terrorist attacks of September 11th in the form of US VISIT (United States Visitor and Immigrant Status Indicator Technology), a biometric screening process involving digital photographs and fingerprints. However, this system has not yet realized its' full potential, in part due to the moral and ethical implications brought on by the capability for its misuse. Biometric technologies in conjunction with "data-mining" software similar to the CAPPS II program must be advanced and incorporated into the security process that is the current reality given the modern terrorist threat. The responsibility of a secure nation is far too large for even the combined efforts of the many intelligence, emergency, and law-enforcement agencies across the country. The average citizen must become a "force-multiplier", able to observe and report on their immediate area for indicators of a threat. Accessible technologies that take advantage of our current communications infrastructure to keep citizens informed of potential threats without violating operational security or creating a culture of fear are necessary to involve and inform the public of imminent hazards associated with potential catastrophes. The nation's telecommunications infrastructure is one of the most advanced and widespread in the world. Smartphone apps that could provide instructions in the event of a natural or man-made disaster, suspect descriptions could be instantly sent out to tens of thousands of subscribers similar to the Wireless Emergency Alerts and Amber Alerts in use by federal law enforcement which has resulted successful return of 495 children within the first 14 years since it's implementation,[31] proving it's effectiveness. Another example is the use of social networking mediums such as Twitter to communicate Homeland Security advisories to followers of the DHS page. This sort of instant communication is critical to informing and involving the public while at the same time making use of the advantages that being a part of a technologically-adept society can provide.

As is often the case with emerging technologies in this field there is the potential for abuse of such far-reaching security systems and privacy concerns voiced by citizens as they undergo increased scrutiny. Once it was leaked that Transportation Security Administration screeners were misusing the images gathered at passenger search checkpoints there was a public backlash resulting in the removal of the devices.[32] This misuse and resulting public outcry deprived us of an otherwise useful tool in preventing the carrying of weapons onboard commercial passenger transport. That is why training programs must emphasize professional behavior along with the ethical and moral implications associated with the use of these technologies. This training must include programs that not only train employees and affiliates of the Department of Homeland Security but also the public. The key is to create training that is both informative and accessible, that citizens will want to participate in given all of the media and entertainment alternatives present in our culture. In addition to instruction regarding the professional and ethical conduct associated with the use of new technology an emphasis must be placed on the continued teamwork of a diverse range of agencies that would typically respond to a threat. Large-scale training scenarios involving multiple agencies that highlight coordination and cooperation in order to be successful are critical in order to challenge organizations thereby resulting in the identification of weaknesses inherent to the system. Intelligence gathered from one location of the country, analyzed by an agency in another, and passed on to another for action is but one example of the type of interagency coordination that must be rehearsed and tested on a regular basis. Ethical dilemmas and so-called "murky events" affecting the training involving any number of hot-button issues, such as religion, with several possible interpretations must be injected into the scenarios. The final outcome must be analyzed and reviewed by every level of each participating agency in order to identify strengths and weaknesses.

The solicitation of recognized experts on a retainer basis to provide fresh insight on potential threats, ethical implications of existing procedures, and cultural awareness training relevant to the field of national security. Subject matter experts not previously associated with the Department of Homeland Security should be invited to debate the merits and flaws of the current system with the goal of producing ideas that will advance forward progress toward the ultimate goal of a more streamlined and competent organization. This "new blood" should be focused on challenging the status quo and standard operating procedure. Differing viewpoints should be expected and encouraged in order to generate robust discussion that will result in positive growth of the organization. The results of these discussions should be analyzed and inserted into the previously recommended training scenarios and computer simulations while categorizing their value to the organization and potential for inclusion into the standard operating procedure.

Concerns over the possibility of drug related violence involving Mexico's drug cartels reaching across the U.S. southern border is yet another point of contention for DHS and CBP. Regional instability, rampant crime, and local government corruption threaten to unsettle the already shaky Mexican foundation. As the violence continues unchecked it is probable that the U.S. will see an increase in illegal immigration carrying the high possibility of criminal or terror related elements using this northward migration as cover for infiltration. The number of Border Patrol agents assigned to Arizona alone had doubled since 2004 and daily surveillance flights along with advances to camera and sensor technology have contributed to the dramatic decrease in illegal border crossings. In 2011, 119,000 illegal aliens were arrested in Arizona down from a high of 610,000 in 2000.[33] Still, over the past decade there has been a sharp rise in the illegal drug trade from Mexico into Arizona. The Border Patrol there has seized one million pounds of marijuana every year for the last few years- four time the amount seized in 2000. Other drugs-heroin, meth are also making it across the southern border in greater quantities than before. Advocacy groups concerned with border security have taken it upon themselves to police the border by placing motion-activated cameras along the border capture video footage of wave after wave of immigrant and drug smuggling groups, often heavily armed, crossing land north of the Mexican border. The U.S. government must attempt a wider range of engagements with government along our shared borders and frequented ports, beyond the current military paradigm, with an emphasis on shared intelligence, better communications, and mutual co-operation as stakeholders.

The evolvement of new technologies, professional and ethical training, and the incorporation of new ideas are key to maintaining an effective security posture and should be given priority when determining budgetary allocations. Technology that takes advantage of the U.S. status as a world leader in the field as well as harnesses the technological ideas introduced by military and private sectors must be actively developed and incorporated. Training that emphasizes interagency cooperation and ties in professional and ethical conduct along with the involvement of the concerned public should be conducted aggressively. New blood, fresh thinking must be brought in and existing procedures must be confronted as if they were under attack. In effect, they are being probed on a routine manner by terrorists with an eye toward challenging existing procedures, identifying flaws in the system and exploiting weakness. It is imperative that we identify and shore up those flaws in our systems, creating a security environment that makes the possibility of an attack so operationally and logistically difficult for the terrorist to effectively execute while shielding the freedoms and values that comprise our democracy.

6
The Culture Of Suicide Terror

In 2003 history repeated itself as the regime of Saddam Hussein in Iraq was rather quickly defeated by a second Coalition effort just over a decade after the first. In Afghanistan, the United States led a coalition-supported effort to defeat the Taliban Emirate of Afghanistan and met with considerable early successes. One of the more extreme tactics that appeared later in these two campaigns included the use of suicide bombings as a tactic by an enemy, desperate and on its' heels. The term best used to describe the one side-effect of these quick military campaigns on a society is cultural trauma. Concisely, cultural trauma occurs when a group feels they have been the subject of a horrendous event, in this case the US led Coalition defeat of the Taliban Emirate of Afghanistan and Sunni political majority Iraq. Many of the significant changes to a culture after this form of trauma include, reshaping of their social and political beliefs, as well as their membership and expressions.

Throughout history suicide as a method of warfare is not new, however it has become a revelation for terrorist organizations. Suicide missions have been used for centuries and include the Kamikaze pilots of Japan, the Leonidas Squadron of Germany and the Viet Minh in Vietnam. Since 2005 the use of suicide bombings by terrorist organizations around the world has increased exponentially. The call to sacrifice oneself for the cause of jihad is viewed as a principle of radical Islam and stressed by many fundamentalist religious clerics while seen as righteous and courageous. Not always was this the case however; Afghanistan saw no suicide bombing attacks against the Soviets during their decade long occupation, no use of suicide bombing during the Taliban conquests from 1995 to 2001, and no more than a dozen bombings from 2001 to the summer of 2005. The mujahedeen fighter and Taliban from those days came from religious orders that believed and taught suicide bombing as cowardly. As a tribal and militant state, under nearly constant turmoil since the mid 70s, the Afghans strictly obeyed these teaching for some time. The use of suicide bombers was believed by many Taliban to be "un-Afghan" like and not in accordance with the code of Pashtunwali. Rather, the insurgents continued to embrace principles supported by the mujahedeen, as they had when battling the Soviet Union from 1979 to 1989; fighters fought to live another day. However, once the United States and its

Coalition took control of Afghanistan, the "living to fight another day" would be replaced by embracing suicide bombing as a form of supreme devotion.

Afghanistan ranks 180 out of 199 nations in the world with regard to unemployment (35% of the total population) and 36% of the population are under the poverty line. They have one physician for every 5000 people and life expectancy at birth is one of the worst in the world with the average person only expected to live about 45 years. Less than half of the men and only about 10% of the women in Afghanistan are considered literate. They are a very young population with a median age about 18 years old and about 42% of the males are under 14 years old. This means that schools, the safest and most prestigious, which are based in Pakistan are tightly controlled by religious groups. The 'madrassas', as they are called, are able to exert considerable influence over a young population which makes it easy to break down older cultural norms against suicide. When you combine all of this with the fact that religious clerics are endorsing suicide bombing as path to eternal happiness in the form of martyrdom, it seems like it would be fairly easy to overcome past teachings. Fear, ignorance, and a perverted sense of pride or belonging are all cultivated into a message that in the histories of most cult or militant leaders is the common denominator in influencing those who are without hope.

Once a forbidden tactic, some jihadists have taken to the suicide attack. Initially, suicide bombers were viewed as cowardly fighters, who were un-Islamic. The Pashtunwali code and Taliban-Deobandi school of Islam considered suicide to be cowardly and those who engaged in it to be cursed. Before the war on terrorism Afghans believed in fighting to live another day. This ideal began to change as the Taliban became less isolated. Not only did the influence of direct contact with Arab Al-Qaeda insurgents help to change the mindset towards suicide bombings, media, in the form of "Iraqi kill videos" and Jihadist tapes, and support from religious leaders were also strong agents for change. This cross-talk of information between Iraq and Afghanistan helped to solidify common tactics and link the two conflicts. In February 2003, Osama Bin Laden sent out a message asking that operatives in Afghanistan and Iraq implement suicide bomb attacks against NATO troops. Over time, there was a cultural change, as Afghans started to see fellow Muslims on martyrdom videos preparing for suicide attacks as a true commitment to Islam. Afghan militants now are instructed that suicide attacks are no longer off limits and are even supported by the Quran.

One former Taliban commander, Mullah Dadullah, was filmed giving passes to heaven for suicide bombers-in-waiting in Pakistan. Taliban leader Jalaludin Haqqani was even said to have given suicide bombers holy water from Mecca to cleanse those who have doubts about the sinful nature of suicide. The acceptance under Islam and the Quran by both Afghan and Pakistani Taliban leaders and the training of children for these missions means suicide attacks will continue for the foreseeable future.

With the insurgence of the United States and its coalition in Afghanistan, Al-Qaeda and other foreign fighters from Iraq seized upon the opportunity to unite Muslims and join their efforts in a global Jihad. This included sharing strategies and tactics, as well as assets and resources. Specifically, the tactical use of suicide bombers in Afghanistan was at first witnessed, analyzed, then embraced by the Taliban in 2003. Drawing upon inspiration from the extensive media coverage following the 9/11 attacks, which was viewed as a successful martyrdom operation striking a highly publicized blow against "untouchable" Western powers, Al-Qaeda demonstrated the effectiveness of this tactic and from the perspective of such extremism resulted in a social change; the embrace of suicide bombings as the ultimate sacrifice in the face of a militarily superior opponent.

While most in the Muslim world at first refused to believe or except this change, as time went on, radical clerics and other leaders embodied this approach and began preaching to the masses. The foundation of this new teaching was paralleled to those giving their lives for a higher cause, the Islamists' fundamental beliefs. From a tactical perspective, the use of suicide bombers is one of the most effective weapons available. Even the mere thought of a suicide bomber instills fear in one's adversary. Thus, after a short time, clerics legitimized this tactic and the Taliban added an addendum in their Layeha-Rule Book legitimizing suicide bombers. This new supreme devotion was validated by Al-Qaeda when they publicly noted on their web site, "While suicide attacks were not accepted in the Afghan culture in the past, they have now become a regular phenomenon". Suicide bombings are now considered one of the most effective tactics used in guerrilla warfare.

Regardless of their motives, the one thing that terrorists in all countries have in common is that they always have had to do more with less. They are typically left to their own devices by low-level leaders and only supplied over-arching strategic objectives rather than specific tactical guidance. Which means that they have to be crafty in order to survive and not get caught. Without someone looking over their shoulder to tell them that they can't do something, they are not hesitant to attempt a new tactic and if the new tactic were a success then word of mouth and the media would spread the knowledge of that tactic. Suicide bombing is a success in the eyes of the enemy. It is low-cost, requiring minimal training by the user who is then often revered as a martyr, whose image is then used as propaganda for additional funding and recruitment. In effect, the tactic pays for itself many times over. From the enemy's viewpoint, the only downside is the potential for public opinion to turn against them drying up those funds and recruiting pools. To date, that has not happened in any significant numbers. Now that certain religious leaders sympathetic to the cause are encouraging the tactic as a sacrifice in the name of jihad there is no counter-balance to keep these tactics from being employed. While security procedures have improved significantly over recent years it is difficult to protect every potential target and this trend will continue to be employed heavily in Asia and carry over into the next conflict.

The mind-set of groups such as Al-Qaeda, Pakistani and Afghan Taliban is such that they have no trouble embracing the concept of asymmetrical warfare. They propagate the myth that that are engaged in a "holy war" and are not bound by any moral or theological restraints because they have the blessing of their god as interpreted by clerics loyal to the cause. The conventional, and possibly dated, tactics of terrorism used in the past such as kidnappings for ransom/demand or hijackings no longer receive the media attention that they once did, especially in the wake of the spectacular attacks that have occurred post-9/11. This media attention is essential for spreading the word of their cause, which in turn leads to additional resources in the way of recruitment, funding, and legitimacy, even if it is criminal legitimacy, on the world stage. The perception that if the enemy, currently Coalition Forces, is stronger, wealthier, and more advanced technologically then the jihadists are justified in any and all means to repel the occupation of their land and apparent subjugation of their people. No longer is any tactic off-the-table or too heinous to be considered when targeting an infidel.

The use of children as foot soldiers or the collateral threat to innocent bystanders will no longer dissuade the terrorist of tomorrow. As we enter into an age of "ultra-terrorism" where each faction attempts to make their mark on the political stage by upstaging the attacks of the past these tactics will escalate in their deadliness. The question is how do we prevent it from reaching these levels? In order to quell this seemingly insurmountable tide it will require a multi-faceted approach involving cooperation among the international intelligence agencies, federal law enforcement in the United States as well as a commitment by the civilian leadership and general population of the affected countries. Finally, the once taboo culture of suicide terrorism in these nations must be changed. This last will be the hardest to accomplish due to the fragmented and tribal nature of familial relationships that has governed these areas for so long.

One thing that is significant and common to most of these countries is the prevalence of extremist interpretations of religion and its significant impact on the motivations of all involved. Like tribal relationships, it knows no political boundaries on a map and is capable of influencing so many by those who are trusted to interpret its intricacies. The perception that these tactics are acceptable must be changed and that can only be accomplished through the channels that first condoned them, the religious leadership. Even fundamentalist clerics can be convinced that there is no honor nor should there be an acceptance of these tactics, especially when the lives of innocents are jeopardized. Respected religious leaders must categorically and publicly denounce the use of these methods before this tactic spreads outside of the religion and is employed by the next extremist group. It is through these elements that the mind-set of acceptance must be altered, and quickly, before it has taken root in the current generation of jihadists as an acceptable and legitimate form of warfare.

As the awareness spreads of the terrorist employment of these tactics, and the security bubble around them is subsequently strengthened, it is likely that the terrorist will shift away from highly visible locales in the major cities and increasingly target areas lacking the proper funding, training, or awareness such as smaller villages and local political leadership in the rural countryside. Al-Qaeda, and the Taliban are increasingly finding it difficult to score any successes using conventional means in the current conflict. Even the ubiquitous improvised explosive device (IED) is beginning to plateau in its effectiveness as tactics, technology, and awareness is racing to close the gap in what was once a highly successful approach to combat. Each success, including those gained through the use of children or female suicide bombers, further justifies their use to propagate the jihad in the eyes of a terrorist.

Extremists will carry on their suicide bombing campaign but there will be an increase in the numbers of women and children being used to conduct these sorts of attacks. The coalition forces in Afghanistan have, for the most part, conducted themselves in a culturally sensitive manner with regards to the people of Afghanistan and as such females do not receive the same level of scrutiny as men do, particularly the military-aged males. The Al-Qaeda and Taliban forces have already identified this weakness and have exploited it on several occasions. In fact, it could be argued that the increase in "insider threat" attacks in Afghanistan represents the next evolution in suicide terror. The only thing that would prevent this in the future is a public backlash against the practice or the use of women and children as suicide bombers. There is much fear among the populace that the Taliban can retaliate against anyone who would denounce them so publicly and those that live outside of the major cities do not have faith in their country's security forces to defend them. The trend will continue toward targets such as civilian gatherings, host-nation political leaders, and examples of Western business and democracy in high-profile areas regardless of a consistent security presence.

Contrary to public opinion, suicide bombers are not psychopaths. Suicide bombers are willing participants or easily coerced persons exposed to an exploitative organization. Al Qaeda's effectiveness in Iraq inspired extremists in Afghanistan by using a broad message of blaming westerners for the world's problems, labeling them as infidels, and calling for Muslims across the world to take up Jihad against them in order to fulfill Allahs' plan. Their propaganda campaign has been very effective at supplying willing and narcissistically vulnerable individuals with the sociological fulfillment and security they crave. The malleable minds of youth are easy prey for extremists. War and economic strife has given youth few opportunities to gain wealth or status for themselves or their families. To these individuals, Al Qaeda membership may seem to provide new opportunities. Terrorist groups blame the west for invading their country, killing their people, stealing their resources, and for driving Muslims to adopt less conservative ways in violation of Sharia law.

From the Afghans' perspective, the West may appear to be the cause of their plight. The US went into Afghanistan to remove the terrorist organization responsible for 9/11. Unfortunately, by doing so, it may have inadvertently created more sympathizers. The U.S. now has the complex task of trying to prevent the reestablishment of terrorist networks while giving the Afghan people back their country. To change their minds, would-be terrorists must be presented with opportunities to work, learn and provide for their family while practicing their customs. The youth need to be taught the value of tolerance, freedom, and civility. Unfortunately, successful terrorist attacks are showcased as a sign of government weakness causing fearful civilians to question the relevance of organizations meant to protect. Specifically, many of the tactics and strategies used by the United States to fight terrorism and the propaganda machine associated with it are formed around political agendas and public opinion.

Al Qaeda's propaganda campaign is quite effective in recruiting individuals as well as gaining the overall support of Muslims in the Arab regions. Terrorist leadership does not predominantly come from the poorest of people but is most often encouraged by the intellectual and mid to upper classes. The people who preach a radical agenda, including the use of terrorism as a tactic and strategy are often the local religious leadership from these nations. Furthermore, these clerics preach radical philosophies to seek out disenfranchised individuals targeting younger males who are uneducated, unemployed, and are destitute.

Al-Qaeda's use of faith to empower and encourage its operatives to engage in suicide operations has directly contributed to its increased acceptance and employment in the wars in Iraq and Afghanistan. The change-agent in this case was the tolerance of suicide in warfare by extremist religious leaders in the Arab community. Coupled with the successes on the battlefield and a successful media campaign spearheaded by Al-Qaeda, these tactics were broadcast world-wide available for viewing, uncensored, 24 hours a day on the World Wide Web. The Internet clips of suicide in warfare hit a mark, by terrifying those that it was intending to terrify and emboldening those that had previously feared the combined military and financial might of the Coalition. The successes involving suicide as a weapon, while initially capturing the world's attention on 9/11, were honed on the streets and bazaars of Iraq. Through the use of the Internet and publicity of the international media, a Taliban force on the defensive and desperate to remain relevant quickly adopted these tactics in Afghanistan and Pakistan.

There are more than 12,000 religious schools in Pakistan, also known as madrassas, many of which engage in extremist teachings and have total control over their student populations preaching violence against the West. The existential drive toward suicide bombings is that of wanting to protect something that is dearer than one's own life. This can be religion-based or secular. Religion can motivate people to kill those they believe are the enemy of god. From the secular view, people who have little status in their society are willing to conduct suicide bombings for the admiration they are given before their attack and to be remembered afterward. Many suicide bombers conduct attacks to provide what they perceive as security and respect for their surviving families. Wealthy backers of Al Qaeda provide not only praise and status to suicide bombers, they also provide money and security to the families after the deed is done. Al Qaeda's extreme interpretation of Islam promotes suicide bombing as a form of martyrdom. Al Qaeda believes that if one infidel, the perceived enemy of God, perishes in a suicide bombing, the bomber is a martyr despite collateral damage or innocent casualties. Extremist teachings bypass the guilt associated with killing civilians or other Muslims by maintaining the belief that it was God's will.

One of the primary tools used to inspire prospective candidates toward martyrdom operations is video on the open Internet showing the beheadings of infidels, successful IED strikes, and suicide attacks. No longer is it just a word from a theological sermon, but undeniable proof of victory and sacrifice against a more powerful foe displayed in full video. A feeling of victimization and fear coupled with the symbolic narratives that idolize martyrdom and the consent of violence contribute to societal approval for these operations. From perceived grievances to the well-executed use of propaganda and the media, al-Qaeda has been able to successfully alter the negative perception. The generation of the proud mujahedeen, who fought to live another day, seems to have adopted a "cult of death" in which the message of martyrdom by suicide has much more meaning and flourishes in myth for the jihadist.

Suicide bombers are no longer viewed with the negative cultural stigma that was once attached to one who would be willing to kill both the enemy and innocents alike. They are revered as heroes in their community and taught that they are not committing suicide but becoming a martyr in a jihad. This principle is analogous to that held in the United States regarding soldiers, police, or firefighters who risk their lives in the line of duty. A police officer that performs his duty when the odds are against him or a firefighter who risks her life to save others is not suicidal. Their actions are viewed just as heroically and with a devotion to duty.

The interpersonal forces involve the drive toward vengeance. Within Afghanistan and Iraq alike, many war survivors have an extensive history of family and friends who have been killed. Al Qaeda's propaganda prays on this vulnerability and blames the war and the resulting death on the coalition and non-Muslims. When minority cultural groups feel powerless in changing their government through other means, they turn to violence to state their grievances. By becoming a suicide bomber, one can avenge their ancestors or attempt to alter the government's actions. Common to many terrorists and suicide bombers is narcissistic vulnerability. Many young adult males find themselves with little meaning or identity in a war torn, economically poor and unstable country like Afghanistan, Pakistan, or Iraq. Like gangs in the US, terrorist groups provide these individuals with purpose and power in an otherwise powerless existence. Those wanting to prove their courage and demonstrate their self-worth to their terrorist group may participate in suicide bombings to feed their ego and establish their identity. A person's exposure to repetitive violence and the option of participating in a terrorist organization increases the likelihood of becoming a suicide bomber. The sponsoring group provides training and materials and validates the ideology of martyrdom fostering a preoccupation with historical grievances by exploiting weaknesses in identity formation. Some sponsoring groups gather children as young as eight in order to expose them to the use of suicide bombs and military tactics. This exposure creates a sociological norm of Islamic extremism, terrorist violence, and suicide bomb tactics.

The broad message of Jihad by Al Qaeda and like organizations has resonated with the desperate Taliban and mujahedeen within Afghanistan. The small Taliban forces cannot fight a conventional war against the coalition, so they must use asymmetric means. Guerilla tactics were first used by the Taliban, but proved not nearly as effective as the suicide bombings carried out by insurgents in Iraq. The Taliban then changed their ideology to fit this effective suicide tactic. As terrorists continue to lose resources and influence, this tactic has become more prevalent. Perhaps the best way to counter suicide bombings is by attacking the previously discussed factors that foster suicide bombing and would require international cooperation to establish a stable economy and government within the countries that are the greatest contributors to terrorism.

7
The Splintering Of Al Qaeda

The group known as Al Qaeda has quickly become famous the world over as a lethal and far-reaching terrorist organization, seemingly capable of conducting operations wherever they choose including Southwest Asia, the Middle East, Africa, and the Americas. Their name has become synonymous with acts of terrorism around the world, inspiring followers and admiration amongst disaffected Islamists seeking to remove Western influences from Muslim countries and establish Islamic regimes in their place. In order to understand the ideology and global reach of this group it is important to understand that it was initially comprised of Muslims recruited from more than 50 countries to fight against the Soviet invasion of Afghanistan. These mujahedeen came from varied backgrounds and geographic regions yet were united by a cause, that of expelling a foreign power from a Muslim land. With so many united under this common political goal, carrying with them a stirring religious fervor, and a strong desire to ultimately be successful about the goal of expelling a superpower it was a natural progression to maintain the momentum that had driven this endeavor to success and maintain this loose-knit conglomerate of devotees to be called upon in the future. Following the defeat of the Soviets, bin Laden wanted the Jihad to continue outside of Afghanistan in a campaign targeting governments that did not strictly follow the tenets of a strict fundamentalist Islamic faith.

While most infamous for the simultaneous terrorist attacks of 9/11, its cells have been traced to acts of terror around the world. Kidnappings, suicide bombings, and plots including Mumbai-style terror attacks and mass-poisonings, its own leaders claim that nothing is taboo as long as it furthers the organizations goals. Extremist religious clerics favored by the organization pardon Al-Qaeda's terror campaign by manipulating the verses of the Quran to excuse its most despicable acts in the name of Jihad. One of its greatest strengths lies in the fact that it does not hold allegiance or ties to any one country but an ideal. As a non-state sponsored organization it is not subject to rule by those leaders or penalties due to international sanction.

While the Arabic translation of Al-Qaeda is literally "the Base", there is no one central base location- the organizations members are the base. Only the high-profile operations are governed with specifics dictated to operatives along with logistical assistance and planning considerations leaving subordinate leaders much room for expansion and creativity. This decentralization allows members to conduct operations based on their own merits while reducing the chances of compromise or detection by the target. Al-Qaeda is known to have cells in approximately 100 countries and is connected to other groups that share similar fundamentalist Muslim views including the GIA, Egyptian Islamic Jihad, and Hezbollah.

By ousting the Taliban regime from Afghanistan and denying Al Qaeda (AQ) safe haven in that country the U.S. dealt the organization a significant blow. Yet this initial success was not immediately followed through effectively and allowed key leaders and fighters to escape resulting in international expansion. With the invasion of Iraq in 2003 AQ members were able to tout their cause as just in the face of what they saw as a religious crusade against Islam. As a result, the group was able to rally supporters from around the globe and become stronger. It has been estimated that almost 30,000 foreign fighters joined AQ's ranks in Iraq gaining valuable combat experience that was to be employed on future battlefields.

The invasion of Iraq inspired the formation of other terrorist organizations that were not able to make the journey to fight instead choosing to carry out acts of terror in their own region. The London subway bombings and the Madrid railroad bombings were both carried out by independent terror cells inspired by the invasion of Iraq. Interpol estimates that there are approximately 40,000 fundamentalist Islamic converts operating in Europe all due to the perception that a campaign is being carried out against their religion.

It is not surprising that there is such a significant pool of recruits for transnational terror groups to draw upon. Wealthy Middle Eastern donors regularly contribute funds toward wide-reaching religious schools spanning the globe. It is common knowledge that a percentage of the rhetoric preached at these madrassas is sharply critical of religions other than Islam and, at times, aggressively hostile toward Western foreign policy. The most excessive among these schools have openly called for religious war against the West as the duty of every Muslim. Individuals are absorbing these extremist sermons, traveling to the warzone and serving their time before returning to their country of origin. These revolutionaries have all the rights of citizens of their country of origin including the ability to travel freely. In the years to come, one of the most difficult tasks for intelligence services will be the identification of the home-grown, foreign trained terrorists living within their borders.

During the last decade, an international effort has contributed to the arrest or killings of much of the AQ's leadership and support network. It has been transformed from a structured organization with definable leadership tiers to an ideological faction. Because of this decentralization it can be everywhere and nowhere at once. This transition of Al Qaeda from a unit that plans, trains, and conducts operations to a spiritual guiding force that inspires others in effect gives the group an immortality that is fed by its own infamy. The group has released audio tapes produced prior to the death of Osama bin Laden that have been edited to bolster his martyrdom in the eyes of his supporters. It is surprising that he did not produce a martyrdom video similar to those made by suicide bombers prior to conducting their operations, Al-Qaeda may have missed an opportunity to allow it's most recognizable figure to have the last word in a message that would have undoubtedly been aired by the media. Even still, through the manipulation of his previous messages and the Internet he may prove to be just as effective an icon in death as he was in life.

The death of Osama bin Laden has forced many of its senior members to gather and select a new interim leader, an Egyptian militant named Saif al-Adel, formerly affiliated with the Egyptian Islamic Jihad. This comes as a surprise to most and could be considered a slight to Ayman al-Zawahiri who is considered to be out of touch with Al-Qaeda's core membership.[34] This selection could not be conducted with the full support of the group leadership due to security concerns, which may lead to further rifts in an already fractured organization. At this point, Al-Qaeda is almost a brand name, so easily linked to terrorism by the media that it will be extremely difficult to claim that the organization is ever truly dismantled. As long as there is one cell, or even one "lone wolf", that espouses the Al-Qaeda name and is willing to conduct operations or preach its philosophy in extremist forums then Al-Qaeda will continue to be a driving force in the world of religious extremism.

The group known as Al-Qaeda in the Arabian Peninsula (AQAP) is actually a sub-sect of the umbrella group Al Qaeda, having sworn allegiance to the terrorist organization in 2009. It opposes the monarchy of Saudi Arabia due to its Western ties and demands the overthrow of the Al-Saud royalty.

Due to Saudi counterterrorism successes, Al Qaeda members in Saudi Arabia have been forced out of Saudi Arabia and have settled in Yemen. In 2009 they announced a merger with the Yemeni AQ branch along with recently arrived recruits from, Iraq, Pakistan, and Somalia to form Al Qaeda in the Arabian Peninsula. One of its most famous members was the American, Anwar al-Awlaki, a gifted propagandist and a source of inspiration for Al Qaeda recruits worldwide. His sermons and operational guidance have been linked to members of the 9/11 hijacking operation and Fort Hood shooter, MAJ Nidal Hassan. As a native of New Mexico, he held dual American-Yemen citizenship and as such, was a special prize for Al-Qaeda before he was killed in a drone strike in Yemen in 2011. With his first-hand understanding of both American and Middle Eastern life he was able to bridge the culture gap and reach out through the use of media to prospective recruits and supporters from both areas.

Some American counterterrorism officials consider this group to be the most dangerous terrorist threat to the United States. Members of the organization have been implicated in the attack on the USS Cole in 2000 prior to the forming of AQAP, shootings that wounded one and killed another US Soldier outside of a military recruitment office, and the failed Christmas Day bombing attempt in 2009 among others. The focal point of the US-Yemen relationship has been counterterrorism efforts aimed at targeting the AQAP organization. In the past, the government of Yemen has downplayed the reported strength of extremist organizations operating inside their country and the influence that they have played on the direction of their operations. US intelligence services have committed to bolstering Yemen's efforts by supplying an influx of money, biometric equipment, training and reinforcing security-related structures within the country. This coordination was leading to some initial successes with arrests of operatives and intelligence leads prior to the uprisings in the Middle East. The government of Yemen has been largely ineffective in countering AQAP's media machine or reversing its propaganda victories. Now faced with the possibility of regime change, western intelligence is concerned that new intelligence relationships will have to be developed once the country political climate has stabilized.

The fracturing of Al-Qaeda is not meant to imply that the group is getting weaker. In fact, it could be argued that as more offshoots of this terror organization begin to appear in Africa and Asia that it is just a matter of a few years before its agents entrench themselves in Western Europe and closer to American interests and citizens living abroad. The French have already begun to target a new figure, Moktar Belmoktar, a radical Algerian and veteran of Afghanistan. Belmoktar lost an eye in that conflict against Soviet forces and now leads the Al-Mulathameen Brigade or "The Brigade of the Masked Ones". This group has been identified as subordinate to Al-Qaeda in the Islamic Maghreb (AQIM) which has aggressively spread throughout the region in recent years. This group has sworn to attack Western interests in the area, particularly favoring the tactic of high profile kidnappings in exchange for the release of their own operatives from jail. Belmoktar issued a warning to Westerners around the world through video posted on jihadist websites, "This is a promise from us that we will fight you in the midst of your countries and we will attack your interests."[35]

It has been said by some that Al Qaeda has been left behind in the "Arab Spring" uprisings that have demanded the usurping of Middle Eastern dictatorships. After all, Al Qaeda claims to represent the voice of Muslim oppression around the globe and appears to be a proponent of the old axiom that change can only come through violent means. In fact, Al Qaeda is attempting to capitalize on these recent changes by claiming that their operatives along with the support of the people are responsible for influencing change in the region. With tumultuous regime change already occurring in Egypt and Syria, demand from citizens of dictatorial governments is growing. For many, the time for a peaceful transition has passed and those involved are too far committed to the change that which has increasingly grown more violent. Backing down at this stage would involve surrender to those nations' militaries and death or imprisonment for its members.

Already heavily active in Yemen, there are conflicting reports that this organization is now reported to be involved in armed engagements with government troops and have taken the city of Zinjibar. The President of Yemen, Ali Abdullah Saleh, has been accused by opposition leaders within the country of handing the provincial capital to extremist militants after the town was seized with minimal resistance seemingly overnight. Similar to their need to establish a state in Mali, AQAP has declared this province an "Islamic Emirate". By establishing a fundamentalist state AQAP seeks to govern in accordance with strict interpretation of Islamic law in keeping with Al-Qaeda's goal of the removal of governments corrupted by Western influence. These uprisings are now being actively encouraged in media releases by the AQAP organization and the words of Anwar al-Awlaki who wrote "The ensuing wars and political turmoil in such states as Libya and Yemen would enable Al-Qaeda militants to recruit, train, and organize in such spaces." From a counterterrorism viewpoint, it is in America's best interest to remain a proponent of stable political governments around the world or at the very least, peaceful and phased regime change.

The conglomerate of tribal networks operating within Pakistan's lawless Federally Administered Tribal Areas (FATA) as a loose alliance of several groups employing the use of terror include the Tehrik-e Taliban Pakistan (TTP), Al-Qaeda, and offshoots of these organizations such as the "313 Brigade". Recognized by the U.S. Department of State as Foreign Terrorist Organizations, the TTP and Al-Qaeda continue to manipulate the tribal population and influence the government of Pakistan through increasingly violent and daring tactics. These groups, although distinct in their individuality, are blended with very similar ideology, goals, and common support networks. The two groups blend well with each other due to their mutually supporting mission. While the TTP seeks to replace the legitimate government of Pakistan with a fundamentalist nation governed under Sharia law, Al-Qaeda seeks to drive all Western, and particularly, American influence from Muslim lands. They often recruit from the same types of radicalized madrassas and unregulated tribal areas seeking individuals disillusioned with their government and receive funding from many of the same sources. Even as the Tehrik-e Taliban begins its rise in status, emulating the growth of Al-Qaeda, talented commanders within its ranks are taking the necessary steps to establish themselves in the hierarchy of terrorist organizations by creating splinter cells with their own fiery message packaged and intended for worldwide media distribution.

The TTP is a loosely affiliated organization of disaffected members of the Taliban predominantly operating in the FATA of Northwestern Pakistan. This group developed in 2007 in the Waziristan region of FATA as a result of several previously unconnected cells of Taliban supporters and sympathizers began to work together due to a confluence of similar goals. TTP was initiated as an "umbrella organization" with representatives from each of the tribes in the region functioning as a *shura* with the stated goals of enforcing Sharia law, expelling the Pakistani government and its' military from the FATA and Swat districts.

With regard to the legal definition of terrorism this organization meets the criteria of a terrorist organization in that it has political goals that it attempts to achieve through violent means or the threat of future terroristic acts perpetrated by a subnational group and guided by the strategic influence of a nonstate entity. Members of Tehrik-e Taliban Pakistan do not feel that the government of Pakistan adequately represents them and as such they resort to terror tactics to draw attention to their cause. An additional benefit for the organizations senior hierarchy is that the business of terror is, at times, profitable. This profitability does not trickle down to the low-level fighters on the front lines. They are provided the bare minimum in terms of weaponry, explosives, communications equipment, and given just enough strategic guidance to carry out missions with long-term goals. The local population often provides logistical support in the form of food, shelter and fuel and when not given freely, it is taken by force, often at the expense of a prominent member of the local community. In the past, concessions ceded to this group in the form of a truce with the government of Pakistan have only resulted in the organization increasing the stakes and ultimately negating the terms of the original agreement.

The TTP, along with Al Qaeda affiliates around the world, were dealt a significant blow when it was revealed that the Al-Qaeda spiritual leader and strategic architect had been killed. Initially, the organization claimed that bin Laden was not dead, referring to poorly altered photographs of the terrorist leader released on the internet as false claims of his death by the United States intelligence agencies. This denial highlights the need within the organization for a spiritual figurehead with which to spread organizational propaganda. The TTP viewed bin Laden as a resistance fighter that was able to stand up the American occupation of Afghanistan and growing influence over Pakistan while successfully evading capture by the combined efforts of a coalition of Western countries. Grudgingly, the TTP was forced to acknowledge the death of Osama bin Laden through the use of several Pakistan news media outlets by claiming that they would avenge his "martyrdom by attacking the governments of Pakistan and the United States and their security forces". It can be safely asserted that this group is attempting to reiterate its relevance within the multitude of terrorist organizations that operate in that part of the world and positioning itself for the inevitable power struggle that is sure to continue in the wake that is left behind after Osama bin Laden's death.

Although they share the name Taliban, which is an Arabic word meaning "one who is seeking knowledge", the TTP should not be confused with the Afghan Taliban despite similar tactics and common resistance to western occupation of Afghanistan and it's influence in Pakistan. Tactics associated with the TTP have included the use of IEDs, complex ambushes, kidnappings, and suicide bombers against government targets. This group receives its funding through several sources in Pakistan, Afghanistan and foreign contributors. The vast production of opium poppies and heroin in Afghanistan, corrupt Afghan and Pakistani officials complicit in their support of terrorist groups in the region and Saudi Arabian charities are but a few of the most notable monetary contributors toward their cause. Income from these charities makes its way to Southwest Asia intended to directly support these *mujahedeen* in their fight against western influence or indirectly under the guise of contributions toward education and then funneled to madrassas with a fundamentalist agenda. Their fighters draw inspiration from figures such as Osama bin Laden, Jalaluddin Haqqani, and fundamentalist Islamic clerics that distort the teachings of the Muslim faith by providing false historical and religious precedent in order to inspire others to accomplish their political goals.

Despite being geographically located on the other side of the world, the TTP seeks to replicate the global reach of Al-Qaeda and has to some extent, achieved success, with the failed Times Square bombing attempted by Faisel Shahzad, identified as a TTP operative. Following this attempt, the TTP was added to the State Department list of FTO's. Although the attack was never carried out due to a faulty fuse within the bomb's detonation system, it could still be viewed as a victory because of how close it actually came to succeeding. Faisel Shahzad, was, by most accounts, living the American dream. Married, with two children, a modest condominium in the suburbs of Connecticut, working as a financial analyst while struggling with the more mundane aspects of life that many Americans contend with on a daily basis. Yet, at some point he made contact with extremist agents and was converted to their radical interpretations of Islamic fundamentalism. Enough that he was compelled to visit his ancestral birthplace of Pakistan and seek strategic guidance and training at a TTP training camp in Waziristan. Upon completion of several weeks of this training he had received enough of a rudimentary knowledge about bomb-making that he was able to return to the U.S., construct a vehicle bomb, select a high profile location that would ensure maximum casualties as well as satisfy the terrorist requirement of geographical significance, arm the device, and walk away. Were it not for a series of fortunate events for investigators, Faisel Shahzad would have never been apprehended as he was just moments away from boarding a flight destined for Islamabad.

The real threat is the potential that others with similar backgrounds as Shahzad could also be manipulated to the point where they would be willing to sacrifice their personal lives for an extremist cause. Realizing the inherent dangers associated with operating as a group, even as small as a cell, terrorist organizations are now encouraging "lone-wolf" operations to conduct acts of terrorism aimed at American interests around the world.[36] These acts are extremely difficult for intelligence agencies to predict and prevent because there is often no paper trail to follow or dialogue to be intercepted. All that is required is one individual to be inspired by an extremist message and the rest is limited only by his imagination. This message appears to have resounded within in at least one man, an Ethiopian immigrant and U.S. Marine Corps Reservist of Muslim faith, who was apprehended in Arlington National Cemetery with Taliban propaganda and five pounds of inert ammonium nitrate.[37]

Following the death of Osama bin Laden and to a lesser extent, the other high ranking members of terror organizations Islamic terror groups around the world have sought to capitalize on the media attention surrounding these events by renewing their calls for Jihad and promising that holy vengeance will soon follow. The lieutenants and captains of these organizations are being promoted through the ranks of their respective organizations through attrition with each death of a previous commander and seek to make their mark on the global stage of terrorism with a media blitz comparable to a movie mogul endorsing the latest Hollywood blockbuster.

Omar Khalid Khorasani, who is considered to be a high ranking commander of Tehrik-e Taliban Pakistan forces in the FATA agreed to an interview with the Reuters news agency in 2010, answering questions posed by the service and recording his responses to DVD, increasing the likelihood that his likeness and message would be televised and made available on the internet.[38] Khorasani claimed that the group was still actively seeking to strike US targets outside of Pakistan and prove to the world and other terror groups that they alone would be capable of conducting operations with a global reach that has, thus far, only been achieved by Al-Qaeda. This sort of rhetoric achieves several media goals for the TTP. First, it makes clear that the goal of establishing a Sharia governed nation under the control of the Taliban has not perished along with the most prominent terror leader in history. Second, this statement reaffirms to the organizations agents, followers, and supporters that their cause is still being aggressively pursued by all cells and that ongoing operational plans, support and most importantly, funding must continue. Third, this statement from a terror leader reinforces the basic message that makes terrorism so terrifying, that the terrorist will never accept defeat and is capable of striking anywhere. The terrorists' dedication to their cause is evident by what is not said- to Khorasani's right sits a young boy draped with ammunition and armed with a Kalashnikov assault rifle. The significance is clear that this group is prepared to continue this war for generations to come.

Khorasani is not alone in his attempt to squeeze a media victory from the death of bin Laden. The head of the little known but violent 313 Brigade of the Harkatul Jihad al Islami, Ilyas Kashmiri, convened a meeting of leaders within the TTP and proposed the creation of the Laskhar-e-Osama, "Army of Osama", which would be tasked with conducting suicide missions throughout Pakistan. This group was to target the embassies and diplomats of several nations, including Saudi Arabia, China, and the United States. Intelligence reports have surfaced that this group has attempted to procure large amounts of poison to be used to contaminate the food supplies of NATO troops in the region.[39] Although there are conflicting reports that Kashmiri was killed in a US drone strike it is still likely that the plans that he set into motion would continue due to the likelihood that success in these endeavors would inevitably result in the strong media attention that a fledgling terror group would require in order to thrive. A victory for any of the jihadist terror collectives is a victory for all due to the impact of terrorism in the media and propaganda disseminated by these organizations. Their methods and goals are so similar that often the Western media will not differentiate between them, labeling them under "catch-all" terms such as Taliban, Islamic terrorists, or the ever-present Al-Qaeda.

The Pakistani military, which is often perceived as being more powerful than the civilian government of Pakistan, and rumored to be shielding some activities of the terror groups that have taken refuge on its soil has not remained silent throughout the country's recent turmoil. In a long-winded press release by the Inter-Services Public Relations wing of Pakistan's military, the members of the 139th Corps Commanders Conference, presided over by General Ashfaq Parvez Kayani, had convened in the wake of bin Laden's death and was referring to the mission as the "Abottabad incident" and that it had consequently resulted in the loss of innocent lives, implying that the United States was indirectly responsible for the subsequent Taliban response to OBL's death.[40] This message further highlights an ever-increasing rift between the Pakistani Army and the civilian government that is attempting to maintain a balance between the historical role and due reverence afforded to the military and the demands of the West, who have a significant and continuing stake in Afghanistan. The conference reiterated the need of the Pakistani Army for economic rather than military aid from the United States, which could be inferred that expenditures would then be assigned by the military without the restrictions of Western oversight. In fact, Western contributions toward counterterrorism efforts in Pakistan, which have been estimated at almost $15 billion in the last decade, only about US $1.4 billion has actually trickled down to the Army while the remaining amount has been appropriated by the civilian government of Pakistan for "budgetary support".

The roots between the Army of Pakistan and the tribesmen that comprise, the Taliban, TTP, and Al-Qaeda run deep and are heavily intertwined. In spite of this, the United States and Pakistan remain reluctant partners in the War on Terror. Pakistan is enjoying the monetary and military benefits that a Western partnership provides while the U.S. desires stability in a nuclear-armed yet fragile region. Anything less than success in Afghanistan and Pakistan threatens to discredit NATO and invite the current model for terrorism to be replicated in other, similarly dysfunctional regions of the world.

As long as the business of terrorism remains an effective tool for those that choose to participate in its conduct it will continue. Factions will splinter, as leaders within these groups attempt to make a name for themselves in their respective region with the goal of rising to prominence on the world stage. The most dangerous course of action would be for these offshoots to determine that they can only be distinguished from their peer organizations through the execution of increasingly violent and spectacular attacks in an attempt to garner media attention. Regardless of the organization that the terrorist is affiliated, the message remains the same. Those who choose to practice it regard terrorism as a means to an end. The threats of violence and the targeting of a nation's government, military, and civilian entities will continue because it has proven effective in the past.

In his final days, bin Laden cautioned AQ offshoots against using the brand name so as not to dry up popular support from constituents disillusioned with their tactics and failures. Regardless of the title, the most hardcore of religious fundamentalist groups share the desire for the expulsion of Western influences from Islamic lands while importing an ultraconserative vision of the religion. In an Al-Qaeda statement announcing the appointment of Aymen al-Zawahiri as the recognized leader of the group, Al-Qaeda took the opportunity to announce that it shared universal goals and was united with other terror organizations around the globe. By citing common hardships shared with embattled states such as Somalia, Chechnya, and the Palestinian territories Al-Qaeda claimed that it "will remain on the path of righteousness as a coherent, solid, cemented rank, with hearts of affinity, and under one wholesome banner, battling one enemy. Even if the names may vary, there is no failing, no hesitation, no surrender."[41]

8
Disaster Theory

The most dangerous course of action for a terror operation would involve attacks using improvised weapons of mass destruction or cyber terrorism upon regional infrastructure. These attacks are likely to have significant impact on human life and recovery. Within each jurisdiction in the United States there is an emergency management apparatus in place that, when integrated properly, is able to cooperate with state and federal disaster management assets. Well in advance of any terror attack there exist a number of preparedness measures that are already in place for natural disasters (hurricane, flood) or industrial accidents (chemical spill, gas leak) that can also be applied to disaster management due to a terror attack.

There are many factors to take into account when considering the most important part of the disaster planning process. One has to consider the most likely emergencies to affect a given jurisdiction, available resources, the level of experience of responders, and the support of the local government among them. But, at its core, successful disaster management can be traced back to a solid plan that is established and rehearsed well in advance of the time that it must be employed. This plan will have no merit without the approval of the local government and implementation of the plan as an authoritative document. Approval often cannot be gained solely on the merits of the plan and implementation, key to its success, will require the support of the community. One important strategy in the population formulation stage is to seek opportunities to work with other stakeholder groups to formulate policies that have a strong chance of being adopted and implemented.[42] There are many competing interests that complicate the formal institutionalization of an emergency operations plan (EOP) within a community.

Leaders in local industry, government, public organizations, and civic groups all have a role to play in the mobilization of their factions in support of plans that would promote their own specific interests thus benefitting the community as a whole. It is these stakeholders that will influence what is eventually accepted as jurisdictional policy and that is why it is critical to network with these contacts and identify mutual concerns that affect both parties. Essentially, the behind-the-scenes politicking is almost as important to the successful adoption of an EOP as the soundness of the plan. The same groups that supported the adoption of policy must then be counted as allies in order to enforce the implementation of the EOP. It will be this relatively small group of leaders that will mobilize the efforts of the community in support of the plan. No plan is perfect; however having a plan that is recognized as the authoritative framework for an disaster response and is actually put to use in a scenario will alleviate much of the confusion that arises during a disaster.

Over time, those who study the science of disaster have developed four fundamental theories that attempt to define man's views on the subject around the world. In an effort to categorize these theories they have been labeled as either acts of fate (or resulting from the will of a Deity), acts of nature, the combined effects arisen from the interaction of nature and society, and social construction. If one were pay attention to the media it would seem that there is a new disastrous event either unfolding or pending almost daily. Increasingly, the media has focused on such naturally occurring weather or geological phenomena as hurricanes, tornadoes, earthquakes, tsunamis, and wildfires that ravage the nations of the earth. Such acts of nature can account for the untold loss of lives and damage that are visited upon our planet with such regular occurrence that they are expected, if not accepted as a naturally occurring fact of life. These events are accepted as the norm and typically planned for in advance by most emergency response agencies.

In our superstitious past the events that unfolded as a result of angry gods or the retribution of nature were thought to be self-inflicted. It may have seemed that we were suffering the wrath of God for some imagined slight or transgression. Even in modern times some of these beliefs persist and can be attributed to the fact that most people hold faith in some form of higher being. This higher form would hold judgment over each of us one day and could conceivably be disappointed in our failures. A minority of the population may take this conviction a step further by believing that this higher power demonstrates his displeasure through karmic acts of nature designed to be a visible symbol of his will on earth. For example, following the Kashmir, Pakistan earthquake of 2005 which was responsible for the deaths of an estimated 79,000 people, some Islamic religious leaders took to the streets and airwaves claiming that the disaster was the divine retribution of Allah for Pakistan's' collaboration with the West. However, if one were to believe that the disaster was God's will then one would approach the concept of risk mitigation entirely differently, perhaps choosing to do nothing at all in the face of His will. Of course, to many, these are outdated beliefs and largely written off as ignorance or superstition under the enlightenment of reason and science. Through the many centuries of combined study and application of informed reason we understand that many of these naturally occurring disasters are the continuing process of the earth "settling" and no amount of penance will influence the outcome of these events. Our sins as humanity are not the cause of these disasters nor are the disasters themselves the resulting effect of our failures.

At times, it may appear that man's interactions with nature may appear clumsy and deserving of the retribution that nature visits upon us in our moments of failure. Mans' dealings with potentially dangerous technologies may be partially to blame for some disastrous events that have befallen us. Hazardous materials that are not carefully safeguarded or handled in accordance with published safety standards pose a risk to all who come into contact with them. Chemical pollution deriving from the processing industry is known to pollute our waters, hazardous biological materials- leftovers from improperly disposed hospital waste are but two examples of the improper interaction of nature and society. Combine the destructive wrath of Mother Nature with the flawed attempts of man to better our lives through technology and the potential exists for cataclysm. One has only to consider the after effects of the citizens of Japan, still reeling from the failure of the Fukushima Nuclear Power Plant following a tsunami in 2011 for an example of the social construction theory of disaster.

Perhaps population growth is to blame for the steady rise in the number of disaster related deaths in the last half century? While it is certainly accurate that there are simply more of us than there were a century ago, after all the population has increased by 4 billion people over the last 60 years with almost half living and working in urban environments. It could be said that this urbanization is a contributing factor in the social vulnerability of these segments of the population because of our increased exposure to technological and industrial hazards. The law of probability is not solely to blame for the growing number of technology related accidents in recent years. The population has developed a sort of "risk-denial" apparent in our casual indifference to risky behaviors and the choices that we make with regards to our places of residence or employment. Even our choices of recreational activities have grown more dangerous, reflecting our laissez-faire attitudes toward risk. The number and many different types of toxic materials that are now a part of our everyday lives has grown exponentially, so much that we are no longer impressed by the sight of nuclear plant cooling towers or industrial facility smoke stacks on the horizon. Our dependence on fossil fuel sources is a direct contributor to the amount of air, water and thermal pollution throughout the world. Our attempts to wean ourselves off of those sources by developing clean energy such as nuclear power carry with them the potential for catastrophe if mismanaged. Risk is an inherent part of our interaction with nature. While attempts to alleviate it may succeed, risk may be unavoidable. That is not to say that we should just give up or use inherent risk as an excuse to assume greater risk than necessary. We should recognize that by recognizing the potential for disaster that we also recognize an opportunity to influence the outcome of such events through our actions.

It is not only the accidental oversight or negligent mishandling of materials that pose a threat to man, but the intentional misuse of technology for the purposes of terrorism or anarchy. Terrorism is a proven tool of power and influence for those who practice it. This tool has proven so effective that it will not go away. To say that one will eliminate terrorism is akin to saying that crime can be eliminated. Terroristic events are driven by societal factors and are conducted with the purpose of influencing the actions of others, usually to achieve a political motive. Attempts by small, disaffected persons to influence the actions of a much larger group have existed for centuries and have proven largely successful while increasingly violent measures have been employed in order to garner worldwide attention to the cause. Chemical and biological agents have been employed with only radioactive material as yet elusive to the rank-and-file terrorist organizations. Terrorist attacks that wound or kill hundreds such as the 2008 Mumbai attacks or thousands as in 9/11 were so successful, from the terrorist, point of view, that it is inevitable that they will be used to inspire future generations of extremists who will attempt to match or outdo these achievements. For all the effect they have on inspiring other acts of terror they impact the victims just as strongly, influencing the response of the impacted government and for this they deserve a classification that is all their own.

Though the theories of disaster could be argued from different viewpoints the fact remains that there will be consequences following these events. One's perception of the root cause may affect the preparation and reaction to the disaster. While it would establish a unity of effort if all affected parties were to agree on the theory of disaster, such an accord is not necessary to prepare an effective response. It is, however, important to recognize the hazards that we choose to accept in the course of our lives. In fact, we increasingly put ourselves at risk for disaster through our own choices and risky attitudes. The choice to live in an area known for seasonal flooding or frequent mudslides can be mitigated somewhat but the hazard can never be fully eliminated. As our everyday lives become dependent upon technology in an increasingly urbanized world we become desensitized to the perils that exist in our lives, both natural and manmade. The dangers associated with the choice to live or work in an inherently hazardous environment can be diminished through awareness, protective materials, or safety protocols but humans are a flawed species. Wherever we are present, so too is the potential for disaster.

Often, in the course of discussions involving major traumatic events that occur to individuals, groups, cities and nations the terms "hazards, emergencies, disasters, and catastrophes" are used interchangeably without any real understanding of the meaning of the words or their proper usage. The evening news is often one of the worst offenders, with anchors and producers that oftentimes sensationalize stories in the name of increased viewership and ratings. In the interest of standardization, it is important for all those involved in the contingency planning and response to a crisis to use the same terminology and with a common understanding of these terms in order to better able to recognize and define the nature of these scenarios.

Hazards pose a potential threat that can be mitigated by identifying, anticipating and implementing risk mitigation measures, also known as hazard adjustment. These are threats that have been previously identified as posing a risk should extenuating natural or man-made events occur. Hazards can be further sub-categorized as natural, technological, or adversarial. Natural, obviously are naturally occurring phenomena that pose a threat either by themselves or in combination with technological or adversarial hazards could potentially bring harm. Floods and wildfires have the potential to interact with technological hazards creating disasters. Technological hazards involve anything that is man-made and without mitigating safety measures could potentially cause harm. Examples include chemical processing facilities and nuclear energy plants. Finally, adversarial hazards are disasters that are initiated by humans and can include acts of terrorism and sabotage.

Emergencies occur with a relative frequency, at least often enough that they are generally predictable and can be effectively managed with local resources and agencies. Without understating the danger to the victims of these events, these scenarios are fairly routine and can be managed through standardized protocols. Examples of emergencies include vehicle accidents, structural fires, ruptured natural gas lines, traumatic injury, and cardiac crises. Most often, local emergency services personnel, fire departments, and police agencies are able to successfully resolve these events.

Disasters are the culmination of the actual occurrence of an event that produces significant casualties and/or damage at a level that exceeds a community ability to cope with the resulting consequences. These incidents exceed the ability of a jurisdiction to effectively manage the aftermath requiring additional resources from outside of the community in order to bring the situation under control. In order to provide a common frame of reference, some examples of disasters that are commonly known include the 1986 Space Shuttle Challenger explosion which killed seven crew members and caused NASA to suspend all shuttle flights for two years, the 1995 bombing of the Alfred P. Murrah Federal Building in Oklahoma which claimed 168 lives and involved recovery efforts from local, state, and federal agencies, severe flooding in New Mexico that occurred in late June of 2012 and was formally declared a disaster by the President making those affected eligible for federal funds to supplement disaster recovery efforts, multiple wildfires that converged to plague several counties and involved multiple emergency relief teams from the state of Oklahoma in August 2012, and Hurricane Isaac, a Category 1 hurricane that left eight dead and thousands without electricity across three states.

The term "catastrophe" should be reserved for only the most severe events, those that have a profound impact on several states and possibly countries. The disaster management requirements to successfully orchestrate and execute recovery efforts will exceed the resources of many local jurisdictions and will disrupt the continuity of many local operations. Examples of these sorts of events may be known worldwide due to the significant numbers of casualties, damage to infrastructure, and economic impact to the regions involved. This list would include the 1986 Chernobyl Nuclear Reactor accident, which resulted in approximately 30 radiation related deaths within days of the event, affected countless thousands of others due to radiation fallout and forced the resettlement of an entire population, the Bhopal India chemical accident in which pesticide was leaked from a processing plant instant killing 3,800 people and thousands more in the weeks and months that followed, 2005's Hurricane Katrina which is arguably one of the most devastating natural disasters in U.S. history, the September 11, 2001 terrorist attacks on America that resulted in thousands of deaths across the nation and sparked two wars involving countries from around the globe, and the 2011 Japanese earthquake which caused a tsunami leading to the rupture of the Fukushima nuclear power facility in an almost perfect confluence of events whose impact affected, in some way, most countries around the globe.

Many changes abound in the field of emergency management with advances in technology, population expansion, and the shifting winds of politics and economics. These changes include how policy is written, how research is conducted, and how responses are being handled. Questions are brought to light such as, are the four fundamental concepts of emergency management (preparedness, mitigation, response and recovery) truly guiding in today's modern world or is it out dated? There is a delicate balance in finding the right level of emergency management and how much of it plays into terrorism and the Department of Homeland Security. Some argue that "Homeland security is a step back from the proactive approaches being recommended today, and it de-emphasizes all hazards other than terrorism".[43] Research is changing and students in academic research are finding there is more to the larger picture than many modern day professionals want to see in the world around them. Many have forgotten the past and only focus on the present, and on occasion the future. Typically, however, these focuses on the future are derived from some kind of catastrophic event having taken place that is forcing them to see a problem or error in the system they have come to rely on. They react to changes in society and bureaucratic changes in government. In fact, the government takes more control of situations and decisions after a disaster has occurred. In trying to come up with answers to how society reacts, how disasters happen, and a variety of other reasons, assumptions and reactions that occur before, during and after a catastrophe, professionals and scholars alike have sought to create one theory about disaster; a "silver bullet", one answer fits all approach, that this will answer specific questions. Unfortunately, the questions are not specific enough to develop a theory. In order to determine what a "disaster theory" might mean or look like, two things must be defined; what is a disaster and what is a theory. An understanding of the two major components of the concept, and an understanding of where the research has come from, can then lead toward a more definitive answer, one that should be strived for and studied, but may never be reached.

To start, theory can be defined, by dictionary definition, as an "explanation based on scientific study and reasoning". However theory can also be arguably defined in other ways. McEntire suggests two different ways of looking at theory; one is that theory is an explanation of preferred or ideal conditions for the society that lives in the world around us. This simply means, from an emergency management perspective, that society does not desire to have devastating disasters that will cost thousands in currency and in lives, but a life free from them. It also suggests that steps be taken to mitigate these disasters from happening, and when they do, working towards a more managed response and recovery effort as compared to the haphazard responses seen in from the past. "Another meaning of theory relates to the entire body of knowledge available in the given discipline", which would tend to fall more in line with a disaster theory as it encompasses many other areas, not just a focus on one specific incident or entity. This is done through a collection of data, concepts, principles and statistics from various areas in society and while there may not be one particular system in place to bring this together under one heading, to find a theory, much research from many areas is required. The research on disaster tends to focus on the behavior of individuals and groups under conditions of stress. While many different sources need to be considered, it is important to note where the information comes from and the biases within it.

The media has one of the largest impacts not only on how incidents and disasters are portrayed at the time of incident, but they also have a heavy impact on how incidents will be remembered. They can frame the incident in one fashion then refocus the blame if they end up being wrong. Hurricane Katrina was an example of this as the national television reportage largely defined the New Orleans catastrophe, particularly since there was no significant federal or state presence in the city for days after the flooding. Only through proper research from more than one source can the truth be derived. Media also has a way of bringing to everyone's attention "how bad it is" by talking to the citizen whom is completely devastated by the disaster. Their quote ends up being the explanation for how bad things are. They can also make the disaster appear to have effected one area of the region and not another. Following the 1993 Braer oil spill of the coast of Scotland the media framed the spill as having a horrible affect on the environment, thus ignoring the human element and the health effects the spill had on those living in the area even though the public health effects were perhaps the most distinctive and significant aspect of the disaster. These media accounts inevitably build what is later studied as the history behind a disaster and the reaction to it.

Students of disaster will have a naturally different outlook and understanding based on their own experiences, observations and research. Goltz explains that in order to understand emergent groups and actions before, during and after disasters, studies of "human interest" articles are more appropriate than articles derived from media motivation.[44] Aside from media outlets, Goltz points out there are two types of sources for information on a disaster. The first is an official source, or one that has an emergency period function. These are the outlets to the media and journalists for their data. The second source is the unofficial source, or "actors" in the incident such as businessmen, and labor unions who do not have any predetermined emergency period function. This is not to suggest that media motivated articles and archives be discarded from research, rather one must understand that they are opinionated and should collect other data to support or deny their findings.

Quarantelli's opening remark, in his writing "Disaster Studies: An Analysis of the Social Historical Factors Affecting the Development of Research in the Area" suggests that not enough research, and data collection has been done in this field. "Almost nothing has been written about the social historical emergence and development of social and behavioral research on disasters."[45] A historical look on how the research was conducted reveals the thought process behind it. During the Cold War, most of the research conducted was supported by the military. This research was based off of wartime assumptions that were, for the time, appropriate given the major threat in the world around the United States. Another reason for this was the practice of appointing Civil Defense Directors who were former high ranking generals and admirals from the military. Their view was mainly but that of the military and wartime threats to the country, there was little view or understanding of natural disasters or society.

Disaster, much like the word "emergency" is difficult to describe. Emergency management has traditionally taken the role of handling disasters from a natural disaster standpoint. Natural disasters created by an ever-changing Earth, are not criminal in nature, they are merely changes in the Earth's rotation, and its environment. "Disasters are clearly periods in which people experience a vast spectrum of intense emotions–anxiety, fear, terror, loss, grief, gratitude, anger, frustration, relief, and resignation–in all their shadings and intensities".[46] Birkland also points out there is a human "dread" of disaster. What is viewed as a disaster to one group may not be a disaster to the entire society. Also in question, is if disaster is something naturally occurring (earthquake, flooding, volcanic activity, etc.) or is it something created by human society and something avoidable.

There are even different views of emergencies. In the cold war era, emergencies were viewed as attacks on the United States by the Soviet Union or China. Many disaster models for planning and thinking were based on military concepts that did not work to address the issues of naturally occurring events such as mass flooding. In the last several years, there has been a digression away from a military view of enemy attack, and a start towards an "all hazards" approach was created. Then as later seen, this view was all but lost with the movement of the Federal Emergency Management Agency being shifted under the Department of Homeland Security in 2003, where the view of a disaster once again came from the stand point of a possible attack; a terrorist attack. An exercise known as Hurricane Pam would point out the weaknesses in emergency planning along the gulf coast, making Hurricane Katrina a reality before even hitting landfall in late August of 2005. This would also show a weakness in the "all hazards" system, pointing to too much focus on terrorism.

Hurricanes are viewed as disasters, but they also create larger disasters, emergencies and other problems. According to the hearing before the committee on Homeland Security and Governmental Affairs entitled "Hurricane Katrina in New Orleans: A Flooded City, A Chaotic Response" eyewitnesses recounted the Superdome as being its own disaster. Thousands of children, along with adults, were packed into the superdome, which quickly lost its ability to remain a sanitary living environment. Food and water supplies ran out early on in the first few days following Hurricane Katrina's landfall, causing a plan to evacuate and relocate to be created. This plan was, however, shut down in short order, when the National Guard reported intelligence of a possible riot in the superdome and that they would not stay to protect the workers. FEMA workers followed suit and left the superdome. The disaster for those in the superdome was not the hurricane itself, but the conditions created for them where they sought refuge.

Yet another view on disaster is the reaction by Miami-Dade County prior to Hurricane Frances making landfall in 2004. Before landfall, the government declared a state of emergency and was added to the list of affected counties provided by the Governor of Florida to the President of the United States. A declaration was issued by the President prior to the hurricane making landfall to help ensure that needed supplies, materials, personnel and other needed resources were in the area and ready to help when the hurricane hit. When Frances did make landfall, Miami-Dade County suffered little impact; the area showed no significant flooding and only received 47 mile per hour winds yet the county and the citizens living in it took advantage of the money provided by the federal government to pay for what little damage (in comparison) they suffered. The truth is the hurricane's eye made landfall some 50 miles north of the county.

Governments have an impact on how disasters are defined and viewed. Government is often detached from certain areas of society and are unable to care for the ecological needs of those societies. Ultimately, it is some decision-making authority that determines the impact of disasters on marginal communities. The impacts of Hurricane Andrew on local fishing communities in Florida and Louisiana are direct examples of this. The storm destroyed habitats, causing fishing areas to become useless to the fisherman who used them to survive. As a result some needs dropped in demand like the bait required to fish and there was a large fear that there would be a loss of jobs. In Florida, the fishing community had a large economic impact on the region, but the state failed to support it properly after the hurricane. The Florida Government made decisions on the industry based on their own opinions and idea of quotas without consulting the users of the industry, while in Louisiana the government listened to its people and helped the fishing industry back to its feet. This was a result of a lack of interest in preparing for hurricanes and understanding the resulting disaster. It depends on the amount, type and direction of pressure on the government to make a decision. They have less understanding of naturally occurring disasters, so there may be a lack of understanding that in fact the disaster created is one based on decisions made after an incident has occurred, and not the incident itself.

The government however is not always responsible for the after effects of an incident, leading to a disaster. Disasters impact different social classes differently. Many times society fails to see the issues at hand before they happen. "Critical to discerning the nature of disasters, then, is an appreciation of the ways in which human systems place people at risk in relation to each other and to their environment, a causal relationship that can best be understood in terms of an individual's, household's, community's or society's vulnerability".[47] The issues come from various areas. Those with very high economical and political status in their community might think they are safeguarded from the rigors of coping with disaster, because they can afford it or have someone else deal with it for them. For this group in society, packing up and leaving may be an option, and then returning once things have been repaired, therefore not viewing an incident as a disaster. On the other end of the spectrum is the at-risk population; elders, the poor, and those with health and mental disabilities who are not in a position to leave their homes or take care of themselves should something happen. To them, a simple house fire that destroys all their worldly possessions and the only food they had can be a disaster. Disaster is based upon perception and represents a disturbance of the normal group and financial patterns of a society. Crisis is synonymous with disaster, and a disaster is probably the event which causes utmost societal disorder and displacement. Disasters have functional and dysfunctional consequences, but who draws the line and determines when things go wrong?

Yet another view that makes defining disaster even harder is the differences in views between responders, decision makers, victims, and the onlooker. In looking at the tragic industrial accident in Bhopal, India in 1984, the perception of the "disaster" was drastically different from the victims and the responders trying to contain the damage, and keep the problem from spreading any further into the community. To the outside eye, looking in on the "disaster" but not impacted by it, things may appear to be normal, or returning to normal following a disaster. They fail to see those who are still suffering from the impacts of the disaster, or in other areas, depending on government input and the socioeconomic structure, projects will be abandon and areas will look like they did when the disaster happened, causing the outside viewer to think that everything is fine.

Society rationalizes what they have been through and the actions that they have taken. Organized people are more concerned with practical action. Again another barrier to defining disaster theory then becomes the study of individual behaviors within society. "There will be a tendency for social scientists to be biased towards rationality by virtue of their training and purposes".[48] There is also the problem of command and control on human systems. It is a fact that people resent attempts to command or control them and makes understanding individual reactions and responses to so called "disasters" that much more important. To understand where a disaster comes from, emergency managers must understand human reactions to the things happening around them, and why humans react the way that they do. Questions must be asked about these human systems, but must avoid an overlying problem in research, that research users tend to ask the wrong questions.

Disaster is based on perceptions, and what people perceive to be devastating to them or a society. Disaster is, in part, determined by sociological contexts. With so many variables applied to the field of emergency management, the professional emergency manager will find it difficult to come to a conclusion on what "disaster theory" is. It is, however, a goal worthy of achievement. The past will not be so easily ignored, the practices of emergency management will continue to change and develop, and a better understanding of society and disasters can be obtained. More important to society today that the specific pursuit of one specific disaster theory is the research and lessons learned from the data collected. Disasters are almost always characterized by a lack of information.

In order to appreciate how population trends contribute to social vulnerability and demand special consideration from emergency managers and disaster responders, one must consider how certain sections of each the public will be affected disproportionately. Factors such as income, ethnicity, or economic viability play a part in contributing to the vulnerability of the affected segment of the population. Segments of the population will be impacted to a greater or lesser degree during a disaster due to these dynamics. Social vulnerability is a reference to a group susceptibility to behavioral changes and the potential for extreme events to alter the behavior of a specified group. Emergency managers must be aware of the demographics of their respective communities in order to be able to address vulnerabilities related to social constraints.

Levels of social vulnerability can vary widely across populations and will create an extra level of complication to emergency operations plans if not seriously considered. Segments of the population most likely to be adversely affected by high levels of social vulnerability must be identified and assessed during EOP development. Losses due to disaster are known to increase due to contributing factors such as population growth, urbanization, economic growth, and social expectations. Age, education, economic stability, and ethnicity are all likely to play a significant role in the behavioral trends of disaster, which affects the EOP concept. These demographic predictors have a proven correlation to the areas that a group has chosen to settle and assume the risks associated with that geographic environment. Those without resources or stable economic options become socially vulnerable and are often limited to residential selections in high-risk areas. These groups are most likely to experience property damage or incur casualties during a disaster because of their social vulnerability and are the least likely to be able to influence the political or economic factors that contribute to their hazard vulnerability.

While this can all be daunting for the emergency manager to consider, there are tools available to assist planners in understanding different social and demographic trends. The Hazards and Vulnerability Institute maintains a social vulnerability index for the United States which measures the exposure of counties to environmental hazards by providing visual comparisons of U.S. counties preparedness and response capabilities while providing suggestions for the more efficient management of resources.[49] The NOAA's Spatial Trends in Coastal Socioeconomics website provides tools to help better understand the social aspects of vulnerability. This tool works by providing planners reports and census data to be used in analysis during EOP development.[50] There is also the NOAA's Coastal County Snapshots, which allows users to analyze a range of demographic data and includes information on critical facilities and land usage information.[51] Because emergency managers cannot directly influence the factors of social vulnerability they must have access to accurate demographical data related to these predictors when preparing the emergency operations plan.

The theories behind why disasters occur and our reaction to them establish the ultimate outcome and how it is viewed within a historical context. Government response to disasters such as the Exxon Valdez oil spill and Hurricane Katrina are remembered in a significantly less favorable light than the response to the British Petroleum Deepwater Horizon oil spill or the terror attacks of 9/11. The importance of social demographics within the affected area, practiced response, legislative agreements, and use of the media to communicate with the populace during and long after the event determine whether the response was a success or failure. This will in turn factor into the post economic recovery timetable, which is an excellent indicator of trade and industry resurgence, critical to the healing process of the affected region. Finally, effective communication, cooperation, and trust between federal, state, local agencies and the civilian populace before the event is the deciding factor in the successful recovery in the aftermath of disaster.

9
The Attack Schematic

The last decade has witnessed an escalation in the number of attacks attributed to terrorism in many countries around the globe. Terrorism has occurred in the United States, Russia, England, Pakistan, Yemen, Saudi Arabia, Mexico... the list is nearly without end. While the actors conducting these attacks differ from region and conflict, many of their methods do not. The methods used by terrorists in the attack and planning processes can be identified and catalogued in an effort to pinpoint weaknesses and lessen their effects. There are many organizations capable of executing a terrorist operation, both state-sponsored and non-state actors, groups or individuals. There are a variety of motivations and the process by which they build up to the point of the radicalized behaviors that come before the attack. What does not change is that once the decision has been made to carry out the mission, the planning processes are remarkably similar. A terrorist attack does not begin at the point of the incident. Those planning such an attack follow a somewhat routine planning method, which is subject to detection by those who know what to watch for. Recognizing these tactics and the behaviors commonly associated with them, allows for one to intervene, and possibly disrupt, the execution of the mission.

Target selection is usually the first in a series of steps leading up to the attack. A list will be composed and potential targets will be reduced based upon suitability and legitimacy until a primary is left upon which to focus. Often, the method of attack has been predetermined based upon available resources, and target selection must then be limited to vulnerabilities based on the attack method. Sometimes, the target is selected first, and the resources are gathered based on operational requirements. This phase of the operation is subject to fluidity and the amount of time required can often vary. Depending on the factors of difficulty and resource availability the mission planning sequence can last from hours to weeks to years.

It is common for those involved in planning an operation to conduct a exhaustive reconnaissance of likely targets in order to ascertain the security procedures and estimate whether they have the capability to successfully conduct the operation. In the event that the target security exceeds the capabilities of the attacking group, that target is then crossed off the list in favor of an alternate. This is the reconnaissance and surveillance stage of the operation and is conducted and in the most successful terrorist operations, it is conducted all the way through mission execution.

Once the target has been decided upon, surveillance will continue, focusing on any information not gathered during the initial observation. For example, surveillance of a facility will necessitate detailed information of passive electronic security measures, structural integrity of the facility, guard or employee alertness, and other routines that are likely to be present during the attack. If personnel were the targets then it would be necessary to identify all points along that individual's common routine. Home of residence, place of business, favored recreation areas all will need to be observed. Attackers will favor areas that absolutely must be travelled in order to reach the destination such as choke points along commonly used routes, especially if they can be controlled while also providing effective avenues of escape. While it is more effective, it is not necessary for the individuals participating in mission execution to actually conduct the surveillance. Several individuals may be rotated through this important, and risky, responsibility.

The individuals that carry out the attack will be occupied by developing skills necessary for the mission such as vehicle handling, weaponry, explosives, language and cultural familiarization. Operatives are usually only informed of their portion of the mission and rarely have access to the complete picture of the operation in the interest of operational security. The planning phase usually ends with a rehearsal or walk-through with as much equipment as will not bring unnecessary attention from security forces. Once planning is complete, logistical requirements met, and participants have been trained, surveillance will continue-often with a member of the actual attack team. A mission that has been planned in accordance with the previously listed criteria has a high likelihood of success and is most difficult to abort once set in motion. Whether the target is an individual, a facility, or an event the mission planning cycle remains largely consistent. Knowing these patterns, a trained observer can now disrupt this cycle.

Only in Hollywood, can one depend on the terrorist plot to be stopped just before it is executed. Security and intelligence personnel must be able to identify and intervene before the attack has reached the execution if there is to be any chance of stopping it. After the first round is fired or explosive detonated, there is little anyone can do but react in accordance with procedure in an effort to mitigate the damage. The plan must be identified early on the preoperational phase, before it is ready to be initiated. Without human intelligence or electronic counter surveillance the only way to detect such an attack will be by noticing behaviors and actions associated with the terrorist mission planning sequence. This is especially critical in the case of the so-called "lone wolf" who will plan and attack a target unilaterally and without communications that can be intercepted.

The surveillance period required to gather information on a prospective target is the earliest point that such an attack could be identified solely through behavior. Hollywood has provided a misconception that the terrorist is infallible, an invisible agent of destruction that can appear, execute his mission, and disappear at will, always one step ahead of security forces. In retrospect, it is more common that individuals tasked with conducting surveillance for the purposes of a terrorist operation are rather careless in the conduct of their duties. This presents a significant vulnerability that can be exploited by alert security personnel. As stated before, the most successful terrorist operations incorporate surveillance of the target into all phases of the operation in order to provide the attackers with the most up-to-date and accurate intelligence regarding movements or changes to security posture. Each of these surveillance missions provides an opportunity for detection, reconnaissance teams to be identified, thereby preventing the attack.

The need to gather intelligence through surveillance in preparation for an attack is almost a necessity in most terrorist operations. This, however, does not mean that the terrorist is proficient at this task. Reconnaissance of an objective is an integral part of the mission planning, allowing a group the opportunity to assess the target for worth, strength, and weakness. Although some may argue that with the advent of the Internet, physical reconnaissance is a risk not worth taking, there is simply no substitute for the information gathered from "boots on the ground" in military parlance. This is even truer if the target is mobile, with varying patterns. While certain Internet sites can provide excellent overhead imagery and even 3D views of terrain from every angle, these should only supplement the planning data and not be considered a complete reconnaissance. Internet surveillance alone would not reveal patterns of security personnel, routines of nearby populace or conditions on the ground that would affect the conduct of the mission.

The amount of time spent on the surveillance phase may vary depending upon the complexity of the mission. An operation involving multiple targets to be executed simultaneously, such as the 9/11 attacks, would require that more time be spent on surveillance than an attack focusing on a single soft target. Complex operations may necessitate weeks or months of surveillance whereas simple operations may have just a few minutes devoted to reconnaissance. In any case, almost all terrorist operations require some form of surveillance, and it is during this period that they are vulnerable.

Given that it is such a necessity for the execution of a successful mission, it is still impressive that most terrorist organizations do not spend an adequate amount of time emphasizing this skill to its members, choosing instead to focus on the kinetic phase of the operation. There is a difference between the "art" and the "science" of any skill. Typically the science teaches the fundamentals, the basics that create a foundation to build upon. The art comes after one has mastered those basics and elevates the technique to an art form. Too many want to practice the art without having first mastered the science. It is no different in the world of terrorism, those lacking the technical skill set to adequately practice this trade are often tasked with gathering the intelligence with which the entire operation is planned. Because of this, they are often deployed lacking technique, adequate procedure, and the finesse that comes to define the art. Yet, they are more successful than they reasonable should be because their targets are even less prepared to identify their sloppy tradecraft. Most targets are aware, in some form or fashion that they could be a target but fall into a mindset of self-denial that it could actually happen to them. In short, they are not really looking for the tell tale signs that would give away a poor surveillance operative.

In order to successfully master the art of surveillance one must be able to effectively display the type of behavior appropriate to the situation that he is in. This is not intuitive and often one must perform in a manner that belies their natural human instinct. Counterintelligence experts in government agencies, the military, and undercover officers in law enforcement undergo extensive training that includes practical exercises that are then reviewed through a detailed After-Action Review (AAR) process before being assigned to work with experienced surveillance practitioners. This developed training reinforces the behaviors necessary to be successful at espionage. Most terrorists never receive this sort of in-depth training, especially if they operate in small cells or consider themselves to be lone wolves.

The core of surveillance is being able to observe someone without getting caught. This, in itself, goes contrary to normal human behavior and the practitioner must overcome natural emotions of self-consciousness and the sense that they do not belong. Often their natural instinct misleads them to believe that they have been spotted, when in fact they have not. These feelings will lead them to act out behaviors that are not in keeping with the environment. Behavior such as furtive eye contact, quick movements in order to escape the object of the surveillance, or an unnatural desire to conceal their face, are just some of the behaviors that manifest due to this unnatural activity. An inexperienced operative will find it difficult to overcome these natural tendencies. Even experienced practitioners often feel these emotions, the difference is that they are in a better position to recognize and control their behavior, maintaining a normal manner despite their instinct telling them to run.

Another mistake made by the inexperienced is failing to get into character for the environment they are observing or assuming a persona that does not fit the environment. The purpose of assuming the persona is to supply a "cover" that would explain why they would need to be at that particular location, performing in a behavior commensurate with their status in an attempt to appear normal. When this is performed correctly the practitioner would appear to fit into the mental image of what is routine for that area by an observer. Examples include individuals who would dress in a manner not in keeping with their "cover" social status or behave in a way that their "cover" would not. The most inexperienced do not practice any sort of cover and appear to be present for no other purpose than to watch.

In addition to the observer who appears to serve only that singular purpose, operatives can give themselves away by appearing to mirror the actions of the target. Moving or communicating when the target moves, going out of his way to make contact with the target, or otherwise acting in a suspicious manner are all indicators. Sometimes these individuals will act in a manner inconsistent with their environment that cannot be articulated but rather "sensed" by the target. The natural instincts that leave the observer vulnerable to detection often serve to warn the target that something is out of place. The practice of good situational awareness does not require one to be excessively paranoid or overly concerned with security. Living under the delusion that there are enemies around every corner or that you are being watched all of the time is not only bad for your mental and physical health but it also leads to poor security practices.

A technique that can be of some assistance to potential targets is to identify specific locations that would likely be under surveillance and then focusing efforts on monitoring personnel who would be in a position to observe those areas. The main entry point to secured locations, doors, or even choke points on commonly used routes. Places that provide the best possible visibility over one of these areas, particularly elevated areas that can overwatch a larger area are preferred as targets rarely look up.

Historically, communications between planners and operatives tends to increase as the time for mission execution draws to a close. There tends to be a flurry of activity such as an increase in training, phone calls, email traffic, and money exchanges as the group finalizes arrangements for the mission and escape. Each of these activities leaves telltale signs that could alert authorities.

The acquisition of weapons is another significant vulnerability to the terrorist. Especially egregious are terrorists of the homegrown domestic variety who tend to aspire to conduct large scale, spectacular attacks that are beyond their true capability. It is common for them to attempt to acquire heavy machineguns, rocket-propelled grenade launchers, and improvised explosive devices regardless of their aptitude at the employment of such devices. Recognizing that they do not possess the aptitude to conduct an attack with such weapons they will often reach out to someone who does, rather than settle on a plan of attack that is within their capabilities. Often, the person that they reach out to is an undercover agent or informant for law enforcement. This need to conduct spectacular attacks that will draw attention to their cause consistently undermines their efforts and exposes them to detection.

The recruitment of members to any aspiring terror group is another cause for concern. Would be terrorists operating in the ungoverned regions of the worst parts of Africa, the Middle East, and Asia are far more likely to successfully recruit from the populace and conduct operations than those operating in the West. With each new member comes the increased risk of infiltration and detection. Every recruit is a potential liability and must be screened. Operational security becomes more critical, and likely to become a failing point, as the time for the operation draws near.

False documentation, funding, resources, and the materials needed to conduct an attack are all friction points in the process. Documents are necessary to execute the mundane but necessary details of an operation. From housing to travel to vehicle procurement these documents will be used and must be able to withstand the scrutiny of an attentive landlord to local law enforcement to customs officials alike. Aside from the need to communicate this is the area most likely to result in the detection of these groups. Secure communication poses a significant challenge for the terrorist, a challenge that only gets more difficult with increased distance between operatives and supporters and the technicality of the mission. The acquisition of funds and need to sustain that funding throughout the operation is closely related to communication in that both require contact with an external source. These factors all pose opportunities for civilians and law enforcement to detect a terrorist operation in the mobilization phase.

The many individual skills necessary to execute the attack are unlikely to be possessed by a single person; rather it is a collective effort. This is one reason why so many attempts at lone wolf terrorism have failed over the years. These skills are dependant upon the type of operation being conducted and vary from kinetic specialties such as bomb building or weapons handling to logistical efforts like funding, housing, and transportation to surveillance and planning. If a necessary skill is not present within the group then members may attempt to acquire that skill through illicit or legitimate means. Consider the 9/11 attackers who paid for aviation schooling in order to learn how to pilot commercial aircraft or the terrorist who joins a mosque in order to expand their support base. Each of has these actions presents a necessary risk and an opportunity for detection.

Conducting operations in one's own backyard is relatively easy for groups such as the Tehrik-e Taliban in Pakistan or Somalia's Al-Shabaab because of the proximity to support networks and resources but when a group attempts to venture outside of their homeland they are more likely to fail. Al-Qaeda has, in some ways, been viewed as a failure in recent years because of their inability to replicate the success of 9/11. The need to project dominance by conducting transnational terrorist attacks is a hubristic notion that has led to the failure of many terrorist plots. Most organizations simply cannot plan, resource, or execute complex global terrorism like 9/11 anymore. However, they should not be underestimated, as they are still capable of causing widespread destruction within their own territories and adjacent regions. American interests around the globe are still susceptible as evidenced by the successful attack on the Benghazi consulate in Libya or the Underground bombings in London. The successful execution of these attacks still projects power in the eyes of the terrorist and his supporters as they are able to influence American policies and highlight weaknesses of a superpower.

10
Globalization And The Proliferation Of Weapons Of Mass Destruction

The United States, and to a larger extent the Western world, currently faces a subtle threat greater than it ever has in history. While arguably a military and, despite recent times, economic superpower, the United States has faced difficulty in stemming the tide of weapons proliferation. Due to changing foreign political tides and fluctuating world economy, the potential for an enemy to obtain a weapon of mass destruction (WMD) is greater than ever before. Globalization is a naturally occurring byproduct of an age in which technology, communications, world economy, and the fear of these ultimate weapons converge to create conditions set ripe for the proliferation of WMD's. Arguments to the contrary, by some acknowledged experts, that dismiss warnings of a new era of WMD proliferation as hyperbole too easily brush aside the overtly -stated goals and covert actions of prominent terrorist organizations and hostile regimes. With the growing number of terror groups who espouse an apocalyptic vision, such as Aum Shinrikyo, there are indications that publicity or political concerns may be overridden in favor of mass casualties as a primary goal of these groups. Although there are still hurdles to overcome for these parties, it is naive to believe that information gleaned from the international intelligence community has been interpreted incorrectly on so many levels. The intent in our preparations, which may be viewed as paranoia by the uninformed, is not to be caught unaware, as we were on 9/11.

During World War II several of the warring nations were seeking to produce an atomic weapon. This weapon would change the course of the war in the favor of whoever attained its power and unleashed it first. As we know, the United States won this vital race (Germany thankfully was overwhelmed and occupied before she could attain the weapon) and unleashed two atomic weapons on Japan forcing her surrender, however Germany did proliferate its secrets, by launching, a few weeks before the end of the war in Europe, a submarine filled with uranium and parts, along with its research to Japan. Luckily this submarine never completed its mission. This is the first example of proliferation. Post World War II existed a Cold War in which such weapons where controlled by nations states such as the US, USSR and UK. The mutually assured destruction scenario kept the threat of Nuclear War at bay all the way until the fall of the Berlin Wall and the end of the Soviet superpower.

There was so much chaos and uncertainty at that time that I believe that, in some way, that chaos prevented the proliferation of those weapons. So many were caught off guard by the collapse of the USSR that the systems were just not in place to move the materials, conduct transactions, provide security, etc. Hindsight being 20/20, frankly it's a miracle that it didn't occur. The chaos, a desperate bid for survival by those with the means, lack of reliable information, the efforts of a few, and a nod from Lady Luck herself all came together to prevent the proliferation of these weapons during those days. We should be so lucky the next go-around.

With the fall of Russia and the fear over newly unemployed nuclear scientists acquiring service with their unique talents across a field of uncontrolled terrorist networks and non-nuclear regimes, concerns were raised over the possibility of an extremist group acquiring such a weapon, either improvised or intact, and prepared to strike against the larger United States or their target of choice. It was obvious that the technologies developed in a post-cold war environment provided the means for those radical extremists intent on using these destructive instruments. Organized crime, money laundering, nuclear smuggling, human trafficking, drug smuggling, and other nefarious activities provided the "means" for non-state actors to access mass destructive weapons and technologies. Nuclear scientists working on the extensive Soviet nuclear program were out of work, thus susceptible to exploitation of illicit groups or individuals. The concern is valid and this writing illustrates the risk of terrorist groups using WMD materials and the unemployed experts to create and detonate a WMD weapon in a western country. President George Bush summarized our fears as a nation in 2002 when he said, "...shadowy networks of individuals can bring great chaos and suffering to our shores for less than it costs to purchase a single tank."

Without these experts it would be impossible to produce an effective product. After all, which presents the greater threat, the components or the experts who know how to employ them? The difficulties in tracking and differentiating between the legitimate and illicit use of these technologies contributes to the Third-Tier proliferation of weapon components. Many of the uninformed do not understand that the individual components are, in many ways, a more difficult problem set for countries than the complete package. The dual-purpose technologies that are so common in the medical fields present a particularly difficult issue in which nations that monitor the practices of international trade can level charges against the presumed misuse of these components, but only after thorough investigation and often intelligence collaboration between countries.

The 1990's saw a departure from the looming threat of nuclear weapons that overshadowed the more readily available biological, chemicals, and radiological elements that can inflict injury and hazards on unprotected personnel. In September 1993, President Clinton addressed the United Nations General Assembly marking the beginning of a formal shift in the U.S. National Security bureaucracy and followed with the signing of Presidential Directive 18, which ordered the Department of Defense to develop a new approach in addressing the increase of WMD.

The sharing of technologies with peaceful intent or the bolstering the defense capabilities of our allied partners holds the likely potential for hostile parties to acquire dual-purpose technology and modify it to suit a need as a WMD component. The horizontal and third-tier proliferation of WMD and its components extend as well to people, possibly the most precious resource. The black markets that inevitably rise as a result of free trade contribute not only to the underground acquisition of technology but also of scientists, technicians, and other specialists with the requisite skill to fit those illegally acquired materials together, for a price. It could be argued that this is potentially a greater threat and much more difficult to regulate.

WMD proliferation efforts have been hampered by the US, for some time but this state-sponsored regulation raises many issues with other state actors. Starting with globalization, the growing security problem faced by recognized nations from non-state actors benefitting from the seams exacerbated by accelerating global politics, trade and industry, and cultural integration. Globalization creates an interesting situation for national security, the faster technology advances; the harder it will be to keep control of information and equipment. It is the process that embodies a revolution in the spatial institution of social affairs and matters, expressed in international or interregional tides and hubs of action, communications, and influence. States are finding it increasingly difficult to police their own people. Advanced technology is making travel, information and weapons flow between states and non-states harder to control, essentially globalization is eroding the ability to wield a preponderant authority over people. A realization that interstate divergence are increasingly discouraged by the devastating potential of prevailing armed forces technology, while intra-state discord involving an insurgency or cultural conflicts are on the upswing. Wars are not being fought between two countries in a conventional manner, they are being fought between conventional militaries and insurgencies; cases in point would be Iraq, Syria, Yemen, Pakistan, and Afghanistan.

Mutual deterrence is a substantial instrument in the mind of countries such as Pakistan and India. The real issue that national security is facing is groups of people who answer to no government. Syria has a large stockpile of chemical weapons. The question becomes, when the current regime is toppled, who will guard and maintain this stockpile? Treaties such as the Chemical Weapons Convention serve only limited value if only states follow them. The concern revolves around non-state actors who are not bound to any treaty. The Global Threat Reduction or better known as Cooperative Threat Reduction (CTR) programs serve the purpose as a proliferation tool, but people like Dr. Abdul Qadeer Khan (Kahn was the head of an illicit proliferation network supplying the nuclear programs of Iran, North Korea, and Libya) and Abdur Rauf of Pakistan erase most of the effort and success of programs like CTR. While globalization creates wealth and the advance of technology, it also creates security risks to the US and other nations. Terrorist organizations and insurgents now have the means and tools from around the globe to wreak havoc on peaceful nations. Conflicts of the past seem so simple compared to the conflicts of the present. We cannot assume that non-state actors will abide by the rules and the regulations that we follow in a time of war.

Instability in countries like Pakistan, and the entire region of the Middle East will remain a gamble for the United States in the years to come. The risk of Pakistan's civil and military regimes collapsing would ignite a conflagration across the region due to the significant nuclear arsenal that would no longer be effectively controlled. Increased instability would likely contribute to a further radicalized Islamist element that would affect U.S. interests in the region. The United States has invested heavily in stability in that part of the world through international peace treaties and partnerships aimed at securing a long-standing peace. But engagements with these governments is not enough, in fact the U.S. should attempt to expand its influence among the general population through public affairs experts, media, and nongovernmental organizations.

As technology advances and information, money, and people's ability to surpass the physical constraints of their state entity, ad hoc interactions circumvent established norms. With the speed rogue entities move, bypass any controls created by a slower moving government, which operates with the confines of law. Equally vexing is the increase of fiscal assets as regulations drive the pirate entities from the surface to black market/

offshore sphere where state power cannot affect. Non-state actors such as smugglers and organized crime syndicates are increasingly becoming an excellent source of illegal merchandise. The sky is pretty much the limit to what smugglers can get his hands on and history has proven that just about anything can be obtained as long as there is someone willing to pay for it. The challenge seems to involve keeping the non-state actors and smugglers from getting possession of materials that could be combined to cause mass destruction.

The proliferation of WMD has come down to extremist ideology to a large extent. Most scientists, who deal with such programs, do so out of a sense of patriotism usually for a state e.g. India, Israel and generally Pakistan, the high-profile exception being A.Q. Khan. Their mission is to provide their nation with a weapon that matches, or outstrips, the technology of their most likely enemy in a war. Such rational and educated professionals can rarely be bought off for profit, they are however susceptible to ideology. Without a state (or a state sponsor) most terrorist organizations will have to rely on third-tier proliferation and will not be able to produce or manufacture weapons unilaterally. Therefore, they have to acquire existing ones, or attempt to produce a lower grade weapon of mass destruction. The dangers of WMD left Pandora's Box in the first decades of the twentieth century, and although we cannot permanently stop the production of these weapons by actors with the resources, we can still slow its spread.

A very small number of regimes aside, very few want these weapons for use in a conventional war. It's the fear that they may be employed against them that directs the motivation to acquire them as a deterrent. Although the Cold War between the US and USSR is over, a Cold War between so many other countries is still ongoing. The Cold War between these states, rogue as they may be, is infinitely more comfortable and predictable than the possibility of a non-state actor acquiring a WMD. These rogue entities are the unknown factor, the equivalent of a madman with a gun.

11
The Psychological Effect Of Weapons Of Mass Destruction On The Populace

Behavioral reactions in the populace that arise from the use of weapons of mass destruction and acts of terrorism have a significant impact on the role of the medical and support systems in place to help citizens recover from such a traumatic event. If you can imagine the psychological impact that comes with a surprise attack in which your friends, neighbors, coworkers, family, and even yourself are maimed or killed without warning then you begin to understand the emotional scarring that would come to define the lives of all involved. The human mind, though significantly evolved from our ancestors, still maintains the primal survival instinct that has allowed us to survive for so long. It is our ability to learn, combined with this survival instinct, that contributes to the manifestations of post-traumatic stress disorder symptoms as part of a survival reflex. Our mind will remind us of potentially life threatening situations regardless of the emotional pain that is generated from these memories. They will scar us and influence our actions for the rest of our lives. Though the exact nature of how an attack utilizing a WMD will vary, behavioral and psychological symptoms from individuals and groups will follow a discernable pattern. When analyzing individual reactions to traumatic events most people will experience three stages, the immediate response, the intermediate response, and the long-term response. Groups may demonstrate signs of mass panic, acute outbreaks of unexplained symptoms and chronic cases of unexplained psychological symptoms.

Individuals will experience a somewhat predictable phased process when dealing with trauma. The first phase occurs in the immediate aftermath of an attack in which affected persons will experience feelings of numbness, fear and confusion. The second occurs in the intermediate period after an attack- usually between one to several months after the event and is characterized by nightmares, startled responses to unexpected events and insomnia. The third encompasses the long-term rationalization process in which the mind begins to settle and cope with the traumatic event. This final phase may last a year or more and typically includes feelings of disappointment in oneself or resentment towards perpetrators of the act or authority figures that failed to prevent it. Medical and support systems are overwhelmed with treatment and care plans of mass patients who display psychological and behavioral symptoms. Most treatments plans are not quick or easy and require a lengthy amount of time in order to be effective. The obvious treatment would include the initial assessment, treatment of unexplained symptoms, and medication however the most important aspect of ensuring the long term psychological recovery is support, counseling and reassurance to all those affected.

There has been much said of the responsive capabilities of governmental response agencies like the Federal Emergency Management Agency (FEMA) in the wake of natural disasters, such as Hurricanes Katrina and Sandy. Most of the response has been negative, despite the sheer scale of their mission. FEMA will not be fully capable, at least in the near future, because their mission is entirely too massive. According to the FEMA website their mission is "...to support our citizens and first responders to ensure that as a nation we work together to build, sustain and improve our capability to prepare for, protect against, respond to, recover from and mitigate all hazards." The 2005 hurricanes Katrina and Rita exposed flaws not only in government disaster response but also more importantly, the complete and total unpreparedness of the general public for the disaster themselves. The public has been cultured to believe that government can care for them, defend them, and assist them in virtually any phase of social and natural disasters and assaults that come their way. It should be painfully clear now that government cannot do so without a multi-tiered response and a somewhat prepared population. The time has come for the citizens of this country to step up and take responsibility for themselves. The government simply cannot take care of everyone all at once. There is something to be said for personal responsibility and independence and we should never allow ourselves to become so helpless that we are solely dependant upon the assistance of federal organizations.

A WMD will have a greater affect on the population than most natural disasters in terms of numbers; a ballistic or explosive event has a more profound impact on victims and the first responders. A common emotional or behavioral reaction by the population after such an attack is to experience a deep loss of confidence in the government or authoritative officials. This is normal as the affected public attempts to psychologically distance themselves from their attackers and authority figures that are meant to protect them from harm. This lack of trust causes emotional stress that lead to post traumatic stressors in victims and first responders.

Considerable psychosomatic and behavioral responses to an act involving weapons of mass destruction are certain; furthermore probable assemblage reactions include mass panic and severe occurrences of medically inexplicable symptoms. Mass panic after an attack creates chaos and unrest in the civil population making it extremely difficult for emergency responders to do their jobs. The events of 9/11 were an example of mass panic; civilians as well as some first responders were unsure how to react to such an event. People were running through the streets while rescue workers without the proper personal protective equipment were trying to save as many people as possible. In addition to the cost of destruction in terms of lives and damage to the infrastructure one must consider the possible weakened state of a community as a result of such an event as individuals focus on their personal needs.

Local Emergency Planning Committees (LEPC) must step in and prepare communities for potential attacks well in advance of these events. The chemical incident in Bhopal, India led to the statutory requirement of local planning committees. According to the EPA web site, LEPC's must develop an emergency response plan, review it at least annually, and provide information about chemicals in the community to citizens. Citizens and emergency hospitals are ill prepared for such attacks, as most weaponized agents that would be employed in a WMD attack are unfamiliar to American doctors. If doctors are not prepared to diagnosis the problem, hospitals will fall behind the power curve.

Although mass panic is typically expected after a major catastrophe, as in a terrorist attack, historical data points to the contrary. Following the Oklahoma City bombing, the Hiroshima/Nagasaki atomic bombings and even after 9/11, mass panic did not occur. Instead, positive, adaptive, and helpful behavior became the norm. This does not mean that mass panic does not occur, it is just not the historical norm. The dissemination of information is an excellent way to mitigate the feelings of panic that arise from an event. In this regard, the mass media can either be used to calm people or it can fuel the fire of panic. Using the media, particularly social media for its speed of message, to disseminate vital information is a key tool in avoiding mass panic.

In addition to standard medical assistance, physicians play a critical role by informing and providing calm capability before their patients during such events. Physicians should be aware of the psychological effects of a WMD event. As a result of the terror and psychological trauma, patients will attribute non-existent illnesses to the WMD event. Even a mass outbreak of false illness is likely to occur, due to panic and hysteria. False reports of poisonous gas have resulted in notable epidemics of psychosomatization in civilians involved in terrorist attacks around the globe. There are numerous other examples where this has occurred in the historical record. Physicians are advised to always show empathy and respect to all patients regardless of the possible cause of illness; failure to do so will likely cause unnecessary tension between patient and physician. In most cases, rest and reassurance will greatly reduce the symptoms associated with panic, anxiety, and PTSD.

Basic sociology can answers some questions relating the behavior of large groups of people in highly stressful panicked situations, also known as mob hysteria. This mob mentality was essentially defined as the behavioral tendency of people, and other social animals, to act in unison with the group in which they are a part. Most sociologists really only apply that line of thinking to the behavior exhibited during riots and the diffusion of responsibility that allows people to act in a manner different from how they would act when alone. Now I begin to wonder if the same attitudes and methods that people use to communicate with one another in crisis situations are the cause of panic due to the lack of reliable information and the need to preserve oneself. Essentially it's a survival reflex, isn't it? The dissemination of information is one key component necessary to the prevention of mass panic. Having said that consider:

1.) What are some effective methods of disseminating information before a crisis that would not exacerbate the problem?

2.) Assuming the crisis involves significant damage to the existing communications infrastructure, how to get information to the people in a timely manner?

It would be negligent to not mention that history is not without case studies involving mass hysteria and the onset of unexplained physical symptoms. These symptoms have been proven to develop into post-traumatic stress disorder in almost one-third of casualties. The medically unexplained physical symptoms have manifested in several traumatic conflicts and terror attacks over the years including World War I, often associated with the first employment of chemical warfare, and the 1991 Persian Gulf War, from which Gulf War Syndrome was born- and to much controversy. Symptoms of fatigue, headaches, respiratory disorders, and memory problems among others continue to plague veterans and survivors of these events for years or decades afterward.

The controversy stems from the disagreement over whether these symptoms are real or imagined. "Shell shock" experienced by veterans of World War I is perhaps better understood now by placing history in perspective but veterans of war in Southwest Asia or victims of terrorist events do not have this lengthy, studied point of view to provide rationale to their own outlook. Do they have a physical cause or are they the psychosomatic result of mass hysteria related to the feared exposure to oil well fires or the aftereffects of burning buildings and jet fuel? Whether the cause is "real" is irrelevant, the symptoms that manifest are just as real as any physical wound with similar debilitating effects. For the 486,000 veterans that have been diagnosed with "Gulf War Syndrome" this malignancy has resulted in an approximate loss of $35,000 a year, per patient, in lost productivity and medical treatment associated with this unexplained illness. The decline in productivity and the ability to interact normally with other members of society will cost the affected public financially and socially in the long term.

In the most general terms, the psychological response to traumatic events has been mapped out and will follow a path from the immediate moment of the event, the intermediate period from weeks to months following, and the long term in which a proper response should focus on recovery. A prepared response will involve a well-trained medical establishment alongside trained and equipped first responders, an informed population that is made to feel that they can contribute to resolving the crisis in a meaningful way, and drawing upon the professional talents and resources of the community. A lack of preparedness for the inevitable psychological toll that is inherent in any attack involving a weapon of mass destruction only increases the destructive capability of the weapon with ramifications potentially lasting the lifetime of all involved.

Physically and psychologically affected personnel will overcome the majority of primary care and emergency care facilities following a WMD event. Weapons of mass destruction along with conventional acts of terrorism are not only selected for their ability to kill or incapacitate while achieving political goals, but also for their ability to sow social disruption by creating a sense of distrust among the population. Did you ever hear the one about 9/11 being an inside job? Then the appropriate psychological effect has been achieved.

A prime example of the psychosomatic results of attacks of WMD is after the Tokyo sarin attack, 5,510 people sought medical attention at more than 200 hospitals and clinics in Tokyo with several hours where only 25% where hospitalized and the others having no signs of exposure were sent home. This overload to the medical and rescue systems sufficiently immobilized the response network in place. The mass panic initiated is a survival instinct in human nature. Such individual and group reactions can only be overcome by concise information, training and rehearsal of response plans. The confidence provided by the visibility of positive actions will greatly lessen the psychological response to WMD attacks. Preexisting physical challenges and mental frailty will be promulgated by the exposure.

The Tokyo subway attack and the resulting "worried well" that overburdened the medical system is an excellent example of how an incident can overload the local hospitals and emergency responders. The post-incident data following the Tokyo attack can help to answer even small-scale incidents and allow one to realize how quickly hospitals and emergency response assets can be overloaded. During an incident of even small scale, anxiety and fear will make people feel like they are experiencing related consequences from the incident that they were nowhere close enough to become affected by realistically. Therefore, an informed public will be a key factor in maintaining public anxiety at manageable levels and allow emergency responders to treat the victims appropriately. Japan has made concrete improvements to its vast consequence management capabilities as a result of these attacks. Many of the lessons learned in Japan also offer insights for the United States. Relationships between various players need to be built at all levels of government; telecommunications infrastructure strengthened; medical surge capacity enhanced; and psychological care capabilities improved.

12
The Chemical Threat

Although chemical agents are perhaps best associated with images of gas-masked soldiers fighting in the trenches of World War I, they have actually been in use by armies for over 2,000 years. In fact, a combination of sulfur and other ingredients, when lit on fire, produced a somewhat effective choking agent used to clear enemy personnel from entrenched defensive fortifications, such as castles during the Middle Ages. The first recorded use of chemical weapons was during the Peloponnesian War when the Spartans deployed wood that had been saturated with pitch and sulfur to produce sulfur dioxide gas. Its primary effectiveness on the battlefield has been as a psychological force-multiplier continuing on through the battles of today.

The usefulness of chemical agents has been proven to be so feared that the United States entered the Convention on the Prohibition of the Development, Production, Stockpiling, and Use of Chemical Weapons and their Destruction, or CWC, on 25 April 1997. The CWC was ratified due to the horrors of human suffering that are brought on by chemical agents, especially those that have been deployed against civilian populations. The United States recognized this as far back as World War I when in April of 1915 the Germans released 265 tons of chlorine that resulted in over 5,000 casualties. Over the years, the use of chemical agents fell out of favor due to their unreliability in warfare. Unpredictable factors, such as the weather, combined with open-air battlefields reduced the effectiveness of these agents, often working against the soldiers that had employed them. Its use in the modern era emerged out of a necessity to break the impasse that had existed as a result of trench warfare. It's ability to demoralize, cause grave bodily harm, and even kill on the battlefield made it appear to commanders on both sides that it could have the potential of a new super weapon, capable of influencing the way wars were fought and won. In spite of the rapid pace of technological advancement that allowed for the development of protective equipment to keep pace with the employment of such weapons, chemicals were responsible for the injuries of almost 500,000 soldiers and deaths of 30,000 more during World War I.

The Germans were quite liberal with their use of gas during World War I, leading Wilfred Owen to pen *Dulche Et Decorum Est* which reads in part:
"But someone still was yelling out and stumbling

And floundering like a man in fire or lime.—
Dim, through the misty panes and thick green light
As under a green sea, I saw him drowning"

A chemical agent is any chemical that can cause death, temporary incapacitation, or permanent harm to humans or animals. Chemical agents are further defined as chemical warfare agents (CW) and military chemical compounds. The subcategorizations of CW agents include choking, nerve, blood, blister, and incapacitating agents. Choking agents cause damage to the pulmonary system and irritation to the eyes. Nerve agents cause acetylcholine to build up in the neural transmitters by inhibiting the release of cholinesterase enzymes. The build-up of acetylcholine causes the over stimulation of muscles and glands, and leading to the inability to breath. Blood agents cause hemolysis of red blood cells, reducing the oxygen carrying capacity of the blood, leading to cardiovascular collapse and myocardial failure. Blister agents cause reddening and blistering of the skin, eye irritation, and damage to the mucous membranes. Incapacitating agents cause temporary physiological or mental effects that prevent a person from completing a task.

These agents can be initially categorized by their physical state and come in several varieties of gas, liquid (most common), solid, or in the case of riot control agents, a powdery substance dispersed with an aerosol. They can be classified as blood, blister, choking, or nerve agents with persistent or non-persistent properties. Named primarily for the effect that they have on the human body, blood agents are fast acting and poisonous when entering the blood stream, typically when inhaled or ingested. Blister agents are named for the extremely painful chemical burns that are often accompanied by blisters to the skin. Choking agents are designed to adversely affect the working lung functions of its victims, resulting in excessive fluid in the lungs and eventually death by asphyxiation. Nerve agents are typically inhaled or absorbed through the skin and are commonly associated with involuntary muscle contractions to include loss of the ability to effectively breathe properly. It is important to note the difference between a persistent and a non-persistent agent. A persistent agent is able to remain as a liquid, without any attempt of disposal, for a period of more than 24 hours. A non-persistent agent will evaporate within that time. The effects of chemical agents include, shortness of breath, coughing, burning of the nose, eyes, and skin, vomiting, loss of consciousness, and death.

There is one very common household chemical that holds a particular interest to potential terrorists considering the production of a chemical weapon- Chlorine. In 2007 Iraq was mired in the middle of an occupation by soldiers of a multinational coalition, rifted by a political power struggle between its Sunni and Shia religious cultures, and experiencing waves of violence by a stalled insurgency desperate to maintain its relevance. The insurgency found that relevance with the introduction and employment of a new tool in its war against the occupiers- improvised explosive devices augmented with chlorine gas. This particular weapon was selected for several reasons: it's availability in mass quantities, its stability for transport and engage targets with minimal chance for detection, and the media attention that would surely result from such an attack, revitalizing the stalled war effort. While initial attempts with this new tactic were poorly executed, subsequent attacks improved upon both design and execution, sending the casualty count into the hundreds. As the threat of this type of warfare held the Iraqi emergency responders and Coalition military forces at bay, the U.S. Department of Homeland Security considered the possibility of its employment on U.S. soil and refined its own emergency response plan. By learning from the tactics of the insurgent, historical uses of chlorine in warfare, and the response of Iraqi security forces and assessments of U.S. military and civilian casualties from local hospitals the United States is more equipped to identify the telltale signs of a pending attack and provide a more effective response should an attack succeed. Awareness of the likelihood of a threat such as this combined with the sharing of intelligence among law enforcement and prompt, factual information with the public is critical to an effective emergency response to any terrorist employment of chemical weapons.

When considering chlorine's potential future applications as an instrument of terror it is important to examine its track record as a weapon. The use of chemicals as a weapon gained notoriety in World War I as a method to sow chaos into the enemy ranks. However, it is not as well known that this use of chlorine was only a natural progression of chemicals in warfare, which had already existed for centuries. This tactic was limited in its effectiveness due to the unpredictability of weather and open-air deployment of these devices. After some experimentation with other munitions containing irritants the German army employed chlorine gas during the Battle of Ypres on 22 April 1915.[52] This first use of the chemical cloud blew with the wind and had the effect of causing a violent fit of sneezing among the frightened French and Algerian troops killing some and causing many others to flee. It was judged to be effective enough to be employed just two days later at the same location against Canadian troops. This second use of the gas forced the Allied forces into a retreat to the town of Ypres. This began an arms race for the dominance of chemical warfare, of sorts, as the French and British began developing their own chemical weapons and protective equipment. The use of these types of agents was popular enough at the time that almost 100,000 tons of chlorine were produced during World War I by the countries involved in the conflict. Of that amount, Germany produced almost 60% of the total amount.

In recent years, chlorine has emerged as a viable option to increase the numbers of casualties added on to already deadly explosive attacks. In fact, the chemical has made headlines as a result of its use by the insurgency in Iraq and several industrial accidents all of which have confirmed its place as a potential hazardous material threat. It is readily available in the United States with a domestic production of over 15 million tons every year and is one of the most common industrial chemicals in the country. Chlorine is widely used for disinfecting drinking water, swimming pools, and in household bleach and when used in the manner it was intended it is a safe form of disinfectant. Most harmful exposures to chlorine exist as the result of swimming pool accidents and improper mixture of household cleaning agents although there have been some larger releases of the chemical from chlorine gas tanks or accidents at industrial facilities. Considering chlorine's potential use as weapon brings to mind the Bhopal, India pesticide accident. Arguably the worst industrial accident in history, the accidental release of 40 metric tons of the chemical methyl isocyanate killed approximately 2,000 people downwind and injured tens of thousands of others.[53] This is the sort of spectacular media attention that drives the mission statement of a terrorist organization.

In 2007, the insurgency in Iraq attempted to bolster the effectiveness of the already deadly improvised explosive device by adding chlorine gas cylinders and other liquid, gaseous or solid toxic compounds. The tactic of the time was to detonate explosive materials in order to disperse a gas or chemical powder in the surrounding areas with the intention of causing secondary injuries. The mentality being that in addition to the injuries from the blast there would also be an atmosphere of terror and intimidation that would spread by extensive and overly-hyped reporting in the media. Steve Kornguth, director of the biological and chemical defense program at the University of Texas in Austin, said the Iraq explosions are not genuine chlorine bombs. "They are putting canisters of chlorine on trucks with bombs, which then puncture the canisters and release the chemical but it hasn't been very effective because the high temperature created by the bombs oxidizes the chemical, making it less dangerous".[54] The initial attacks of this type were crude, resulting in few injuries from chemical component of the explosive, but due to the media attention and fear generated by this new component it is was widely reported as the most damaging weapon in the insurgents arsenal. No matter the crude status or ineffectiveness of the chemical weapons used by the Iraqi insurgents the concern is the psychological impact such a weapon would have if used within the US.

Although chlorine attacks in Iraq took a drastic decline after mid 2007 the US still took preventive measures. Law enforcement set up an operation to show just how easily a terrorist could acquire materials for a deadly chemical strike. Undercover police bought chlorine online without providing identification and watched as a truck delivered the chemicals to a Brooklyn warehouse. The operation determined that terrorist in the United States could acquire large quantities of chlorine without being detected by law enforcement or intelligence agencies. While there was no specific threat of chemical attack, the police department increased the priority of screening shipments of chlorine after the increase in homemade chemical bombs in Iraq. This department then lobbied the Department of Homeland Security to implement stricter regulations for chlorine sales. A DHS spokesman, Russ Knocke, stated that Homeland Security had been undertaking an array of methods to enhance the security of the nation's domestic supply of chlorine.

In 1995 the Japanese religious cult Aum Shinrikyo initiated a terrorist chemical attack of the nerve agent Sarin on the subways of Tokyo. A variety of factors led to the cult's selection of Sarin as the agent of choice including a fear of persecution by the Japanese government and a the belief held by it's leaders of a coming Armageddon in which the cult would rise to world prominence.[55] Sarin is classified as a nerve agent originally produced as a pesticide in the late 1930's. Harmful exposure can occur through ocular contact or inhalation. There are several mechanical methods of detection available to the military and equipped HAZMAT units including M22 alarm systems and M8/M9 papers among others. Sarin is colorless and odorless but can also be identified by the manifestation of its symptoms including runny nose, water eyes, difficulty breathing, headache, and nausea. Those exposed for a significant period of time will likely lose consciousness, experience involuntary muscle spasms, respiratory failure, and death. Responders to a terrorist attack involving chemical weapons should protect themselves by wearing appropriate protective equipment including chemical-protective over garments, respirator, facemask, gloves and impermeable boots. Atropine is an effective nerve agent antidote that must be considered for the protection of medical personnel and treatment of casualties. Patients should be removed from the source of contamination, preferably upwind or outside of structures to an open-air environment. In the event of a gas exposure, decontamination begins by first removing the clothing of the victim followed by showering with soap and water diluted with hypochlorite.[56] Sarin is considered to be a non-persistent agent likely to evaporate in one to two hours at temperatures beginning at 122 degrees Farenheit.

Historically speaking, the dispersion of chemicals as part of a terrorist attack has resulted in the deaths of very few people. For example, Ramzi Yousef employed chemical terrorism in 1993 when cyanide was combined with explosives that were then detonated at the World Trade center. This attack resulted in six killed and approximately 1,000 wounded, however the cyanide, which was destroyed upon the initial blast, created none of these casualties. The Japanese Sarin gas attacks that occurred in 1995 resulted in the deaths of 19 and injury to approximately 1,000 passengers, a relatively small number to the tens of thousands traveling through the subway at that time.[57] These chemical attacks were successful in one respect: they drew widespread attention and fear among the populace as concerns about a new wave of radicalized "mega-terrorism" spread through the media. In the case of the Iraq chlorine attacks, the majority of the casualties could also be attributed to blast injuries, not chemical effects. The numbers of injured persons are highly likely to increase in the event of an attack involving chlorine, especially after prolonged exposure, but exposure must be at very high concentrations in order to result in death. A Department of Homeland Security scenario developed in 2005 considered the potential casualty count from a terrorist attack and subsequent destruction of a large chlorine container facility and estimated that it could lead to approximately 17,500 deaths and over 100,000 hospitalized.[58]

Chlorine is used extensively throughout the United States and there are significant raw materials available that a terrorist organization could employ in a device. Stocks of these substances are typically poorly guarded. Although there are significant sources of materials available to terrorist organizations to construct IED's using chlorine, means of dispersing the gas using explosives are inefficient. The Iraqi insurgency's reaction to this problem was to increase the scale of the explosive device rather than find a way to make the device more efficient. It is most likely that the detonation of an explosive next to chemical will also result in the destruction of a large portion of the chemical element, with some of the remaining substance being dispersed and still posing a threat. The devices used in Iraq were poorly designed, resulting in the burning off of most of the gas before it was able to properly mix in to the air. It is highly likely that the explosion would accelerate the spreading of the agent causing the substance to dissipate faster than it would after a straightforward chemical leak. This offers a partial explanation as to why the weaponisation of chemicals is so difficult. Chlorine that is dispersed in an explosive detonation is not likely to be present in immediately fatal concentrations. The shrapnel created by the initial explosion is still the most immediate threat to life.

In most forms, chlorine is a greenish-yellow gas with an asphyxiating bleach-like odor. Because chlorine gas is heavier than air it is subject to moving downwind and downhill, concentrating in poorly ventilated and low lying areas. Depending upon the amount released the gas could be expected to dissipate to levels within acceptable health parameters in about an hour. There are exceptions however; the release of extremely large amounts in combination with cold weather in confined areas would increase the amount of time for the gas to dissipate on its own. In liquid form it can produce skin burns equivalent to frost bite and burns to the eyes ranging from minor eye irritation to severe corneal burns. The effects of exposure to the gas form vary depending upon the age and health condition of the persons involved. For example, an individual with a pre-existing lung condition would be more severely affected than one without. Symptoms to exposure from non-fatal amounts include a sense of asphyxiation, chest pain, vomiting and nausea. Victims of a chlorine gas attack should be immediately moved away from the source of the contamination. It is not necessary to decontaminate victims who are only exposed to chlorine gas and are without irritation of the eyes and skin. Water or saline are sufficient to flush and remove traces of the chemical. There are no specific medical tests that are able to identify chlorine injuries. Careful attention to patient symptoms, combined with a steady flow of information between first responders and hospital medical staff may be the only way to confirm the presence of chlorine following an attack. After non-fatal exposures the recovery time is fairly rapid, although some symptoms may persist for up to two weeks. Medical care over the long-term is generally not necessary for most exposures that result in negligible or even marginal effects. Casualties who are treated and then recover from the most severe effects may potentially develop chronic pulmonary medical issues

Contingent to the prevention of such a terrorist scenario is to first minimize the possibility of terrorists gaining possession of weapons, explosive devices, and the freedom of maneuver to reconnoiter potential targets. There are several practical obstacles to a terrorist deployment of explosive involving chlorine. One must consider where a sizeable amount of the chemical could be stored without detection, the preparation of a large delivery container; target reconnaissance and rehearsal all pose significant challenges for a terrorist cell. An explosive device that is constructed and prepared away from a populated area has to be moved into the population center, during which time there is a risk of a premature detonation. The addition of chlorine to an explosive is unlikely to significantly improve the lethal capability of attacks unless the design is modified to either include a greater amount of chlorine or be more selective in the target site selection process, all of which create additional hurdles for the terrorist to overcome. Chlorine production and storage facilities must be made aware of intelligence suggesting that a terrorist organization is seeking to improve the effectiveness of an explosive device with the use of chemicals. A close working relationship between facilities of this type, local and federal law enforcement must be established and maintained on a regular basis. Also, management of these plants should prepare to work with local hospitals and provide information as to the nature of the chemical compounds at their facilities in the event of a future industrial accident or attack. From the perspective of the emergency responder priorities should include alerts to area hospitals, activation of hazardous materials response teams, law enforcement support in traffic and site control, and providing notification to the public regarding what actions to take. Although attacks involving chlorine have so far resulted in limited success, attempts at more sophisticated devices have the potential for more devastating effects. Because of its toxic properties and wide availability, it should be expected that large amounts of chlorine would continue to be sought out by terrorist organizations for use in combination with explosive devices.

Regarding the credibility of the global jihad's intent and capability to employ chemical weapons it is important to note that there is a clear difference between the two. While the intent is clearly present and encouraged among those circles, it is not matched by the capability to carry out such an attack. Perception of the true nature and seriousness of a threat will often not match the tactical reality. Following the spectacular attacks of 9/11, which caught the civilian populace and most of the intelligence community completely unaware, there was a need to absorb as much information as possible about the shadowy jihadist movement. In an effort to prevent another such attack, every scrap of information that could grant some insight into this organizations future plan was scrutinized, dissected, and partitioned off to adjacent agencies in the spirit of cooperation and hope of preventing the next wave of attacks. Some of these leads would pan out, allowing for a successful and crippling invasion of Afghanistan and overthrow of the Taliban and Al-Qaeda strongholds and safe houses. Many other leads would not. In the early days of the US invasion of Afghanistan the videos that purported to show the testing of chemical weapons on dogs by Al Qaeda scientists combined with intelligence that jihadist recruits had received training in the manufacture of such weapons was enough to spark fears that this may be the clue that could prevent the next attack. While the intent was clear, the assumption was made that Al Qaeda possessed the means and technical knowledge to produce and field an effective device. Was it responsible to possibly divert resources to investigate leads on the jihadist development of these weapons? Absolutely. We ignore these signs at our own peril and unfortunately that means that we are often relegated to searching for the proverbial needle in a haystack. Hindsight is always 20/20 but if we do not pursue these courses of investigative action and a device of this type is employed we would have no one but ourselves to blame. The potential for an attack involving a chemical weapon should be ranked in between nuclear and biological, with biological being potentially the easiest to produce and employ and nuclear being the most difficult. The videos, jihadist manuals, and interviews with captured terrorists and insurgents all point to the same conclusion: Al-Qaeda has a definite interest in employing chemical weapons and is actively pursuing the resources necessary to produce an effective weapon of this type. The key word being "effective".

In 2002, another subway attack was planned. This time, it was to take place in New York City and was to be carried out in 2003 by an Al-Qaeda cell based in Saudi Arabia using hydrogen cyanide gas. Fortunately, the attack never happened. CIA officials who briefed the US government did not know why Zawahiri cancelled the attack. On the basis of the projected 3,000 casualties, it is speculated that Zawahiri was planning something far larger to follow the 11 September 2001 attacks. There is one likely reason why the attack was called off. As the senior operational Al-Qaeda leader, Ayman al-Zawahiri called the shots for Al-Qaeda. When he was informed of the planned attack, it is hypothesized that he was concerned that the attack would not be as spectacular as the 9/11 attacks and could be considered a let down in the shadow of that success. The fact that the attack was called off should not be used as an indication that Al-Qaeda has given up on producing chemical weapons. There are numerous examples, both before and after 9/11, of terrorist groups possessing both the recipes and compounds such as ricin and cyanide salts that can be used in manufacturing chemical weapons. While it may never be known why Al-Qaeda called off the attack, it is possible that the leadership was aware of the limitations of their chemical weapons program and preferred to wait until a more effective weapon had been developed or acquired.

Chemical agents may be broken down into various categories, dependent upon how one wish to view their threat, usefulness or effects. Chemical agents have been defined as chemical substances that are intended for use in military operations to kill, seriously injure, or incapacitate humans or animals through their physiological effects. This definition is significant in that an agent is defined as separate from a substance. The term substance is used to define the basic makeup a particular chemical whereas the term agent is used in this context to define the implications of the use of a particular chemical for a defined purpose. Chemical substances that have a benign and useful agricultural or industrial purpose, such as an herbicide, are defined by their useful application when growing crops, protecting plants from harmful insects or in the production of manufactured good. A chemical becomes an agent when its properties are applied for use in military operations in order to shape an enemy's abilities or capabilities.

Chemical warfare agents are man-made, supertonic chemicals that can be dispersed as a gas, vapor, liquid, aerosol (a suspension of microscopic droplets), or absorbed onto a fine talcum-like powder to create 'dusty' agents. Chemical warfare agents are classified by physiological affects on humans, their physical state, and tactical use. There are four different basic classes of CW agents; choking agents, blood agents, blister agents, incapacitating, and nerve agents.

Choking agents, such as diphosgene and chloropicrin, damage lung tissue and can eventually cause asphyxiation. Choking agents are non-persistent designed to kill by swelling the membranes of the nose, throat, and lungs in effect choking the person to death also known as "dry land drowning". These agents are primarily inhaled and affect the tissues of the respiratory tract. They can cause fluid to fill the lungs, which will cause respiratory failure. One of the dangers associated with this agent is the fact that the complete affects of the agent can be delayed for up to 72 hours after exposure. There are two choking agents: CG (Phosgene) and DP (Diphosgene). CG was used in WWI and is a colorless gas with an odor of new mown hey or grass. An estimated 80% of the chemical fatalities in WWI resulted from CG. DP is very similar in all areas to CG except one of its symptoms is a tearing effect making it easier to detect than CG.

Blood agents, including hydrogen cyanide and arsine, are essentially poison to the blood and can disrupt the physiological processes blood is vital to such as cellular respiration. Blood agents are non-persistent chemical agents absorbed into the body by inhalation and can be dispersed by mortar, artillery, rocket, and spray. AC can be a gas and a liquid that can be absorbed through the skin but is highly volatile making it very difficult to weaponize. However AC can be very deadly in closed spaces (a form of AC called Zyklon B was used by the Nazis in their gas chambers). The symbols for the blood agents are: AC (Hydrogen Cyanide), and CK (Cyanongen chloride); Symptoms of blood agents are rapid breathing, giddiness, headache, vomiting, convulsions, and a respiratory failure. If the person is exposed to a large amount of blood agent they will simply collapse and die and there is no medical treatment that can help; if the exposure is small the treatment will be to speed up the body's own ability to excrete cyanide and bind it to the blood. These agents affect the ability of oxygen to attach to hemoglobin. Unfortunately with these agents, death is a significant possibility. One of the easiest ways to recognize the symptoms is by the appearance of pink skin that is similar to exposure to high levels of carbon monoxide or if there is a change in the patient's respiratory pattern.

Blister agents, including mustard gas and lewisite, can cause irritation, inflammation, and ultimately damage exposed tissue on a human to include skin, eyes, the nasal passage, and airway. Blister agents can be a gas or a liquid; they received their name because of the type of wound they leave (burns and blisters). These are tissue-damaging agents that can cause serious damage to internal organs, eyes, and the respiratory system; the effects of exposure do not occur until 2 to 24 hours after exposure. The Germans in WWI first used blister agents in April of 1915 in the town of Ypres. A cloud of yellow and green would hit the troops, sowing panic, as they would run back to their camps. Symptoms can be mild aching eyes, a lot of tears, inflammation of the skin, hoarseness, coughing, sneezing or severe blistering of the skin, nausea, vomiting, and diarrhea with sever breathing difficulty.

Incapacitating agents when administered in a low dose cause effects similar to a psychotic disorder or the loss of feeling, paralysis, and rigidity; they also cause the person to have trouble making decisions. These agents can also cause unconsciousness, hallucinations, and coma and can remain with the effected person for one to three weeks. These agents can be delivered via bombs, spray tanks, and missiles and are excellent candidates for a terrorist weapon due to their ability to be dispersed with improvised devices.

Nerve agents disrupt nerve-impulse transmission in the central and peripheral nervous systems, causing convulsions, and death by respiratory paralysis. Focusing on the militarization of chemical agents, they are classified within a set of physiological parameters that relate to the manner in which they affect humans. They appear as a colorless to brown liquid and may have either a fruity odor or no odor. These agents affect the neurotransmitters along the nerve pathway, which can cause the body to excrete large amounts of saliva and nasal discharge or have constricted pupils affecting vision. The only antidote is to administer Atropine, 2PAM Cl, and the anticonvulsant medicine Valium.

The U.S. military further broke the classification of agents into two distinct sub-classifications, chemical warfare agents and military chemical compounds. Military chemical compounds may also, to a lesser degree, fall into the category of chemical agents, but are generally used as harassing or obscuring agents, not as compounds that are intended to kill or cause permanent damage to a person. CW agents can also be classified further into the tactical use of the agent. The terms 'persistent' and 'nonpersistent' describe the time an agent stays in an area. Persistent CW agents can have long lasting affects up to several days or weeks. The ideal use of persistent CW agents by an enemy is against the physical environment and to hinder logistics, command and control, and operations. Nonpersistent CW agents are fast acting, highly lethal, and generally disperse the affected area in a short period of time. Due to the lethality of nonpersistent CW agents, they would be almost always be used by adversaries (whether state or non-state actors) against personnel to produce casualties. While CW agents are classified by the amount of time the agent will affect an area, both persistent and nonpersistent classes of CW agents can have devastating effects on operations tempo and cause casualties, including fatalities.

Chlorine is a choking agent, which can cause damage to the lungs, irritation to the eyes and the respiratory tract, and pulmonary edema. Chlorine as an agent, known as Cyanogen chloride, is a colorless gas that is classified as a lachrymatory and irritating agent. Chlorine, due to it's industrial uses and ready access for this purpose, may be a primary target for terrorists and should be guarded when stored in large quantities.

About 70 different chemicals have been used or stockpiled as chemical warfare agents during the 20th century. The earliest target of chemical warfare agent research was not toxicity, but development of agents that can affect a target through the skin and clothing, rendering protective gas masks useless.

The lines that separate the battlefield and the homeland are growing thinner and harder to distinguish as we move from nation-state warfare to hit-and-run terror driven warfare. The line is blurring between who the target is in an attack and with whom one is actually fighting. The implications of a chemical attack that is successfully carried out in a major metropolitan area are such that the impact may have far reaching results well past just the area affected. The causational impact of the fear-based portion of the attack may in itself be the result that the terrorist is working toward. If a population thinks it is no longer safe to go to their place of business, then business will come to a halt. The secondary, or causational, impact would be a heightened sense of fear within the effected community as well as the surrounding communities that would then fear an attack in their own area of operations. A person who fears the consequences of going to work more than the consequences of not going will usually chose to stay home rather than face the potential hazard of an attack. This alone will accomplish the terror that the terrorist wishes to inflict.

Military chemical compounds are not as toxic as CW's, but have similar effects. They fall into the following categories; respiratory irritant agents, RCA's, smoke and obscurants, and incendiary materials. RCA's are chemicals that cause lacrimation and at low doses cause tearing of the eyes while higher doses cause pain or vomiting. Respiratory irritants cause sneezing, coughing, nausea and overall bodily discomfort. Smoke, obscurants, and incendiary materials can cause respiratory irritation, but the general effects are as they are so named.

Chemical weapons and military chemical compounds have several factors that limit their duration of effectiveness, including the method of dissemination (deployment) weather and terrain condition, and the stability of the agent. The methods of deployment in the field are vapors, liquid, or aerosols. Released as a vapor, the initial cloud expands and cools, becoming heavier, keeping its form as a vapor. Aerosols are fine particulate mist in a liquid or solid form that behaves like a vapor. Liquids can be absorbed

and adsorbed by surfaces that can later become a vapor and off-gas causing a hazard. Weather and terrain conditions are influencing factors such as
wind, temperature, humidity, vegetation, soil and contours of the terrain.
The United States along with many other countries have begun to eliminate
their stockpiles of these types of weapons. In fact many Americans don't
know that there are at least nine chemical stockpile / destruction sites located from Maryland all the way to Oregon. By October 2010, according to
government documents, 80% of America's stockpile of chemical warfare
agents and weapons had been destroyed. The creditability of a jihad global
chemical attack is relativity small.. The nature and scale of such a threat often does not match reality. Although chemical attacks are proven difficult
to successfully orchestrate, the priority of these threats should continue to
be taken seriously. The capabilities of the global jihad movement are most
likely overstated when compared to their actual ability to effectively employ
chemical weapons as part of their arsenal. The likelihood of the global jihad's
ability to deploy a chemical weapon appears to be slim but it cannot be
ruled out. The desire for the jihadist is strong and would only increase their
credibility as a terrorist force. Although there has been evidence of training
and the wish to produce such weapons, the logistical support appears to
be lacking. In addition, there are three main obstacles that face the global
jihadists' when it comes carrying out these types of attacks. First, they have
to obtain the agent, second they have to distribute the chemical effectively
without contaminating themselves and third they must avoid law enforcement authorities the entire time prior to any planned attack. The jihadist
aspiration to produce chemical weapons is, at this time, beyond their logistical capability.

While Al-Qaeda currently lacks the technological capability to produce a chemical weapon powerful enough to achieve the desired effects,
this brings into question the possibility of a terrorist organization using already existing chemical production facilities to engineer a chemical disaster.
Such disasters are already on record as being capable of creating nightmare
scenarios for civilians, emergency responders and, and governments. The
Bhopal disaster in India comes to mind. While terrorists did not engineer this
event it must certainly have been on the terrorist radar for the sheer scale of
anxiety that it caused. Current terrorist capabilities may fall short of actually
producing their own WMD's but they are not averse to using our own facilities against us. What if just one of the aircraft involved in 9/11 had struck a
nuclear power plant in Kansas, or perhaps the CDC in Atlanta? The terror and
subsequent second and third order effects resulting from such a scenario

would have been far more widespread than they actually were on 9/11. As we must consider all of the preventative measures that must be undertaken in an effort to make our citizens safer I am reminded that it is not the fear of what we know that causes us to lay awake in our beds at night, but the fear of all the things that we do not know. That is the true victory in terror, its ability to modify our behavior even when no direct action has been taken.

13
Case Study-
Jordanian Terrorists Attempt Chemical Attack
Amman, Jordan 2004

Terrorism requires adaptive and creative forms of thinking along with a willingness to blaze a trail where none had previously existed. In the last decade terrorists have employed increasingly sophisticated measures in their attempts to operate undetected by intelligence agencies and law enforcement. In April of 2004 Jordanian intelligence agencies and elite counterterrorism units thwarted a terrorist plot to initiate an attack involving explosives augmented with chemical weapons on three political and national security related targets located in the political center of the country.

Jordan's elite counterterrorism unit, Battalion 71, operating under the authority of the Royal Jordanian Special Operations High Command, was able to intervene and capture or kill all of the terrorist cell operatives within hours of the plan being uncovered by intelligence agencies. Just before two Al-Qaeda inspired cells were scheduled to activate a high explosive attack with chemical weapons against three nearby targets in a simultaneous raid against a country that it viewed as too closely tied to the West. Their targets included the Office of the Prime Minister, the Dairat al-Mikhabarat (the General Intelligence Service), and the Embassy of the United States.

Earlier that month, Jordanian police moved to intercept three vehicles transporting a cargo consisting of more than 20 tons of explosives and industrial chemicals near the town of Irbid. Upon questioning, the drivers confessed to involvement in a larger plot to launch an attack in the Jordanian capitol. A known Al-Qaeda affiliate, with ties to Abu Musab al-Zarqawi, was identified as the head of two terrorist cells that were planning the attack. It was quickly established that Azmi al-Jayousi was in the process of establishing an operational base in the Marqa district of Amman, an area known for it's dense population, poverty, and anonymity. It was determined that al-Jayousi would be unlikely to willingly surrender despite the setback of losing the recently captured materials. It was the assessment of the GID that al-Jayousi would attempt to reacquire the materials and proceed with the attack as scheduled.

Interrogation of the captured drivers revealed that the cells were very well organized, which created a significant challenge for authorities to plan a counterterrorist operation. Perhaps most significantly, the cells had established a sophisticated communications plan built upon a system of interconnected cell phone communication using mobile phones acquired on a burgeoning second-hand black market. This required counterterrorism officials to have accurate intelligence as to the current location and status of both cells, and all members, before moving to stop them. Once action had been taken, it would be necessary to move against all members near simultaneously.

Al-Jayousi had selected a densely populated urban environment located within close proximity to a school for his safehouse causing concern over potential civilian casualties should the police raid not occur as planned. Operational planners made the decision to move under cover of darkness against the safehouse, minimizing the chances that civilians would be caught in the open in the vicinity of the building. At approximately 2 a.m. the counterterrorist team secured the rear exits of the building and established an inner and outer cordon around the immediate vicinity while the entry team announced its presence in a 'tactical call-out' operation. The terrorists inside responded with a hail of automatic machinegun fire, wounding a member of the team. The decision was quickly made to enter the building and within moments the cell was neutralized, killing one suspect while successfully capturing al-Jayousi, his wife, and children.

The safehouse was quickly exploited by the Jordanian counterterrorist unit who identified large amounts of explosives and initiation devices that had been purchased and manufactured by the cell along with small denominations of currency including Euros, Dinars, and U.S. Dollars, laptops, passports issued by various countries, and weapons. Captured training videos indicated the terrorists' encouragement of using 'human shields' when conducting operations, hence the reason for the family present at the point of capture.

Interrogation procedures were immediately implemented and al-Jayousi revealed details of his relationship to Al-Qaeda, his training in Central Asia, and operational financing from Syria. Despite intensive efforts he would not disclose the exact location of the second terrorist cell complicating efforts to action before their next scheduled communication, a scant six hours away. Using a captured cellphone, the team was able to lure one member of the second cell to a public area located in the Hashemi district and arrest him.

This man was identified as the head of the second cell and he quickly gave up the location of the other safehouse as well as the fact that he was expected to report by phone to the cell within 15 minutes. The counterterrorist unit was immediately redeployed to the district and began the process of isolating the target house. Once again, the cell had selected a densely populated district in a poor community located near a school. Knowing that the cell had been in the process of preparing for an attack using explosives and industrial chemicals the government decided to evacuate nearby residents and students at the school. Once this operation was complete, and the cell was unaware that their location had been compromised, the counterterrorist team moved on the safehouse location. Realizing that innocents may be located within the house, a hostage negotiator initiated contact with the cell employing a psychological tactic involving Muslim religious themes against suicide and murder. This tactic was unsuccessful and the terrorists opened fire on the teams securing the compound perimeter, injuring another member of the unit. The unit employed canisters of tear gas in an attempt to draw the cell members out of the safety of the building. While the canisters sowed confusion among the ranks of the cell members the team gained entry into the compound and, within seconds, killed three members of the group.

Once the site had been secured intelligence agents were able to pour over reams of information collected by the cell and piece together the complete plan for the attack. The cell had amassed approximately $250,000 from various sources and purchased vehicles to be used as logistical and diversionary support as well as the actual mission execution. Almost 70 different forms of industrial-grade chemicals had been combined with conventional explosives in an effort to enhance the explosive effect of the bombs and disperse a toxic cloud of chemicals throughout the city, creating a mass casualty incident. This tactic had been previously employed by Al-Qaeda in the 1993 attempt to topple the World Trade Center towers in New York with a mix of explosives and cyanide gas. Fortunately, in the WTC attack, the initial explosive destroyed the chemical component during the initial blast.

Over the course of several weeks, the cell modified several vehicles to conceal the explosives and increase the effectiveness of the blast upon detonation. The largest vehicle was selected to breach the entry gate of the government compound and modified with a heavy steel skirt to protect the engine from gunfire and act as a ramming tool. The plan called for a small, and highly maneuverable, sedan to initiate gunfire on the guard outpost at the vehicle entry control point while three modified trucks traveled in trail and rammed the compound gate. The lead truck would select whichever building presented itself as the most accessible target while the other two vehicles would drive as close as possible to the remaining two buildings and all would detonate their explosive payload.

Analysis of the plan, after the fact, reveals that the objective of the terrorists to create as many casualties as possible in a tactic reminiscent to the September 11 2001 attack, and the bombing in Madrid, as well as the objective of the failed London subway bombing. This incident tells us that the terrorist group had a vast array of resources, capabilities, and associations in order to accomplish their goal with a limited amount of money and technology. The terrorists were committed to their course of action and willing to die than surrender going so far as to include their families in their scheme. The cell demonstrated an effective appreciation for operational security with their elaborate communication plan and the use of untraceable cell phones. The choice of target would have struck a blow to the Jordanian government, its security apparatus, and a high profile representation of Western interests, the American embassy. The use of chemicals to augment the destructiveness of the blast and cause additional injury underscored the terrorist ingenuity to increase the lethality by using unconventional methods. While the tactic of using simultaneous attacks has allowed the terrorist to initiate high-profile operations despite their meager resources. In the future, it is likely that terrorist cells will continue to seek additional materials, like chemical weapons, to supplement their operations.

The terror cell eliminated while preparing for the massive chemical attack in Amman, Jordan was versatile, technologically proficient, and prepared to die in order to carry out their mission. The targeted compound, housed the Jordanian Office of the Prime Minister, the Intelligence center of the Jordanian government, and the U.S. Embassy- all high profile and located within close proximity to one another, making them an attractive objective for any group wanting to send a message to the United States and government of Jordan. Jordan, has long held close political ties to the West as well as a standing peace treaty with Israel, both of which are considered threatening by the views of some extremist Islamic organizations and countries. The willingness to not only action against this political hub but increase the destructive blast with chemical additives and inflict civilian casualties with toxins underscores the message to governments and civilians that cooperation with the West and Israel will make like-minded countries acceptable targets, as well. The targeting of civilians and use of chemicals is designed to bring attention to their message and increase political pressure by civilians and against governments with warm views toward such cooperative efforts.

The initial intercept of the trucks carrying the explosives intended to be used in the attack occurred in the town of Irbid, which had become a crossroads of sorts for jihadist fighters, because it lies at the intersection of routes trafficked by fighters traveling to Iraq through Syria and those traveling to Lebanon for guerrilla training. The group had chosen safe houses in well-populated but poor districts where jihadists had been known to frequent since the 1990's. Family members were chosen to live with the cell members to decrease the likelihood of detection by maintaining a sense of a normal functioning family as well as possibly serve as human shields in the event of detection.

The captured cell leader, Azmi al-Jayousi, claimed close ties to Abu Musab al-Zarqawi, who at the time was the operational head of Al-Qaeda in Iraq. It is said the Zarqawi envisioned the attack and coordinated with al-Jayousi to finalize the planning and oversee its execution. Approximately $250,000 was allotted for this mission to provide for all logistical and sustainment until mission completion. The group was largely able to remain self-sustaining throughout all stages of the operation, including initial planning, resourcing, reconnaissance, weapon and explosive acquisition, and final planning until capture. This ability to self-sustain decreased the opportunities for intelligence services to intervene along any of the points of detection commonly associated with the terrorist mission sequence. The groups' technical proficiency is evident in its ability to manufacture explosives and initiators as well as safely transport such a massive quantity safely and undetected through two densely populated districts. Its modifications of vehicles were designed to not only conceal their true cargo but aid in breaching the reinforced entry points of the compound and increase the effectiveness of the blast.

The selection of sulphuric acid to the explosive components used during the planned attack was meant to supplement the caustic effectiveness of the blast. This acid is corrosive, causes severe burns, and is harmful if inhaled. While sulphuric acid is known to industrial nations as the largest volume chemical produced in the world, it is more familiar to the rest of us as the result of propanethiol S-oxide gas contained within onions and when combined with the moisture in our eyes it produces minute amounts of sulphuric acid which causes the burning sensation in our eyes. The choices of acetone and nitric acid are known in chemistry circles as highly volatile "hypergolics" and ignite, creating a fiery explosion when mixed in an 85/15% solution. Trained chemists are advised to only combine these chemicals under controlled laboratory conditions with appropriate protective equipment and following approved recipes, belying the scientific capability of the group.

Items that could not be built by the cell had to be bought using the $250.000, most of which was in small denominations of Euros, Dinar, and U.S. Dollars increasing the chances for acceptance and decreasing the opportunities for a financial trail to be traced regardless of the dealer. Mobile phones used for inter-cell communications were purchased used, from the black market, and completely disposable. A frequent communications plan requiring constant assurance that members had not been compromised meant that Jordanian intelligence had to be sure of the location of all cell members before initiating against any of them. The availability of passports provided a means of escape for surviving members should the plan be carried out or if the plan were halted prematurely.

People who do not have a credit card, or do not have the financial resources for a typical service contract turn to secondary market phones with pre-pay plans and are ideal target audiences creating a demand for throw away phones. The cost for secondary market phones is about $15 including service. Most people buying these phones are not committing a crime, but it is an industry terrorist and others of ill intent are keen to take advantage. Closing the gap on this risk would be difficult without treading on civil rights issues. In the U.S., those on public assistance are eligible to receive a free cell phone with 250 monthly minutes. Battered women's shelters provide free cell phones for a victim to call 911 if in an emergency situation. Phones are donated in most cases and service is donated for tax deductions or federal subsidies. Perhaps this is a potential solution to track phones domestically and reduce the demand for throwaway phones.

Jordanian intelligence agencies wee able to act quickly and decisively to intercept the members of the cell before they were able to execute their mission. Effective interrogation techniques combined with thorough site exploitation allowed for the unit to piece together the plot and associated members of the group. Battalion 71 recognized the potential danger to civilians in the vicinity of the target houses and moved to quickly evacuate them while establishing an effective isolation of the safe houses and preventing escape. Once it became clear that the cell members would not willingly surrender and were using family members as shields the counterterrorist teams employed tear gas canisters in an attempt to minimize collateral damage and prevent the loss of innocent life before forcefully moving on the cell.

This case illustrates that a terrorist cell will do business or develop partnerships with anyone necessary to accomplish their goals as evidenced by the two separate cells, the quantity of materials, and money found at the site. It is commonly believed that terror cells act independently with no single organization working an entire plan. Each separate cell has a part of the plan, therefore if one cell is stopped another may be able to pick up or replace where the former left off. Terrorists will trade with anyone to get what they need to complete their mission whether or not they have the same agenda. The capabilities of the terrorist should never be underestimated. Although they are typically one part of the "whole" the thought and expertise that goes into the planning of an attack is carefully orchestrated.

Following the McVeigh bombing in Oklahoma City, a lawsuit was filed against the chemical company that supplied some of the explosive ingredients for their negligence in detecting an unusual purchase pattern by the mombers. Although the suit was dismissed, it highlights the need to secure the supply chain through transparency and diligence. Purchases of large quantities of industrial chemicals, such as sulphuric acid, by private parties should be carefully scrutinized by government agencies for signs of potential terrorist activity. Many companies are considering the implementation of fraud detection departments, not only to prevent financial fraud, but also to detect unusual and suspicious activity.

The cost of launching an attack, such as the planned Jordanian attack, is comparatively inexpensive. Terror groups will continue to attempt to circumvent the guidelines and regulations adopted globally to detect unusual transactions. On the months following the signing of the Patriot Act the banking industry had to completely revise their daily procedures. Cash deposits, personal checks, or withdrawals over $1,000 required a lengthy forms and identification verification process. Some banking institutions implemented the thumb print verification system in order to establish an identity trail. Anything under that dollar amount was not considered an issue and could be moved around undetected. Individuals depositing checks for $999 committed many fraudulent acts on personal and small business accounts after 9/11. While the check was on hold the perpetrators would withdraw the available amount of $599 before the bank recognized the check bounced. This, in part, is how money laundering schemes and employment scams work. Although there is a different criterion for dollar amounts on types of deposits or withdrawals, the principal of the banking process remains the same. By withdrawing small amounts over a long period of time, or making multiple smaller purchases of a chemical compound or equipment-spreading it across multiple vendors would go virtually undetected. The trick for law enforcement is to identify where all of the points of probability meet and act upon those areas.

Estimates by Jordanian intelligence members revealed that if the plan had succeeded the civilian casualty figures would have measured approximately 20,000 killed. Al-Qaeda has a history of planning large-scale simultaneous attacks involving Western targets and without regard for the loss of civilian life in the targeted zone. It can be surmised that, due to its geographical location and cultural significance to Jordan, Amman will continue to remain a hub for radical Islamic groups with ties to major terrorist organizations. Human intelligence, and specifically the ability to extract this information from captured cell members and quickly distribute it to counterterrorism forces in the field was essential in the successful disruption of this attack.

14

Case Study-
The Mubtakkar Device
Saudi Arabia, 2003

In February 2003, five men were arrested at a traffic control point while attempting to cross the King Fahd Bridge between Bahrain and Saudi Arabia. One of these five men had strong ties to a Bahrain-based terrorist cell, which in turn, had ties to Al-Qaeda. Bassam Bokhowa, a driver with the group, was investigated and linked to six jihadists in Saudi Arabia, who were also later arrested. It was discovered during the investigation that the Bahrain terrorist cell was planning to launch a cyanide gas attack on the New York City subway system. The plot was discovered when a computer was seized from the Saudi apartment of Bokhowa, where the schematics of a then-unknown device was discovered. The device was called Mubtakkar , or invention in Arabic. It was comprised of readily available material and could easily be constructed within minutes and placed near ventilation ducts, and in theory, was designed to asphyxiate its victims. The device could be used with or without a detonator, and the detonator would be used to break the inner containers, mixing the chemicals and creating a gas.

Al-Qaeda experimented with cyanide gas prior to 9/11 according to Millennium bomb plotter ,Ahmed Ressam, during testimony in his trial. He revealed that cyanide was mixed with sulphuric acid and placed into a box. The box was then placed into a room with a small dog, and revealed that the dog died shortly after the experiment was terminated. This experiment along with other factors more than likely was the reason Al-Qaeda called off the attack. It was also revealed during the investigation that when the Bahrain cell asked Al-Qaeda permission to carryout the attack the number two man, Ayman al-Zawahiri called off the attack stating "we have something better in mind".

It is most likely that Ayman al-Zawahiri called off the planned gas attack on the New York subway system because of the limitations of the device. It is important to recognize that, in the context of the time, Al-Qaeda was still riding the wave of infamy generated from the 9/11 attacks, which were still very fresh in the minds of most Americans and much of the world. It is possible that the jihadists were aware that this mubtakkar device would not work as advertised and were willing to wait until a more effective weapon had been developed or acquired. Anything less than the spectacular attacks of 9/11 may have been considered a letdown, or even failure, in comparison. This is a group who, at the time, thought that they could bring down the combined nations of the world by generating fear among their citizens wanted to capitalize on the "success" of 9/11. Al-Qaeda had spent a significant of time emplacing operatives and conducting reconnaissance for such an attack, all the while expending finite resources. Aside from money, it is difficult to emplace knowledgeable and willing operatives in the United States without at least the strong possibility of detection. To expend those resources, all the time spent refining a plan, as well as reveal their target on an attack that would have been considered only partially successful may have been viewed as wasteful. Al-Qaeda still viewed their organization as being on the offensive and able to bide their time until the conditions were set for the next big attack. Not realizing that their organization would quickly, and publicly, be dealt blow after blow to assets and personnel around the world as nations cooperated to stem the jihadist tide.

Jane's determined the described device as "lacking in detail", probably more effective as a concept than ready for deployment. Such concepts still need refinement and experimentation, which is not easy to accomplish while attempting to maintain a clandestine operation. The limitations of hydrogen cyanide (HCN) gas coupled with the difficulties in concentrating it to a form strong enough to do more than sicken many, makes it the wrong choice for such an attack. The problem with using HCN is that it is only lethal in high concentrations and is known to dissipate quickly upon release. While the chemicals to produce hydrogen cyanide are readily available, the delivery method to produce the number of casualties to have any sort of significant impact is not present. Intelligence agencies cannot overlook the pace by which technology is growing nor the advancements made by terrorists as they develop more efficient deployment methods for chemical attacks. The mubtakkar device is a prime example of how terrorists refine their methods in order to produce as many casualties as possible.

Cyanide, in gas form, would be most effective in an enclosed area. Most subway stations are well ventilated to reduce fumes from the trains, lowering the impact of the attack. Cyanide gas is lighter than air and prone to dissipation. The amount of cyanide gas required to cause a significant amount of damage would be logistically difficult and problematic to deliver. Historically, cyanide poisoning has resulted in a low death count, but high on minor illness and injury counts. The majority of victims had low exposure to the gas and would have been treated for rapid breathing, dizziness, weakness, headaches, nausea, and vomiting.

It would be very difficult to keep public transportation moving if security measures similar to airports were put into place given the current technology. It would be cost prohibitive and impractical as there are countless stops along any given route. Many train platforms within subway stations are often tied into the same air systems as the buildings overhead and pose an additional risk to be considered. The lack of sealed doors on trains combined with emergency fail-safes that automatically open doors at stops would allow for air to ventilate and reduce gas concentrations to less-than-lethal levels.

The details for the planned device itself were flawed, too nonspecific and too generalized, allowing for the possibility of misinterpretation as to exactly how the device may be built or employed, probably decreasing its effectiveness. This device has appeared in various forms in several terrorist manuals, both in print and online, since 2005 and seems to continue to be circulated by jihadists in a manner similar to "The Anarchist Cookbook" by would-be revolutionaries and curious teens in the early '70s. While just the knowledge that terrorists are exploring this line of thought is enough to guard against, this particular design has not been fully explored- nor is it ready for prime time.

What should be of greater concern is the inflammatory language that often preempts the detailed instructions for building the device. "Within these pages is the great victory ... what we wish is that it becomes the deciding factor in the victory of the believers", followed by an eight page manual with 34 diagrams that illustrate the steps and components required for assembly of the device. The manual consists of six chapters that not only explain how to build the device but offers advice on target selection and weapon emplacement advising that it should be used in the vicinity of central air conditioning units and by emergency exits.[59] The religious themed introduction offers insight into the future of terrorism and their intent to seek out more effective forms of chemical warfare, "Lethal gasses are among the most effective, most frightening, most affordable, and most reliable weapons." A manual such as this provides the impetus for future evolutions of the tactic.

It is highly likely that Al-Qaeda monitored the execution and effects from the Aum Shinriyko subway attack, although widely publicized at the time, but have quickly receded into memory because of the low numbers of actual fatalities. If you were to go outside the circles of those who study the methodology of terrorists and ask them to recall any details of the Aum Shinrikyo cult you would likely get a blank stare, while images of 9/11 are indelibly associated with Al-Qaeda and burned into the psyche of most Americans. Al-Qaeda leadership at the time wanted to remain associated with high-profile successes rather than high-profile failures.

Now mostly removed from Afghanistan, not to be confused with the Taliban, Al-Qaeda splinter groups are eking out a living in the FATA of Pakistan and the Horn of Africa, trying to gain a foothold in Yemen and Mali while expanding their influence throughout Asia. It has not attained the levels of terrorist supremacy that it once aspired and is increasingly shifting its strategy away from transnational in favor of regional terror. Al-Qaeda is not gone but now exists as just a shadow of its former self, only able revel in its former glory. Even Bin Laden himself, advised jihadist leaders against operating under the Al-Qaeda name in his final days as he realized that it had been too closely tied to Islamic radicalism. Perhaps now its' greatest strength is its ability to inspire future offshoots of "the base" that seek to become the next Al-Qaeda. Chemical weapons, in their current level of complexity, that are employed by terrorists are far more effective for the psychological costs associated with their use rather than any tangible effectiveness in terms of fatalities. Subways, government buildings, and places where large numbers of civilians gather will continue to be selected as targets for chemical attacks due to their enclosed spaces and the perception that they are poorly ventilated and prone to human congestion. Federal buildings associated with the economic and political stability of the West will also be lucrative targets, forcing the American and host nation governments to spend gross amounts in personnel, finances, and resources in their defense.

15
The Biological Threat

In the late '70s an exiled Bulgarian writer drove to the BBC overseas radio services to broadcast a radio show on Radio Free Europe and the BBC. His name was Georgi Markov, once a very prominent writer in Bulgaria and adored by the elite of the Bulgarian society. On September 7, 1978 Markov parked his car along the Thames River due to the difficulties in finding parking near the BBC; as he walked toward the BBC he felt a sharp jab in his thigh, looking back he noticed a man picking up an umbrella apologizing; thinking nothing of it Markov continued on with his day. Later that night while at home he began to run a fever; his blood pressure fell, finally two days later his heart gave out. Before he died he was able to tell his wife about the strange incident in front of the BBC with the man and the umbrella. Once Scotland Yard heard this information they had Markov's body x-rayed; they found a small metal pellet the size of a pinhead with four holes drilled into it; these holes contained ricin. The KGB has used these types of tactics for years, some may remember Alexander Litvinenko the form Russian KGB Lieutenant Colonel who was poisoned with thallium back in 2006.

References to the KGB's use of biological weapons brings to mind spy thrillers such as the James Bond series of books and movies. To think, that these tactics are in use today by these organizations is both exciting, from an espionage-thriller point of view, and more than a little scary. But reality can be a bit darker than anything imagined by novelists or screenwriters. For example, a declassified article produced by the CIA envisioned the potential use of biological agents by terrorists in the 21st century. To summarize the article, advancing technology combined with the technological gap in our ability to detect these agents have the potential to create biological weapons suitable for the desires of either a rogue nation-states or the extremist seeking to make a permanent mark on world events.

Diseases can now be engineered to be far more lethal than anything occurring naturally. The very same research techniques intended to map the biological complexities of a bacteria in order to better protect us from the next outbreak of influenza or AIDS are also currently in use to produce the most malicious organisms known to man. Fiction can help us conceptualize such world-altering events for without it, I otherwise would not be able to imagine a world with an engineered disease capable of wiping out 99%

of those infected. Think of Stephen King's "The Stand", where the author lays out the subtle spread of a bio-engineered "super-plague" as it spreads undetected around the world through a series of interstate highways and international air travel or more recently Steven Soderbergh's "Contagion" as the face of human interaction is forever changed due to a pandemic. Then think back to the fear that gripped Chinese authorities and the world with the spread of the SARS virus and the real-world uncertainty and suspicion as legitimate journalism and rumor fueled by fear collided, igniting debate over whether the disease could have been a fluke of nature or an intentional act of terrorism.

In the mid-1990's, Larry Wayne Harris became one of the United States most wanted men by obtaining biological agents and expressing an intent to engineer a regional crisis. Mr. Harris came to the attention of several local and federal law enforcement agencies when he was arrested for the purchase of a biological agent with the intent to use it as a weapon as well as misrepresenting himself as one who was qualified to handle and study biological agents for lawful purposes. He began to demonstrate an interest in biological agents while serving in the military as a mechanic, stationed at the U.S. Army's Aberdeen Proving Grounds- known for it's classified research on a number of defense related projects. After leaving the military, Harris continued his obsession with biological warfare (BW) agents and claimed to work at several highly classified BW laboratories, both real and fictional. He maintained that his knowledge of such agents resulted in employment by the Department of Defense, civilian BW think tanks, FBI, and the CIA. Mr. Harris' military records and statements by federal officials discount his claims of highly classified employment with any such agencies confirming only that he has sought out civilian education in the microbiology field at Ohio State University.

He made claims to personal acquaintances of apocalyptic scenarios involving BW agents unleashed upon America by foreign governments and statements indicating that he was capable of teaching American citizens the weaknesses within their society through the deployment of such agents. Harris had made several attempts to procure biological agents through his employment at a civilian research laboratory, all of which were denied because he lacked the credentials, the facilities, or the need to properly study such agents. He then manufactured the necessary credentials at a local printing shop by way of a fabricated office memorandum letterhead, an act that must now be considered a laughably bizarre breach of security protocol were it not successful. The faked memorandum was enough for the biological agents to be shipped to Mr. Harris' home address, as requested, and may have gone unnoticed if not for his own impatience. After waiting only five days, Harris contacted the shipping company to complain about the slow pace of his order and an attentive customer service representative alerted the authorities to his suspicious inquiries.

After a through investigation by officials it was determined that Mr. Harris was more likely seeking fame and credibility through a series of misrepresentations of himself and his professional skill than any real plausible threat. After this determination he was released on probation, which for almost two years he kept up with the requirements of his release and claimed to have reformed his behavior. In actuality, he had continued with his obsessive and delusional activities and established relationships with the right-wing religious group, Christian Identity Church that maintain apocalyptic ideologies and the racist paramilitary group, Aryan Nation. In 1998, he was arrested based upon information from an informant who claimed that Harris was in possession of a weaponized strain of anthrax and had intended to deploy this agent upon an American city. Subsequent research determined that the anthrax strain was harmless and commonly used in veterinary vaccines.

There are several common motivational factors associated with individuals and groups considering the use of biological terrorism. Of these criteria, Larry Wayne Harris met a number of of them, and in retrospect, was flirting dangerously with the actual employment of a biological warfare agent. He had formed relationships and had, in fact, become a trusted member of the higher echelons of militant groups espousing racist and apocalyptic beliefs. He had apocalyptic visions, which were tied to a deep sense of paranoia that he sought to confide in others, and failing to find the level of commitment in his beliefs that he was seeking, sought to convince others by initiating these actions himself. His sense of grandiosity led him to claim employment with highly classified groups within the Department of Defense, FBI, and CIA, working on projects that were "too classified to reveal", according to informants. These statements were apparently used to lend credibility to his professional microbiology experience, which was lacking the credentials to work for any of the aforementioned agencies on any of the projects that he claimed. Harris wanted to show America that it was unprepared for an act of biological terrorism by committing such an act and setting himself up to be the individual who had predicted it in the first place. In a sense, he fancied himself a savior from an act of terrorism that he was willing to commit.

Incidents of biological terrorism, both at home and abroad, have highlighted America's vulnerability to these asymmetrical forms of attack. Recipes for a growing number of biological agents, coupled with detailed recommendations of how to deploy them, can be readily located with a quick Internet search and a general understanding of high school level science

In the past, terrorist groups such as Al-Qaeda have focused on large-scale spectacular attacks designed to sow terror and garner worldwide media attention. However, there is evidence that these groups may shift their strategy from high profile attacks to small-scale targeted attacks in an effort to report any type of success. In light of this information law enforcement, first responders, and health care facilities in smaller rural areas not known for high population density should begin to assess their own security environment and prioritize training and resources for such an attack.

The 1984 case of the Rajneeshees religious cult is one documented case of a successful biological attack to occur on U.S. soil. The cult devised a plan to control the outcome of a local election, and thus gain political power, by disseminating a strain of liquidized salmonella at restaurants in a small county in Oregon. The idea was to sicken enough of the local populace so as to render them unable to vote in the election and allow the small population of the cult to influence the election results. Approximately 751 local area residents were sickened by this poisoning, although none fatally.[60] The specific form chosen by the group was the Salmonella agent in a liquid form, dripped across the salad bars of local eateries with an intended oral method of delivery. The agent was meant to be incapacitating, as opposed to lethal, as is common with most agents with an oral delivery method.[61] Liquid forms of biological agents have very limited properties that can be detected by the human senses. They are typically of a viscous consistency similar to whole milk, and most biological toxins resemble the color of bacterial liquids ranging from off-white to amber or opaque. The symptoms of salmonella poisoning include, fever, diarrhea, and abdominal cramps and typically last less than a week.

The immediate priority for first responders in a biological attack is self-protection. The use of a protective mask, over garments and breathing equipment and possibly preventative prophylactic treatment with antibiotics will be necessary, at a minimum. Any casualties incurred as a result of a biological attack will require the same forms of treatment as those who had contracted the disease by natural means. In the case of salmonella poisoning, it is not typically fatal, with the exception of the very young or old who are at the highest risk. Rehydration to replenish liquids lost as a result of diarrhea and normal food intake coupled with antibiotics in only the most severe cases will effectively treat the disease. The site of a salmonella attack can be decontaminated with the application of high intensity water pressure with chlorine or bleach additive.[62]

Most emergency response planning for a terrorist incident has been concerned with overt attacks, such as large-scale simultaneous bombings, however there are indications that some terrorist groups would be willing to cross the threshold from these conventional forms of warfare to more unconventional methods. In the past 30 years the world has seen the attempted use of chemical and biological (CB) terrorism by a number of non-state actors and terrorist organizations. The Rajneeshee cult in Oregon in 1984, the Aum Shinrikyo cult in 1999, and the mass poisonings of hundreds of school-aged children in Afghanistan are all examples of CB terrorism. The question of CB terrorism is no longer "if", but "when" will the next attack occur and what form will it take? Arguably successful, when considering the psychological impact and media response of these attacks, and a stark reminder to the world that terrorists are capable of striking at a variety of targets of their choosing, sending the message that nowhere is safe.

Biological warfare (BW) agents are living microorganisms, such as bacteria and viruses, and nonliving toxins that can cause illness and disease usually resulting in death. The effectiveness of BW agents are exponential compared to chemical warfare (CW) agents in that generally speaking, a smaller amount of a BW agent can have a greater impact on more casualties than a larger amount of a CW agent. Pound for pound, BW agents are extremely more effective than CW agents because of their lethality. BW agents are classified into two different categories, pathogens and toxins and can further be subcategorized in contagious and noncontagious categories.

Anthrax, the plague, Q fever, tularemia, smallpox, and equine encephalitis fall under the pathogen category of BW agents. While the plague and smallpox are highly contagious pathogens, Q fever and anthrax are non-contagious BW agents. Botulism and ricin are two examples of BW toxins. Transmissibility, vaccination, and routes of infection are all factors taken into account when an adversary attempts to engage in BW. They are unique among the CBRN threats in that they cannot be detected by human senses, existing without a detectable scent or taste and too small to be seen without laboratory equipment. Most biological agents are at the mercy of weather and meteorological conditions affecting their ability to take root at the site of a deployment.

The most likely, and dangerous, method of exposure is by inhalation. Biological agents inhaled, bypassing our body's natural defenses such as skin, and then settling in the lungs. Due to the difficulty in effectively disseminating BW agents, there is only one known case of a BW agent being used in the US. The current level of sophistication for many biological agents is low, but there is enormous potential–based on advances in modern molecular biology and drug delivery technology–for making more sophisticated weapons.

The insidious nature of biological agents coupled with the fact that symptoms may not show up for hours, days or even weeks is the single most important factor that make them so dangerous. This makes the trace back process to the point of contamination, and then to the perpetrators, unimaginably difficult. Biological terrorism has, in fact, been the progenitor of a new type of criminal investigation, that of the field of biological forensics.

There are 4 basic building blocks that make up a biological threat, these being:

1. The Agent–this is the actual pathogen or toxin that is the hazard. An agent may be an incapacitating agent or it may be a lethal agent. An incapacitating agent causes harm, sickness or some other modifier to the target, but generally does not kill the host unless the host is predisposed to being harmed by the agent, as is the case with the very old, the very young and those who have a weakened immune system prior to infection. A lethal agent is one that generally kills the host.

2. The Delivery System–this is the means or mode by which the agent is brought into contact with the host to be infected. The delivery system may be in the form of munitions, an aerosol producing system or a directly infecting means, such as a dead body or a stagnant body of water.

3. The Delivery–this is the actual vector to host contact itself, the passing of the agent from the delivery system to the host. The delivery may be an aerosol that has been released from a delivery system that is inhaled by

the host, or a liquid that the host ingests or even a vector delivery, such as the bite of a mite or a mosquito.

4.Meteorological Conditions–this is the pattern of conditions that influences the spread of the agent over the area being contaminated, and is specific to the direction and speed of the wind, the amount of sunlight (UV) exposure, the temperature (inversion) of the area and type of area where the agent is released (out of doors versus the confined interior of a building).

The effectiveness of an attack, release or accidental exposure of a biological agent is dependent upon the synergistic effects of these four building blocks. An example one could examine would be the aerosol delivery of Q-fever through the use of a commercial sprayer in an open field containing cattle. If the agent were sprayed on the field during a high wind, say greater than 25 mph, the likelihood of mass infection would be minimal due to the agent losing its physical integrity. All of the building blocks need to be in place in order to attain the maximum impact.

Biological weapons may be employed in various ways to gain a strategic or tactical advantage over an adversary, either by threats or by actual deployments. Like chemical agents, biological weapons may also be useful as area denial weapons. These agents may be lethal or non-lethal, and may be targeted against a single individual, a group of people, or even an entire population. As a tactical weapon for military use, a significant problem with a biological warfare attack is that it would take days to be effective, and therefore might not immediately stop an opposing force. Some biological agents (especially smallpox, plague, and tularemia) have the capability of person-to-person transmission via aerosolized respiratory droplets.

The CDC categorizes biological agents in the following manner:

Category A is defined as- the U.S. public health system and primary healthcare providers must be prepared to address various biological agents, including pathogens that are rarely seen in the United States. High-priority agents include organisms that pose a risk to national security because they

- can be easily disseminated or transmitted from person to person;
- result in high mortality rates and have the potential for major public health impact;
- might cause public panic and social disruption; and
- require special action for public health preparedness.

Category B is define as second highest priority agents include those that

- are moderately easy to disseminate;

- result in moderate morbidity rates and low mortality rates; and
- require specific enhancements of CDC's diagnostic capacity and enhanced disease surveillance.

Category C are the third highest priority agents include emerging pathogens that could be engineered for mass dissemination in the future because of

- availability;
- ease of production and dissemination; and
- potential for high morbidity and mortality rates and major health impact.

As recently as 2006, Fox News reported that the leader of Al-Qaeda in Iraq, Abu Hamza al-Muhajir, authored a message to all of the "faithful" calling for scientists and explosives experts to participate in the jihad by using their unique skills to prepare an unconventional biological "dirty bomb" to be detonated in the United States. This is in contrast to the groups' doctrine before 9/11 that called for the attainment of CBRN weapons more as a deterrent against the conventional capabilities of U.S. and Israeli forces, as opposed to a weapon optioned for a first-strike.[63] Modern terrorism, involving independent cells guided only in the strategic sense rather than given more specific tactical guidance increases the likelihood that members of an organization which acquires biological capabilities will be far more likely to use them without provocation.

The acquisition stage of biological weapons is, in fact, not the most difficult step for a terrorist group because many potential agents have valid uses in the industrial sector and are relatively available. In addition, the wealth of information available through online sources makes the ability to acquire biological cultures, dissemination components, or the sharing of information related to a successful terrorist operation easier today than ever before. Twenty years ago, the most provocative terrorist plots were more a display of technological gullibility and wild ambition whereas today's groups are more technologically savvy and able to communicate successes, failures, and new ideas instantly through the Internet.

In comparison, any attack involving a biological agent is likely to be conducted in a clandestine manner, allowing for the agent to spread undetected throughout the populace. This form of an attack present unique challenges requiring that emergency planning procedures are prepared with a more direct involvement with the public health network. The dissemination of a biological agent as part of a terrorist attack is not likely to be immediately detected due to the period of incubation between the initial exposure and the manifestation of symptoms. Physicians and other health care providers would likely identify the first casualties of such an attack. For example, patients would begin showing up at local area hospitals, clinics, and emergency rooms complaining of symptoms that would develop, over time, to the final stages of the introduced disease. By the time that the symptoms were recognized and enough cases were confirmed, the disease would likely have already spread through person-to-person contact and the responsible group would have already escaped. There would only be a limited window of opportunity for the health officials to determine that the even is not a naturally occurring phenomenon, a biological attack has actually occurred, identify the source, and prevent further casualties by the distribution of mass vaccination treatments and an information awareness campaign.

Some chemical agents can also be introduced via contaminated water or food sources. In the northeastern provinces of Afghanistan, there have been several mass-poisonings of school-aged children by an unidentified group opposing the education of young girls. These poisonings have sickened hundreds and created a climate of distrust and fear among the community. Like the aforementioned biological attack scenario, this incident highlights the need for swift diagnosis of unusual health problems and the sharing of that information with the health care infrastructure. The early detection and rapid response to both chemical and biological attacks is a critical part of the public health response organization, which exists to protect the public against any suspicious health episode.

The skills, methods of detection, diagnosis and resources that are required to detect the symptoms of disease as well as the patterns of injury caused by the accidental misuse of chemicals are complimentary to those used in the detection of a terrorist biological or chemical attack. However, responding agencies must also take into consideration the additional features that a terrorist attack may entail such as the intentional infliction of hundreds of casualties, the use of conventional explosives to disguise and disperse the agent, or even a combination of these tactics across multiple locations, simultaneously overwhelming emergency and health care services.

The overwhelming majority of chemical and biological attacks have been crude, utilizing agents such as arsenic, potassium cyanide, salmonella, pesticides and other ingredients known to have dual-use properties. While unsuccessful in creating large numbers of casualties they have been effective in creating a disproportionate psychological effect on the population. More powerful agents have been deployed only rarely, by the Aum Shinrikyo cult and during the Anthrax letters incident of 2001, with enough of a potency to cause fatalities. These two incidents had one thing in common, a well-funded and equipped weapons program with the freedom to experiment and more fully weaponize an agent prior to deployment. In the current security environment it is far less likely that a terrorist organization would enjoy the freedom to develop a weapon without fear of exposure. Therefore, it is most likely that future CB incidents by terrorist organizations would continue this trend of simple, makeshift delivery devices and agents that are effective at sowing terror while causing low numbers of actual fatalities.

There are numerous potential chemical and biological agents that could be used and the health care structure must be prepared to resolve crises that would occur as a result. Priority must be assigned to focus preparedness efforts on agents that would have the most significant impact on the public health and security of the citizens of the United States. Highly contagious agents as well as those that can be weaponized for dissemination by aerosol currently display the characteristics desirable for a terrorist attack and should be the primary focus of preparedness efforts. Preventative detection measures and awareness of the features of biological agents should be essential and regular training among health care workers should be standardized across the U.S. The health industry must have increased ability to investigate suspicious events and inexplicable illnesses and communicate their findings to other providers and public officials. State and regional laboratories must be augmented to quickly identify biological agents not commonly used in the U.S. Primary to these efforts is an all-inclusive training plan aimed to guarantee proficiency in health preparedness as it relates to biological terrorism and cooperation at the highest levels of local, state, and federal agencies.

Aside from the dangers associated with the risk of exposure to responders and health care workers is the possibility that they may be the target. The Occupational Safety and Health Administration (OSHA) recognize that employees are at severe risk and have established safety practices designed to mitigate these risks. Approximately half of the United States has adopted state plans approved by OSHA.[64] Most of these plans closely follow the recommendations made by the agency but differ in the way they are enforced or the exact standards to which they are upheld. This still leaves 25 states without these standardized procedures or methods of enforcement. A nationally recognized standard is still in need of development and approval. The responsibility for the health of American citizens is still predominantly an issue for individual states. This creates issues with not only a non-standardized response but also implications for differing responses to a bioterrorist event that spreads across state boundaries. Undoubtedly, national resources would be requested but through different channels and in ways that would further complicate an already complicated event. One agency that would almost certainly be involved in investigating any incident would be the Center for Disease Control. However, unlike national criminal investigative agencies, the CDC must be requested first by the state before they are authorized to launch an investigation, slowing down the response time.

Frustrated response times to bioterrorist attack due to miscommunication and inefficiency between local, state, and the federal government have already been the subject of numerous reports and papers all with varied suggestions on how to improve upon this mismanagement. In fact, one such working group identified that although the National Response Plan calls for the Department of Health and Human Services is intended to be the lead agency meant to coordinate directly between state and federal levels during a bioterrorist event it must manage an 'umbrella' of smaller agencies. The working group found that there was no specific team or response effort designed to provide medical care to large numbers victims until almost 48 hours after the initiation of the event.[65] While, as representatives of the federal government there is an inaccurate assumption that they are the cavalry, prepared and capable of bringing organization and streamlining the response of such an event. In fact, they would have an extremely limited ability to improve the medical fields response to large numbers of casualties.

Further complicating matters are concerns over funding, cost-effectiveness, resource management, command hierarchy, and compatibility between the many agencies involved in a response at every level. There are many agencies with regionally organized command structures however, most of these were developed independently of one another and their primary mission is other than response to bioterrorism. Efforts to improve coordinative efforts between them are underway but are not extensive. Many analyses of whether it is worth the effort to regionalize responding agencies conclude that there would be many benefits to such a daunting undertaking. These benefits would most likely manifest in the form of improved triage, distribution of vaccine, investigatory procedures, security and emergency management, as well as cost-effectiveness when training emergency services personnel and standardization of training. By enforcing the coordination of these agencies at the federal level, all would benefit from the implementation, improved communications, and increased performance of these limited assets.

Recent incidents as well as continued threats of CB terrorism by hostile organizations against civilians have exposed vulnerabilities in nations around the world as well as underscored the need to augment our ability to detect and manage the outcome of terrorist actions. A nationally standardized set of response protocols for the prevention and response to chemical and biological terrorism would streamline the process to share intelligence and limited assets. The CDC, in cooperation with Department of Justice and state agencies, should be afforded the opportunity to better assist and work more closely with the populations that they are designed to protect. CDC scientists and advisors could maintain small teams that work regularly with local governments on the state level so that they can gather information, advise appropriately and request necessary assets from the federal level. The population must be protected from a widespread range of potent CB agents, including those that have been engineered for military use. Systems that emerge as a result of the preventative measures against biological terrorism can perform in a dual-purpose capacity. They serve to quickly detect unusual outbreaks of disease and streamline the response to health emergencies such as naturally occurring pandemics. Even without the threat of imminent war, a prepared national defense structure functions as a deterrent against hostile nations. In the same way, investment in a well-prepared health-care system will provide the best deterrent against biological terrorism.

16
The Choice Of Anthrax As A Weapon

To date, the most highly publicized, and successful use of anthrax has been attributed to Dr. Bruce Ivins. A seven-year inquiry conducted by the FBI concluded that Dr. Ivins prepared the anthrax powder and mailed it to several media organizations and two U. S. Senators in 2001. Following the highly publicized anthrax letters event, the FBI Weapons of Mass Destruction Directorate responded to 2,500 reports of the use or threatened use of anthrax or other biological agents and became an incredible drain on resources, manpower, and time.[66] The fear caused as a result of the 2001 anthrax letters continues to this day. It is becoming more common for law enforcement to respond to hoax threats pertaining to the ubiquitous "white, powdery substance". Whether the subsequent investigation reveals these materials to be a real biological threat or a hoax it is undeniable that they disrupt emergency services in the area and pose a potential threat to the responding agency. The threat of a bioterrorist event, particularly anthrax, is so grave that seemingly anyone with a envelope, a grudge, and any "white, powdery substance" is capable of delivering a terroristic message that serves a reminder of how unprepared we all are to face this type of danger. Besides the drain on investigative services and hazardous materials agencies there is also the psychological impact on those targeted, intentionally or unintentionally, as they often undergo weeks of tests and months of medical treatment just in case theirs is a legitimate biological incident. Critical to deterring terrorists from effectively deploying anthrax as a weapon is the information available to the public and medical support personnel, including the methods for detection and avoidance, individual protection, and proper decontamination procedures.

There are several factors that make a biological agent an enticing weapon of choice for a terrorist group. Availability or ease of production in ample quantity, ease of dissemination, lethality or the ability to inspire a terror effect in the populace all must be considered by the prospective terrorist. Biological agents become candidates for terrorist use based on their ability to incapacitate or kill their target. It is not always necessary to have a lethal ability in order to achieve success in the eyes of the terrorist. The ability to inspire fear, panic, and gain the attention of the media while appearing to strike at the target of their choosing in spite of existing security measures is often sufficient. An effective biological warfare agent must be able to be disseminated in the air by using commercially available equipment, such as industrialized aerosol sprayers or similar device. For example, an aerosol sprayer could be mounted vehicle, such as a car, boat, or airplane and operated upwind of the target, allowing the wind currents to disseminate the agent over a large area. Another scenario involves introducing the agent in an enclosed space such as an office building where it could infect all who occupies that area. There are few bacteria that have been deemed to be of any military significance. In fact, among several thousand identified strains, only approximately 100 have determined to be pathogenic, anthrax being one of them. The spore itself is quite resistant, able to withstand extremes with regard to temperature, arid or moist conditions. Some pathogens are capable of toxicity producing disease and possibly death.

A terrorist attack involving a biological agent would be a complicated affair as the attack could go unnoticed for days or weeks. The delay of symptoms, possibly preventing any warning to the populace or preparation for treatment to begin, would further increase the likelihood of casualties. It is essential that public health information be communicated to the public in an expeditious manner as a risk mitigation component. Recent incidents involving anthrax or the 2003 Severe Acute Respiratory Syndrome (SARS) outbreak suggest that the public response depends upon the quality of information provided, specifically whether the information appears to be scientifically reliable, from a credible source, and distributed in a timely manner.

Anthrax is caused by the Bacillus anthracis microorganism and primarily manifests itself in humans in three forms, cutaneous, gastrointestinal (GI), and inhalational anthrax. It is capable of being transmitted from contact with infected animals, ingestion of their meat, or aerosolized spores. The soil of both domestic and wild animals, mainly cattle, horses, pigs, goats, and sheep, is known to be a reservoir for anthrax. Contrary to a widely held belief, humans are not able to contract anthrax directly from soil. The symptoms of anthrax depend upon the method of transmission. Symptoms of cutaneous anthrax include swelled, necrotic ulcers covered with black scabbing on the surface of the skin and if left untreated has a fatality rate ranging between five and twenty percent. The accidental ingestion of anthrax is known to cause oropharyngeal or gastrointestinal anthrax the symptoms of which include fever, difficulty swallowing, and nausea. Once the bacteria has incubated within the host, the virility of symptoms increase to include abdominal pain, bloody vomiting, with the possibility of septic shock or even, and death. In the case of inhalation anthrax, the initial symptoms would include fever, severe fatigue, chest pain, difficulty breathing, and death. The typical incubation period for anthrax spores range from two to seven days, although periods lasting up to 60 days have been reported. Transmission of the bacteria between humans is extremely rare, although clothing and soil infected with anthrax may remain contaminated and susceptible to transmission for years. Depending upon the form it takes, anthrax is known for its potentially high fatality rate, measuring approximately 40% to 50% percent even with medical care.

Potential delivery vehicles for terrorists include improvised bomblets, point release or an aerosolized airborne line release. The intentional contamination of food or water must also be considered as a delivery method in the event of a terrorist attack. In 2010, a study was conducted with the intent of identifying potential mitigation measures to prevent the spread of anthrax during a terrorist attack. Using an imitation anthrax spore released within an office building, researchers were able to create an effect similar to the intentional release of an anthrax agent. In less than five minutes, the spores had spread throughout the entire building via a series of ventilation ducts. It was found that attempts at lessening the spread of the spores by closing doors or disabling the air ducts were ineffective.

Considerations at an incident site involving a biological warfare agent should include the attempt to identify the agent through sampling, control of the site as a biological hazard and crime scene, decontamination and treatment of exposed victims at the point of injury in preparation for movement to the next level of medical care. A secure health care facility and organized staff is critical to the effectiveness of any disaster response scenario resulting in significant numbers of casualties. Medical personnel must be concerned with not only the risk of contamination at the site but also the potential for a continued spread of the disease and decontamination sites and treatment facilities. A clear understanding of the fundamentals of decontamination procedures during a bioterrorist attack will minimize the probability of the continuance of the disease among patients and medical personnel.

Throughout the epidemic of SARS in 2003, there were over 8,000 cases of the disease reported worldwide. In Canada alone, there were 351 cases reported, and of those 72% contracted the disease while in a health care facility. 45% of those to contract the disease in Canada were health care workers, underscoring the grave risk to medical professionals by an infectious agent. Publicly available information will be necessary to encourage awareness of the signs and symptoms of anthrax exposure. There isn't much known about the variables that may affect the willingness of medically trained personnel to render aid to patients during a bioterrorist event. Of critical interest is the willingness of first responders and physicians to expose themselves to harm in order to treat patients who may have come into contact with anthrax. A 2010 survey of medical professionals found that those with the greatest knowledge of the symptoms and treatment of anthrax were 50% more likely to come to work in the face of such an attack than those who felt uninformed. Of that group, 37% were willing to treat patients supposed to be infected with the disease, and 28% would treat patients confirmed to have been exposed. The implication is that increased knowledge among medical professionals would likely increase their willingness to treat those infected during a biological attack involving anthrax.

The notification of transportation providers, such as airlines, the public and further coordination between health and federal agencies must be planned and rehearsed prior to an attack. Site decontamination must be a coordinated effort between the Environmental Protection Agency, the Center for Disease control, and local Hazardous Materials teams. Because anthrax is an enduring organism it is not likely to be rendered inactive by the environmental conditions alone. Extensive cleanup operations will be necessary including environmental testing and closure of contaminated areas possibly requiring the long-term relocation of civilians and rerouting of traffic patterns with a significant economic impact. There would also be long-term health impacts that would arise from such an attack including the medical measures that would be taken to prevent further increase in symptom lethality or spread of the disease. Many would be sickened, disabled, or killed due to exposure. Combined direct and indirect costs associated with physical and mental treatment following an attack coupled with the economic costs from loss of consumer confidence would be astronomical.

Depending upon the release area and patient symptoms at the onset of the disease in the event of the terrorist employment of anthrax, it is likely that experienced clinicians would detect the use of an anthrax agent rather quickly. Emergency room physicians, hospital personnel, and infectious disease specialists should be able to readily identify the symptoms of the disease and cross-reference that information with the spread pattern of patients across a wide selection of the population demographic. Laboratory resources to diagnose suspected preliminary symptoms of anthrax are available at most public and private laboratories, combined with an increased awareness of the disease following the 2001 anthrax letter attacks, has increased the likelihood of rapid detection in most American cities. Agent detection and sampling at the point of introduction site combined with a joint hazard assessment conducted at the local and federal levels will confirm the presence of anthrax allowing for a response to be mobilized.

Anthrax does have several available vaccines and antibiotics that are well tolerated by humans, provide lasting immunity, and are effective. A controlled study involving mill workers found that the anthrax vaccine effectively protected approximately 92% of those in the study group. An increase in the antibody production to the disease, commonly regarded as a measurement of effectiveness, found that 91% of adults who had received the vaccine demonstrated an immune response after just two doses and a four-fold enhancement in antibodies after three doses. Concerns that adverse human reaction to some of these treatments has proven largely unfounded. Studies have found that adverse reactions to many of these vaccines are comparable to reactions observed when inoculated from diphtheria and tetanus toxins or influenza. Although no significant effects have been reported on a regular basis, there are still concerns that rare side effects will still occur.

A bioterrorist attack involving anthrax is a credible threat within the United States The capacity to prevent the release of anthrax as a terrorist weapon lies with local, state and federal authorities and include the requirement for laboratory strains of the organism to be controlled, the identification and registration individuals with the scientific skill and laboratory access required to produce and refine anthrax to an aerosolized form. Information is the most critical aspect to minimizing the chances for a successful use of the agent. In spite of advances in technology and measures designed to detect the spread of anthrax, it is still the prepared physician that will be most likely to detect the illness caused by an intentional exposure to biological agents. An informed public, in cooperation with emergency personnel and medical staff is the most critical component of a successful counterterrorism campaign aimed at the prevention of the bioterrorist use of anthrax.

17

Agro-Terrorism

When the American public thinks of a potential terrorist attack it's usually in the nature of a bombing, considering that it is the terrorists' mostly likely (and comfortable) course of action. Despite the threat of terrorism and the occasional foiled plot most don't consider the possibility of eco-terrorism or agro-terrorism. However, the threat is very real. According to a CRS report for congress in 2004, "agro-terrorism is a subset of bioterrorism, and is defined as the deliberate introduction of an animal or plant disease with the goal of generating fear, causing economic losses, and/or undermining stability." In fact, the agricultural sector would be especially susceptible to disruption resulting in disastrous consequences for the economy of the United States and a ripple effect throughout the world body. Approximately 13 percent of the Gross Domestic Product and 16 percent of employment comes from this sector of the national community. In Midwest America, a regional area measuring just 200 square miles houses roughly 70 percent of cattle intended for slaughter. An intentional act of bioterrorism or a naturally occurring outbreak would cripple the production, processing, and distribution of agricultural products with an economic impact of almost $51 billion dollars annually and a worldwide loss of confidence in American exports.

The world, as a whole, will continue to think of conventional attacks long before they consider bioterrorism when the word "terrorism" is used. Terrorists have had a long and successful history with conventional explosives, even more so than the kidnappings and hijackings that were so prevalent in the 70's and 80's. The fact is, that although there have been some attempts to employ methods of bioterrorism; none of these attempts have resulted in success in the way that was intended. Without that precedent for success or available information for terrorists to learn from, many are hesitant to branch out with experimental methods. There are going to be some entrepreneurs in the extremist circles who will attempt to make this happen but they currently have a lot of obstacles to overcome. Assuming the goal is to create terror for the purpose of influencing U.S. international policy, causing economic damage, or fatalities then they still have to employ an agent far more virulent than what has been employed in previous attempts at bioterrorism.

The potential threat of a bio attack on U.S. agriculture would not be terribly difficult for an eco-terrorist group or a foreign terrorist organization to achieve. This, in fact, is true considering the majority of agricultural facilities and or small family owned farms that supply America's supermarkets lack the necessary means to defend from such an attack. Take a look at farms in general, the majority of crops are in large opened, unsecured fields, and livestock, if not in opened fields are housed in open air barns/pens which can easily be exposed to airborne pathogens. Livestock are normally confined in areas numbered in the hundreds to thousands waiting to be slaughtered, processed, and distributed which can result in large-scale contamination. Another issue with livestock is they are routinely commingle with livestock from other facilities that can result in dissemination of deadly pathogens across the countryside, which in turn makes it more difficult to contain.

Many scientists widely accept the view that livestock herds are much more susceptible to agro-terrorism than crop plants. This is because of livestock that are unvaccinated or not routinely screened for disease. Livestock that are infected can act as a vector and continue to carry and transmit the disease to uninfected livestock, and when transported to locations with other livestock that can later facilitate an outbreak. However, when dealing with plant pathogens isolation is limited to a smaller area, making an outbreak easier to control. Some plant pathogens also require certain environmental conditions in order to spread. Therefore, the spread of plant pathogens by a terrorist organization is less feasible.

The use or consideration of such weapons by a nation-state has been mostly stagnant since the ratification of the Biological and Toxins Weapons Convention in 1972 in which many countries stopped producing and destroyed stockpiles of biological weapons. Despite the lack of bio-weapons used against agricultural targets, the uses of chemical agents have been used more frequently. For example, the use of Agent Orange by the United States during the Vietnam War to destroy undergrowth and ultimately destroyed some crops. The use of this agent proved its effectiveness, but resulted in harmful long-term health effects on American soldiers who served in Southeast Asia.

The economic effects of a agro-terror attack could result in negative consequences to the U.S. and ultimately the world economy. First, the cost of containing the virus, decontamination, and the loss of production; second, the loss of exports due to countries preventing potentially contaminated food from entering their country; third, the federal and/ or state governments could ultimately absorb the cost in eradication and the high cost of containment of such viruses. The bioterrorism threat to food and water supplies is a very real and credible threat in today's world and is already considered a reality today. You can make this argument by pointing out that it has already occurred in attacks dating as far back as WWII, with the release of Glanders upon the Russians by Japan, or even further back to the sixth century with the contamination of water supplies by the Assyrians with rye ergot, or around 300 B.C. when the Greeks were known to put human and animal corpses into their adversaries water wells.

Without a doubt, terrorist groups have considered America's food and water supply a potential target. But the question is, is it feasible? Nation states have developed the capabilities to severely corrupt another country's food and water supply, but only to be used in the event of a large-scale regional conflict. Does a small-scale operation, even with the support of a shadowy government, have the ability to make it real? There is a considerable amount of media coverage and thought that gives credence to the idea that a terrorist organization would 1.Have the desire to use biological weapons 2. Have a vulnerable target 3.Have the technical capability to deliver this agent to the target 4. Have the finances to logistically support such an operation 5. Acquire or develop the agent. There are several steps along the path to a successful bioterrorist operation and every one of them involves the risk of failure.

The success of the Rajneeshee cult poisonings or the Hanakam group following WWII were small-scale and would not be considered successful to a group intending to significantly harm the population or economy. Currently, there aren't many historical trends for the terrorist to draw conclusions from due to the lack of successful bioterrorist attacks whereas conventional weapons are known to be effective, easily acquired, and more familiar to the terrorist. The support of a state-sponsor removes some of the potential friction points from the plan but opens up said state to repercussions in the form of alienation and overwhelming retaliation on a number of fronts beyond conventional military.

There are many points in the food distribution network that are vulnerable to disruption. Crops and livestock, the processing and distribution process, transportation, storage and retail facilities are all possibilities that are vulnerable be exploited by a terrorist group. Although the awareness is there, the expertise is not always present to advise the agricultural industry of necessary steps to upgrade security. While federal agencies such as the

Food and Drug Administration and the United States Department of Agriculture have published inspection guidelines and identified potential targets, they do not have the authority nor do they have the necessary expertise to enforce recommendations to security measures as they apply to the agricultural industry. In fact, the onus is now on much of this critical industry to "police" themselves.

The problem is that government can only regulate business, they cannot tell them how to conduct their business. Although there are many food production associations that work with the government establishing safety measures, not all producers are willing to join those associations and adhere to the strict guidelines. There are professional associations that partner with the FDA to develop guidelines for food safety and self-police their members who are then granted the right to display the associations' logo on their packaging. I recognize two problems with the effectiveness of professional associations self-policing members. If a consumer is unaware of the member certification label and does not know what it means, they probably will not look for that label to ensure they are buying a product embracing safety or quality values. The other problem is that membership into an association is voluntary. Without buy in from the supplier (which is usually coincides with consumer demand), the system of self-policing will not work.

Many of the entities involved throughout the supply chain are unwilling to commit to protecting food quality and safety that goes beyond current FDA requirements. In another report, a well-known egg hatchery holding 7 million chickens and responsible for the production of 14.5 million eggs daily was found to house those chickens in unsanitary conditions, creating a disease risk and affecting the quality of eggs produced. One of the most disconcerting findings surrounding this egg producer was that a majority of the employees were undocumented migrant workers. Although most undocumented workers are not a threat to national security, they are often underpaid and uninsured, living in substandard conditions, creating opportunities for corruption. A terror group could offer incentive for facility access or the introduction of an agent into the food and water supply.

The threat is considered a reality because there are already documented cases of agro-terrorism around the world. There have been attacks on food supply dating back to ancient civilizations such as the Fifth Plague referenced in the Christian Bible (Ex 9:3). In the 1970's Israel faced a contaminated orange crop that reduced exports significantly. In 1989, the United States detected contaminated Chilean grapes suspending imports that cost Chile and estimated $200 million. The list goes on.

❖ ❖ ❖

There are extremist groups that do not care about the ramifications of bioterrorism. It is those unpredictable elements that we guard against when we envision and rehearse against terrorist scenarios. In one such exercise the U.S. Government Accountability Office found that the agriculture sector accounted for about 13 percent of gross domestic product and 18 percent of employment making it a potential economic target.[67] The threat is to be taken seriously as this report determined that there were vulnerabilities in the control measures designed to protect the food supply. Most notably, the Customs inspection stations located a ports of entry around the U. S. were simply overwhelmed, preventing thorough screening. Even recent technological assets, designed to increase the screening capabilities were not common at all Customs screening locations and were not operated around-the-clock. Without these checks in place the United States is vulnerable to pathogens that may be intentionally be introduced to infect livestock or destroy staple crops. The report found that in some smaller countries, scientists, students and laboratory workers had access to facilities that contained high-risk pathogens increasing the likelihood that a non-state actor could acquire them.

In addition to the terror threat there are also legitimate concerns of natural catastrophes that pose a threat to the food and water supply. Climate change is occurring more rapidly than previously thought and will likely have significant implications for national security. Agriculture production often occurs in geographically vulnerable areas exposing food sources to flooding, rising water tables, or drought. Water limitations in these parts of the country negatively impact the economic development and business growth within agriculturally focused communities. Improved capability for risk analysis in environmentally susceptible areas will stave off natural disasters before they become catastrophes. Climate change can impact the United States by modifying trade and migration models, influencing those outside the affected area due to our increasingly interwoven supply chains.

The Public Health Security and Bioterrorism Preparedness and Response Act of 2002 makes it a federal requirement for community water facilities to objectively assess their vulnerabilities to a potential terrorist attack and develop contingency plans against such a threat.[68] These plans must then be filed with the Environmental Protection Agency and are then exempt from public distribution through the Freedom of Information Act. Given what is currently within reach of most terrorist organizations, the threat to our water supply remains only a threat. Many details still need to be worked through in order to initiate a successful attack. As the terrorist works on these details, a host of officials with far greater resources from law enforcement, intelligence services, even local municipality water treatment facilities are aware of the potential danger and considering how best to close the potential vulnerabilities. That is not to say we can all sleep soundly in the knowledge that none of these scenarios will ever become reality. We must continue to adapt and evolve our preventative measures from detection of any plot to stopping the attack at any one of the detection points along the way to the actual attack.

18
The Radiological Threat

For a very long period in American history it was feared that our enemies would announce their arrival on our soil with a devastating nuclear attack as an overwhelming show of force. This trepidation was a holdover from the Cold War era of mutually assured destruction and seemed to fade with the fall of the U.S.S.R. in the early '90s. Then came the chaos in the aftermath of that collapse with rumors of Russian generals with access to these superweapons seeking to sell them to the highest bidder in a last-ditch cash grab before the rug was pulled out from underneath them. But this trepidation can be somewhat allayed by the knowledge that nuclear weapons are highly technical machines that require extensive preventative maintenance and are extremely difficult to transport undetected. Most terrorist groups are without the extensive resources of a nation-state and must be content to do more, with less. They still desire to control the fear and awe that a nuclear weapon encompasses but they do not have the capability to build, maintain, transport, or detonate one of their own. According to Tucker, "A terrorist group that does not commit acts of terrorism or gain recognition as a feared opponent of the establishment has lost its reason for existence".[69]

Terrorist organizations have proven to be resourceful and coupled with the fanaticism that the new breed of transnational terrorists are becoming known for it is not surprising that they would take a device as complicated as a nuclear weapon and break it down to its most simple parts and then seek to use those components that are within their reach. Although the initial blast is still the most destructive aspect of a nuclear weapon, after the explosion there are still the effects of ionizing radiation left behind. It is recognized that these particles have common applications in the industrial and medical fields and are much more likely to be obtained by a terrorist network than a functional nuclear weapon.

To this day whether it be due to a stroke of luck, great national intelligence and security, or a little bit of both, there has not been a nuclear terrorist strike on American soil. While certain groups have shown great interest in obtaining nuclear materials to create a dirty bomb and use it against America, the actual manifestation of these desires and ideas has not occurred yet. This is quite surprising given the vast resources and availability of radioactive material. Radiological materials are very abundant throughout the world, and are classified by their use. Civil nuclear facilities can emit radiation from the production of power and the processing and disposal of nuclear waste. Radiation is present in industrial and medical settings due to radioactive equipment being used in these facilities. Radiological weapons, including radiological exposure devices (REDs), are specifically designed to destroy and cause casualties by releasing radiological material. A more "commonly known" form of radiation comes from depleted uranium, which is a byproduct of the uranium enrichment process. According to the military's' Joint Publication 3-11, the planning and consideration of radiation exposure is the most important part of planning for chemical warfare agents, biological warfare agents, and radiological material simply because radiological material is present in so many areas. With the presence of radiological material in industrial and medical devices, communications equipment, and depleted uranium, the Joint Chiefs took extra consideration in their recommendations to commanders.

Ionizing radiation can be comprised of several types of particles: alpha, beta, gamma, and neutron. These particles can be delivered by several methods. Explosive radiological dispersal devices (RDD) are perhaps the most likely method that a terrorist would use to spread radioactive particles. This device consists of a comparatively weak explosive component meant to disseminate the particles over a wide area rather than cause destructive damage. It is likely that emergency response services would become quickly overwhelmed with casualties and damage control allowing these particles to spread, assuming cooperative weather conditions, and be inhaled by all near the scene of the blast. Since a terrorist group has not yet acquired RDDs and their use has not become common it is unlikely that radiological detection equipment would be readily employed at the site. Another effective method would be the employment of a device emitting high energy and a radiological component that would expose those in the vicinity to particles, also known as a radiological exposure device (RED). This method is not as effective as an RDD because exposure levels are not likely to be significant enough to contaminate those in proximity.

In regards to terrorism the threat is not so much from nuclear weapons as it is from Radiological Dispersal Devices, which is defined as any device, including weapon or equipment other than a nuclear explosive device, specifically designed to employ radioactive material by disseminating it to cause destruction, damage, or injury by means of the radiation produced by the decay of such material. RDD's are a low-technology device that may use biomedical sources, industrial radioactive material, and/or radioactive waste as its core element in the device. Another means of employing radioactive material as a weapon is by use of a radiological exposure device, which is defined as a radioactive source placed to cause injury, illness, or death.

Radiological materials that can harm biological functions are broken down into four types of radiation known as alpha particles, beta particles, neutrons and electromagnetic radiation. These are further broken down into two subcategories, particulate and nonparticulate that cause damage by passing through cells and disrupting the normal cycle or killing the cells. Particulates consist of alpha particles that are slightly penetrating and found in polonium, uranium, plutonium and americium elements. Since they do not possess penetrating characteristics they only affect the cells immediately next to the particle. The affects are localized yet the danger comes from the fact that most alpha emitting particles also emit gamma radiation that is very penetrating and can cause long-term damage to cells. Alpha particles travel at speeds in excess of 5% of the speed of light, but they interact with matter very heavily, and thus at their usual velocities only penetrate a few centimeters of air, or a few millimeters of low density material such as the thin mica material which is specially placed in some Geiger counter tubes to allow alpha particles in. Alpha particles do not penetrate skin and cause no damage to tissues below. Some very high-energy alpha particles compose about 10% of cosmic rays and these are capable of penetrating the body and even thin metal plates. However, they are deflected by the Earth's magnetic field and then stopped by its atmosphere.

Beta particles are emitted from an atom nucleus as it tries to stabilize itself. They are the leftovers from the fission of heavy nucleus atoms, and include plutonium. Some of the leftover elements are Cesium-137, Strontium-90, and Iodine-131. Beta particles can penetrate deeper than alpha particles. A burn mark may be seen on the external skin where contamination has occurred and much more damage has been done deeper in the tissue. Internal ingestion will cause a sphere of damage around the area. If it is ingested, the damage will follow the digestive tract and damage cells along the way. Beta radiation consists of an energetic electron. It is more ionizing than alpha radiation, but less than gamma. Beta radiation from radioactive decay can be stopped with a few centimeters of plastic or a few millimeters of metal. It occurs when a neutron decays into a proton in a nucleus, releasing the beta particle and an antineutrino. Beta radiation from linac accelerators is far more energetic and penetrating than natural beta radiation. It is sometimes used therapeutically in radiotherapy to treat superficial tumors.

Neutron radiation is much more damaging and is the result of nuclear fission and fusion. They can change the atomic make up of atoms, thereby making them unstable and radioactive. The nonparticulate category consists of electromagnetic radiation. Gamma and x-ray from a nuclear reactor accident or nuclear detonation are the most common form of these. Because of this, entire body exposure to these if an individual is near the event. Both of these rays have no mass and travel at the speed of light. Neutrons are categorized according to their speed. Neutron radiation consists of free neutrons. These neutrons may be emitted during either spontaneous or induced nuclear fission, nuclear fusion processes, or from any other nuclear reactions. Neutrons are the only type of ionizing radiation that can make other objects, or material, radioactive. This process, called neutron activation, is the primary method used to produce radioactive sources for use in medical, academic, and industrial applications. Even comparatively low speed thermal neutrons, which do not carry enough kinetic energy individually to be ionizing, will cause neutron activation.

X-rays are electromagnetic waves with a wavelength smaller than about 10 nanometers. A smaller wavelength corresponds to a higher energy. Soft tissue in the human body is composed of smaller atoms than the calcium atoms that make up bone, hence there is a contrast in the absorption of X-rays. X-ray machines are specifically designed to take advantage of the absorption difference between bone and soft tissue, allowing physicians to examine structure in the human body

Gamma radiation occurs to rid the decaying nucleus of excess energy after it has emitted either alpha or beta radiation. Both alpha and beta particles have an electric charge and mass, and thus are quite likely to interact with other atoms in their path. Gamma radiation is composed of photons, which have neither mass nor electric charge. Gamma radiation penetrates much further through matter than either alpha or beta radiation. Gamma radiation can travel for many meters and can travel many centimeters into the body. For this reason it is often called penetrating radiation and the best type of defense against this type of radiation is lead, steel and concrete.

Radioactive particles are most dangerous when they enter the body through the eyes, nasal, mouth passages or damaged areas of the skin and settle in the lungs or blood stream. Those exposed to radiological threats can minimize their risk of contamination by evacuating the scene as quickly as possible and shielding themselves from the particles with appropriate protective clothing and shelter. There are various materials that are capable of shielding an individual from the effects of radiated particles. Unbroken skin is capable of stopping the effects of alpha particles while aluminum and lead are sufficient to stop beta and gamma rays, respectively. The most effective material is concrete, which is capable of shielding the effects of all radiological particles. Health effects depend upon the amount of exposure and time spent in the affected area. The first symptoms of radiological exposure are typically flu-like and include, nausea, vomiting, and diarrhea and can appear in as little as a few minutes or manifest after several days. Skin discoloration resembling sunburn accompanied by itching and swelling can also occur. Anyone experiencing these symptoms must immediately seek medical attention. The U.S. military recommends certain basic standards of proficiency for civilians to be able to operate and survive an NBC environment. Chief among these is to be able to identify the signs and symptoms of an attack involving a NBC agent, followed by the ability to properly don protective clothing, seek shelter, and decontaminate once the threat has passed.

Depleted Uranium is quite popular among conventional militaries around the world and is widely available in the tank graveyards of wars past, making it a readily available resource for potential terrorists. Depleted uranium (DU) arises as a byproduct of the production of enriched uranium for use in nuclear reactors and in the manufacture of nuclear weapons but, the United States and NATO militaries used DU penetrator rounds in the 1991 Gulf War, the Bosnia war, bombing of Serbia, and the 2003 invasion of Iraq. Another use of depleted uranium is in kinetic energy penetrator s anti-armor rounds, such as the 120 mm sabot rounds fired from the M1A1 and M1A2 Abrams because it is ideal for use in armor penetrators. These solid metal projectiles have the speed, mass and physical properties to perform exceptionally well against armored targets. The use of DU in munitions is controversial because of questions about potential long-term health effects. Depleted uranium was used in a number of weapons systems like the A-10, M1A1 main battle tank. The M1A1 had depleted uranium 105mm rounds as well as depleted uranium armor. But depleted uranium has had other uses in the past such as in dental porcelain, trim weights in aircraft wings and was used in boat keels. But do to the health considerations the use of this type of metal has been scaled back and in most cases it has been stopped completely. Normal functioning of the kidney, brain, liver, heart, and numerous other systems can be affected by uranium exposure because uranium is a toxic metal. It is weakly radioactive and remains so because of its long radioactive half-life but, the actual level of acute and Chronic toxicity of DU is also a point of medical controversy. Exposure can be harmful to the kidneys, brain, lover and heart and has been blamed for cancer in many gulf war veterans. It can also cause genetic defects in those who have been exposed. The United States still has DU in storage cylinders which when disposed of will cost roughly 15 to 450 million dollars.

Depleted Uranium (DU) is the "leftovers" after the uranium isotope 235U is enriched for use in nuclear power plants. According to the World Health Organization (WHO), DU contains three times less 235U than natural uranium, and subsequently is less radioactive than natural uranium and the radiation dose from DU would be 60% of a radiation dose from natural uranium of the same quantity. While DU does emit radiation, there are practical uses for DU due to its high density. DU is used as counterweights in aircraft, radiation shields in medical radiation therapy, militarily as defensive shields and also in penetrating ordnances. The health effects of exposure to DU can be numerous, however most of these effects are largely speculation and are considered to be nondeterministic health effects. The WHO also states that the main effect of DU exposure on humans is on kidney function. It is also believed that exposure to DU could potentially cause lung cancer as well as erythema.

Radiological materials cause physiological damage through the ionizing effects of neutron, gamma, beta, and/or alpha radiation. Some radiological hazards include any electromagnetic or particulate radiation capable of producing ions so as to cause damage, injury, or destruction. Radiation exposure may result from dispersed radioactive material in solid, liquid, gaseous, or vapor form or it may result from discrete sources, such as a radioactive source concealed in a high traffic area. Any alpha, beta, gamma, and neutron source may present a potential radiation hazard. Characterization normally includes identifying the radionuclide or ionizing radiation type and half-life of the source, quantifying the dose rate, and determining how the dose rate will change over time.

The U.S. government and American people need to have a conversation about radiation terrorism before the next attack. The easiest way for such a conversation to take place is through solid reporting and discussion by the news media. It is possible that a terrorist event could involve the introduction of radioactive material into the food or water supply, using explosives, dynamite for example, to scatter radioactive materials, called a dirty bomb, the destruction of a nuclear facility, or exploding a small nuclear device. Although introducing radioactive material into the food or water supply most likely would cause great concern or fear, it probably would not cause much contamination or increase the danger of adverse health effects. Radiation accidents are the most likely events that threaten US forces and civilians. A radiation accident is a situation in which there is a real or suspected unintentional exposure to ionizing radiation or radioactive contamination. Over the years there have been over 400 such accidents in the United States.

From the terrorist perspective, the most difficult part in resourcing a terrorist radiological attack is the procurement of the materials in a large enough quantity to be effective. Terrorists are currently hindered by the stringent regulations currently placed upon materials and devices that use radiological particles as a key component. These items must continue to be safeguarded in a responsible manner by the authoritative regulatory body. Regulation is our best weapon in defending against the use of radiation by the terrorist. Couple that regulation with the abject fear that people have when dealing with radiological events and the case can be made that terrorists may be looking at alternate sources for materials that may be used to perpetrate a terrorist act. One does not have to create a fission or fusion reaction in order to place radioactive isotopes into a bomb. The ability to use medical or mining grade materials will suffice in many of these instances and allow for a terrorist group to create a dirty bomb.

Because of the nature of radiation, it can be used in small quantities to mix in with the primary explosive device and create the fear and panic associated with a nuclear event. The public does not really know or care about the difference. The public will perceive a bomb explosion as a tragedy, but will react to a bomb explosion that has a radioactive component with abject fear. It is the nature of the unknown that causes this panic, and the drive one feels to seek out medical attention. With a typical kinetic bomb one is either hurt or not. If one is bleeding or feels the effects of the concussive nature of a bomb there is a need to self-identify the wound and seek medical attention. With the introduction of radiation the population that is affected becomes much greater, and the radius of those who feel they are at risk expands greatly. The incidents of those seeking treatment would also increase greatly causing panic at most medical facilities, many of which are ill prepared to handle an influx of so many people with "worried-well" symptoms.

One of the greatest dangers associated with a nuclear material release is not just the immediate release of radioactive material, but the residual radiation. If there were a nuclear explosion, the largest number of injuries would not be caused by the blast, flying debris, and heat but radiation that would contaminate the environment for years to come. There are also the hazards associated with the soil and wildlife in the affected area.

According to the Joint Service Publication *Treatment of Nuclear and Radiological Casualties* in one of the few recorded incidents of terrorists actually using radioactive materials, Chechen rebels placed Cesium-137 in a busy Moscow park in November 1995. The Environmental Protection Agency classifies Cesium-137 as a metal that may be stable (nonradioactive) or unstable (radioactive). The most common radioactive form of cesium is cesium-137; due to its strong radioactivity it is very useful in industry. This threat may prove very viable should terrorist organizations acquire materials and individuals with the knowledge to construct and store such devices in the future.

It is essential that action must be taken in order to prevent an act of radiological terrorism. There are organizations actively seeking to acquire the radiological materials and dispersal devices required to disseminate these particles. Around the world, there are many sites that contain the materials necessary to develop a radiological weapon and, in spite of the threat, many of these sites lack adequate security measures to prevent the theft of these materials. It is internationally recognized that these sites are potential targets for terrorists but there is a dangerous lag in the sense of urgency necessary to protect the material. In many of the industries operating in smaller countries around the world security measures are sometimes perfunctory and often take a backseat to commercial profitability. A current UN Security Council resolution calls for "appropriate effective" security measures to be in place surrounding these materials but that leaves a lot of gray area as that definition leaves much open to interpretation. Shared databases of intelligence about the terrorist threat and incidents are, for obvious reasons, an excellent measure to prevent future theft. Once these measures are in place then their must be a sustained commitment to maintaining these preventative techniques as long as the potential threat exists, long after the terrorists are no longer making the sensationalistic headlines that are the norm today. Selection and training of the "right" personnel, maintenance and upgrades of security equipment, and a sincere effort by all parties involved to protect these materials from the terrorist is required in order to improve upon our current security posture. I recognize that many of these suggestions sound a bit naive as all of this hinges on cooperation between nations around the world. In fact, that may be the most difficult obstacle to overcome. There will be holdouts such as isolationist regimes like North Korea or an emerging nuclear-armed Iran and they will obviously not be willing to be forthcoming with details regarding their nuclear security program. But, if a sincere effort is to be made to secure these materials then they must be involved as well.

19
WMD Detection, Protection, And Decontamination For The Civilian

The government has spent a great deal of time, effort and treasure working out best practices for the detection and avoidance of CBRN events, both actual and forecasted. The main focus of effort that the military has applied resources toward has been the avoidance of the CBRN threats that exist in combat as well as demilitarized areas of operation through the use of intelligence gathering and avoidance measures. The avoidance of CBRN threats are broken down, according to the U.S. military, into three distinct phases consisting of preattack, during attack, and post attack measures that each have their own unique procedures to follow. While these techniques were originally developed with the military in mind, at the time the most likely to face this threat, they can still be applied to civilian use. Associated with avoidance of a CBRN threat is the effective detection of a possible hazard, which naturally means that avoidance has been compromised. The effective detection of a CBRN hazard varies with each of the threats denoted by the acronym CBRN, which are:

Chemical:

Detection of chemical threats is accomplished through a multitude of techniques and procedures using various chemically reactive tests as well as electronic means. These devices may be through the use of M256A1 kits, ICAM, ACADA and M8 detection paper.

Biological:

Biological agents may be introduced to the area of operations through the use of aerosol, vector or covert methods and may be detected through the use of an alert medical infrastructure and other means. The best means of protection is through the identification of the dispersal method and elimination of this threat. Another method of combating a biological threat is through the use of vaccinations and wearing of protective outerwear. By their very nature a biological threat may not be detectable until after the symptoms of the attack present in the affected victims.

Radiological:

The best possible way to protect personnel from a radiological or nuclear threat is through the use of shelter and limiting the amount of exposure that a person has to the radiating effects of such a threat. A radiological or nuclear attack may be detectable by the characteristic mushroom cloud of such a bust and measured through the use of nomograms.

Nuclear:

This form of attack involves the actual detonation of a nuclear device. While the actual blast would have catastrophic effects for all in the blast radius, many more casualties would be sustained in the months and years afterward due to the side effects of radiological fallout.

The most fundamental aspect of detection and avoidance involving the effects of a CBRN attack is awareness. A general understanding of what CBRN agents are, how they are likely to be employed, and what happens to them after they are released will significantly increase the probability of survival. One must be aware of their surroundings, the environmental conditions, the symptoms, nearby emergency response assets, and the ability to evacuate the affected area. Prior to any attack there are several preventative measures that can be taken to minimize the subsequent effects. The preservation of food, water, equipment, and protective clothing must be considered. Likely targets such as events attracting multiple civilians, structures that create a congested environment for personnel, significant dates such as holidays or anniversaries of prior attacks must all be assessed for their target potential and prioritized for response.

Once the attack has occurred these measures must immediately be initiated. Effective communication must be available, trained, and rehearsed in order to engage first responders in an efficient and timely manner. CBRN threats to the United States constitute an issue of concern since 9/11. The prevention of these events has been the focus of much legislation, including the Bioterrorism Preparedness Act of 2001. If prevention fails, the capability to dispatch informed first responders within minutes following a CBRN event would save lives.

Biological agents can be broken down into two sub-categories: pathogens and toxins. Pathogens are often naturally occurring infectious agents that are capable of causing disease in humans, animals, or plants such as bacteria or viruses. Toxins are poisonous substances that are produced as by-products of the microorganisms (pathogens), plants, and animals. Biological agents will likely be delivered by one of three methods, each designed to get the agent inside of the body by targeting a specific entry point. Aerosol dissemination will most probably occur by vehicle mounted aerosol generator that could be initiated upwind of the target zone on ground, in the air, or over water. In any attack involving an aerosol delivery system, the agent will travel downwind at the rate of the wind speed and will spread out over distance affecting a broader area. The most dangerous areas will be those closest to the initial deployment point as the cloud will remain at its most concentrated at that area. The further the cloud travels, the more meteorological conditions, settling, and the effects of terrain will have an impact on its effectiveness. Burst-munitions capable of exploding and disseminating the agent over a wide area is the second most likely method, although in addition to the weather and terrain conditions, the likelihood that some of the agent is destroyed by the initial blast must also be considered. Finally, the spread of an agent by vectors, such as fleas, lice, or mosquitoes is a possible, although unlikely. Infecting the vector, containing it in a suitable delivery device, and then transporting it to the transmission site all pose significant challenges for the terrorist.

In the event of an attack with radiological properties, the fallout zone will be the most contaminated area affected. In order to predict where the fallout will most likely settle, one must consider the winds aloft as well as surface winds, as the two may differ. Areas affected by fallout should be avoided if at all possible. This fallout may be visible during daylight, appearing as dust-like particles or precipitation. Personnel in the area of fallout should take cover, protect all exposed skin and not ingest or inhale these particles. While the military and emergency services personnel are properly trained and equipped to coordinate an effective post-attack decontamination following the use of CBRN agents, the average citizen is usually ill prepared for an event of this significance. The use of commonly available tools must be considered when preparing for a potential terrorist attack. Soil is an excellent substance used for protection from radioactive particles as just three inches (8 cm) is capable of reducing the radiation dose by up to one-half. Brushes and vacuums can be used in combination with hot water and detergent to begin the decontamination process on personnel or surfaces. If shelter were available in a contaminated area, it would be advantageous to remain and improve upon its protective qualities rather than risk contamination during a hasty evacuation.

Shelter management teams should find suitable protective facilities against radiation to ensure continuity of operations. During the attack personnel should seek radiation protection shelters immediately, or if not available seek ditches, depressions, or other shelters to minimize exposure. Personnel should don all available protective equipment, perform self and buddy aid, and ensure closing doors/windows and sealing with plastic if possible limit exposure. After the attack CBRN cells will monitor radiation and decontaminate affected personnel, equipment, and the area. Local health agencies may also direct the distribution of iodine tablets.

As I was conducting research for this book and considering what data was most appropriate to share with the reader I was struck by the shear volume of information available. I felt that many military field manuals and digests were the most informative with a brief summary of the methods of dispersal and types of agents followed by preventative measures, and actions to be taken during and immediately following an attack. Most of these manuals follow basically the same layout with about the same type of information. But manuals covering chemical attacks consisted mainly of approximately 50 pages of reporting procedures basically geared toward the military. I am aware that these are military field manuals and that the majority of information will be geared toward service members but I am always considering how best to inform the general civilian population as they will likely be the target of a terrorist attack in the United States. The wealth of reports and formula for predicting size and length of dispersal clouds or rates of nuclear fallout will not be of much use to the average citizen in the event of an attack.

I wanted to learn more about what is being done to prepare the civilian population for this type of an attack. It is without a doubt the responsibility of the government to supply the population with factual information prior to the threat, trained first responders and necessary equipment during the threat, and appropriate facilities, medical supplies, and security until the threat has passed. But, I also believe that some burden must also rest on the shoulders of the responsible citizen. Civilians have a duty to seek information, prepare within their means, and have a plan in place. A recent survey of families by the DHS and the American Red Cross determined that only about half had prepared any kind of a disaster plan and just under a third had any kind of a disaster kit. Local emergency departments will be as prepared as possible in the event of a disaster scenario- but the many citizens who are unprepared will hamper their efforts. The information is out there (mainly on the internet) but I believe that there is almost an aversion to prepare until the threat appears to be imminent. It is highly likely that there will be no warning in the event of an attack. I have heard talk, in recent years, of government-subsidized disaster kits but how many civilians would take advantage of such a program if it were in place?

Our military has the ability to detect and defend against chemical or biological agents, but what about or civilian first responders? Should there be a chemical attack on a city our firefighters and EMT personnel would be some of the first on the scene. The Department of Homeland Security has the BioWatch program that monitors air samples in select cities but we really don't have any other way to detect if a scene is safe enough to enter. As of now, BioWatch detects a threat agent within a few hours up to a day after the agent has been released. The government is working with Department of Defense and other agencies to fix this problem, hopefully before an attack occurs.

Chemical detection equipment (CDE) is an essential component of hazardous material (HAZMAT) emergency response. This equipment could detect the harmful agent and define the area of exposure. Chemical detection paper is a very sensitive technique for detecting chemical agents. It is one of the least sophisticated and thus least expensive methods of detection. M8 and M9 chemical agent detection papers, commonly used by the military, are available commercially to HAZMAT response teams. Detection systems must exhibit high sensitivity for the biological agents because of the agent s low effective doses. Sensitivity can be defined as the smallest amount of target agent that gives a reproducible response above the system noise for a detector. Other variables contributing to the effectiveness of detection of biological agents are the detection processes itself and the efficient use of consumables in the field. Radiation detection devices must be able to detect the presence of radiation in the environment, on the surface of people (external contamination) and inside people (internal contamination). There are many types of radiation detection devices but no single device can detect all kinds of radiation and no one device is useful in all situations.

The presence of chemical, biological and radiological threats can be ascertained only by a limited number of means. For the purposes of chemical and biological threat detection the use of detection sensors or detectors that are designed for their specific task can prove paramount. The presence of such threats can also be determined by being cognizant of casualties caused by such threats, though the former method is obviously preferred.

It is important to keep in mind, in regard to biological threats, that detection of biological materials is a significantly greater challenge because the availability and accuracy of biological agent monitors used throughout the public safety community and healthcare system could be characterized as random at best. Detection of radiological threats, on the other hand, may be a bit more difficult to discern initially. The onset of symptoms of personnel exposed to radiation is often delayed because radiation dose must first accumulate in the casualty, the rate of which depends on the duration and amount of exposure. While difficult to notice when exposure may have initially occurred, vigilance in the use of the detection systems that are available would undoubtedly serve to effectively mitigate the affect of radiation exposure by, at the very least, limiting exposure time and thereby reducing the potential dosage.

As detection of chemical, biological and radiological threats is improved and as situational awareness and communication procedures are enhanced and honed, avoidance becomes significantly more expeditious and effective. Avoidance of chemical, biological and radiological threats can be a very simple procedure. If adequate detection systems are utilized, and a contaminated area is identified, avoidance can be executed in one of a few ways depending on the situation. For airborne threats wind direction and speed as well as other factors such as temperature must be taken into account in order to predict if the threat will be carried into the area. If this is a possibility, the area may need to evacuated and later decontaminated. One of the most important and basic elements to avoiding exposure to any of the aforementioned threats is the use of individual protective equipment.

There are several basic fundamentals inherent in the overall process of protecting civilian communities from the dangers of terrorism involving an CBRN weapon. First is assessing the enemy's capabilities and most likely courses of action. Authorities have a finite number of resources that they must allocate in areas where they will be of the most use and must consider many aspects while focusing their energies on the terrorist most likely course of action. Emergency planners staff support to the emergency commander analyzing the threat from a medical perspective while evaluating the environmental and occupational health risks in the area. Their guidance will be based upon the intelligence gathered and will be projected based upon the agents likely to be used, duration of exposure, and concentration. Once these capabilities are assessed emergency services must inform their personnel, first responders, local hospitals, and the civilian population of the measures to take in the event that the plan is enacted. Once the Incident

Commander has initiated his basic protection measures he will instruct his support staff to develop a risk assessment, recommendations to mitigate risks to an acceptable level, and the implement the measures that will have the most significant impact on improving survivability rates. This risk assessment must take into account and balance the need for individual care against the achievement of a military task that might involve life-threatening activities.

The potential for terrorists to employ a weapon with CBRN capabilities creates significant challenges for emergency response planners as a covert attack could occur at any time. Incident response commanders have a responsibility to their subordinates and the public to ensure their units are proficient in carrying out their duties in spite of the CBRN threat. Regular sustainment training must be conducted to ensure confidence in both individual skills and equipment. Equipment must be readied, NBC survival and decontamination skills must be refreshed, and actions must be rehearsed if at all possible. A professional, well trained, and well-equipped force will have the confidence of the civilian population and minimize casualties while bringing order to the chaos of such an attack.

Something that may not be considered is the psychological reaction to NBC protective uniforms and equipment by the professionals who wear them and the civilians that see them. Research from several medical journals confirm that the use of some of these items evokes reactions of fear and anxiety in others because of their association with chemicals in warfare. Younger emergency responders display symptoms of anxiety when conducting proficiency training with this equipment, most likely due to inexperience and the claustrophobic feelings common with this type of protective equipment. Chemical and biological warfare agents provoke psychological worries because they contaminate the air that is necessary for the most basic function needed for life- breathing. When responders and civilians without protective equipment think about the effects of these agents they feel powerless and that nothing is within their span of control. Also, lack of confidence in their equipment or their proficiency in using it also can contribute to a sense of hopelessness. Terrorism using these types of weapons is likely to produce many more casualties from psychosomatic stress than actual injury from exposure, similar to the "worried well" phenomenon common in the civilian population after exposure to a traumatic event. Reactions of hyperventilation, compulsive obsessions with decontamination, claustrophobia, and the need to hoard protective items of equipment are common when operating in a contaminated environment for an extended period.

During the 1990 Persian Gulf War where there was a significant concern of chemically armed Scud missiles, there were several accounts of soldiers failing to take necessary precautions during missile alerts because prior alerts had been uneventful. There were also accounts of soldiers prematurely injecting themselves with atropine to ward off the effects of chemical agents and preventing other soldiers from entering protective shelter after the alert had been sounding fearing contamination. It is to be expected that within a civilian population there would be similar adverse psychological effects from the prospective use of these weapons. Of the over 5,000 patients treated a hospitals following the 1995 Tokyo subway sarin nerve agent attacks, 73.9% displayed no symptoms of exposure to the nerve agent, instead they were concerned of the possibility that they had come into contact with the agent.

The United States and our partners face a spectrum of challenges, including violent non-state actors, hostile states armed with weapons of mass destruction, rising regional powers, emerging space, cyber, and technological threats, natural and pandemic disasters, and a growing competition for resources. These adversaries will use unconventional warfare to pursue ideological and political goals, and they are willing to use CBRN weapons to cause catastrophic effects. The increasing availability of highly destructive technology combined with a variety of weapons and means of delivery from state and non-state actors greatly exacerbates the problem. Adversaries may deploy CBRN weapons and devices to inflict casualties on civilian populations, degrade instruments of national power, or counter U.S. military superiority. A trained, integrated, adaptive, and innovative force that deters enemy use of CBRN weapons and, should deterrence fail, safely and effectively performs its mission in a CBRN environment.

Decon kits are issued to individuals and groups to protect them from CBRN hazards and are manufactured in models to decon skin, decon personal equipment, and decon larger equipment such as vehicles. Personnel are also issued Nerve Agent Antidote Kits, (NAAKs), which contain two autoinjectors, one being atropine and the other being pralidoxime chloride. In event of a CBRN exposure, particularly a nerve agent, the NAAK must be used immediately to survive the exposure. A new type of drug tablet called the Nerve Agent Pretreatment Pyridostigmine (NAPP) is in the trial phase, and if approved will be issued to emergency responders and will be taken as needed based on possible exposure.

Contamination by a CBRN agent will be avoided at all costs, however there may be times when contamination is unavoidable. Decontamination procedures must them be initiated in order to minimize the risk to other persons as well as make equipment serviceable for future operations. Not all levels of contamination are equal; ranging from immediate contamination, which minimizes further exposure and spread of the agent to a clearance decontamination consisting of a methodical process intended to reduce the threat level to the lowest detectable level. Typically, other chemicals are employed for the purpose of decontamination, particularly if the agent used was also a chemical. By forcing a reaction between the chemicals, the intent is to neutralize the harmful effects of the original weapon. The physical removal of the agent may be required, often common cleaning chemicals such as soap or bleach can be used to physically remove an agent.

Nature has its own effective method of decontamination relying on the natural properties of environmental conditions to cleanse an area in a process known as weathering. Weathering involves the process of evaporation and precipitation to reduce or break up a contaminant to the point where it is no longer a threat. This process is the simplest form of decontamination for large areas, land, and large structures. However, weathering is also a time consuming process in which the environmental conditions may not be conducive to decontamination efforts, in which case the forced removal of the agent may be necessary in order to expedite the neutralization process.

The decontamination process must be prioritized beginning with people before moving on to equipment. This immediate decontamination is carried out with the intent to save lives and allow for the further use of critical individual items of equipment and systems. Flushing of the eyes with water as soon as possible followed by a wipe down of the contaminated individual within 15 minutes of exposure is a critical survival skill that will prevent further injury. Vehicles should be washed down within one hour of contamination.

Depending upon the CBRN agent released will determine the most effective method of decontamination and length of time that the agent maintains harmful qualities. For example, biological and chemical warfare agents typically survive days or even weeks under optimal conditions while radiological agents can still pose a threat for years.

There are four major types of decontaminates. They are natural decontaminates, standard chemical decontaminates, miscellaneous decontaminates and developmental decontaminates. Natural decontaminates include weathering, earth, fire, water, and soil. A few things that are significant to note of this category are that ultra violet radiation from the sun has the ability to destroy most biological agents, burning is an effective means of eliminating certain agents and facilitates dispersion by wind though a significant downwind hazard is created. Water can be used to flush agents from surfaces or hydrolyze certain agents; however, any remaining residue will still pose a hazard until it too is removed. Also, using approximately four inches of earth to cover a small area of chemical contamination is a useful means of sealing the contamination or absorbing it so it may then be removed. Standard chemical decontaminates include STB, high-test bleach, and reactive sorbent powder. Significant of this category is that, while very effective, STB is quite damaging to most electronics and corrosive to metals so application of this decontaminate may be limited. The miscellaneous decontaminates include many common household type materials like soap, bleach, ammonia, degreasing solvents, and so on. The commonality of these materials is likely the most important thing to keep in mind. Finally, developmental decontaminates seem to be among the most applicable to the military. This category is important to the decontamination and clean up of spills and personnel exposure.

In today's global threat environment, the capability to reduce hazards of any given type or severity must be available to a vast array of organizations and people. Civilian law enforcement, emergency management, and safety organizations must all be, at a minimum, aware of their options when confronted with such hazards. Simple household solutions exist to mitigate many common hazards. For example, caustic soda, which is commonly known as lye will destroy G agents on contact and hasten the hydrolysis of lewisite and mustard. An alcoholic solution of caustic soda will decontaminate BZ and VX agents. Lye is fairly easy to obtain can be used to decontaminate some significant hazards. Soaps also provide a very convenient means of decontamination. Soap is also useful in removing chemical residue hazards.

When planning for a mass decontamination following the terrorist use of a CBRN weapon there are several points to consider. It can be expected that there will be many more patients seeking treatment who are not contaminated than those who are contaminated. It is estimated that there will be an approximate 5:1 ratio of non-contaminated vs. contaminated personnel, however they should all be treated alike placing a higher strain on already stretched resources and personnel. Because the most important factor in decontamination is the quick and thorough removal of an agent, the exact method used is not as important as the speed by which it is removed.

Due to common availability of water in large quantities, mass decontamination can be most effectively accomplished with a water shower system. The use of water for flushing is generally considered the best method for decontamination. If it is available, the use of soap adds a marginal improvement by dissolving oily substances as is common in some chemical agents. There are two main disadvantages to using soap. First, there must be enough on hand for use by all. The time required to disseminate it to the affected public will take up precious minutes in an already time sensitive task. Two, soap may actually hydrate the skin, potentially increasing the damage caused by some blister agents. The decontamination process should not be delayed in order to add soap or other cleaning additive. While bleach has been considered as an additive to be used when treating in a mass casualty scenario, it is generally not recommended. Bleach must be diluted, the exposure time to a patients skin is considered excessive, and it is not medically recommended for use near eyes, mucous membranes, or wounds.

The decontamination process must be initiated as soon as possible to ward off the further damaging effects of the agent in use. In a mass casualty event there is a necessity for the patients to be triaged and prioritized for decontamination. Patients closest to the point of release, with physical evidence of exposure, and non-ambulatory patients with serious medical symptoms should all receive special consideration for prioritization. The expedient physical removal of an agent from the victim is the most important action of effective decontamination. Physical removal includes scraping or blotting the agent from skin, the use of absorbents to soak up the agent, disrobing, and showering with large amounts of water. Disrobing and removing contaminated articles of clothing is a critical part of the decontamination process, beginning at the head and working down to the feet. Following a attack, agents may still be present, especially if the attack was initiated inside an enclosed structure. It is likely that toxic levels of the agent will remain trapped inside the fabric of clothing and will continue to affect personnel even after they have vacated the site of the incident. The act of disrobing further reduces possible agent exposure and effects among victims. First responders must remember that they must also undergo the decontamination process in order to avoid any serious side effects from secondary transfer exposures.

Protection is critical to the survivability to any group or community. Unfortunately, it seems that in today's society, there is not an awareness of attacks involving weapons of mass destruction. While the logistics of an actual attack are quite a hindrance to any groups interested, people should not interpret this being so unlikely that it would never happen. Communities should expect and rely on the government to handle the overall big picture management of a disaster, however they should also take their safety and security into their own hands as well. People don't need to be prepared for nuclear winter with years worth of stockpiles, or build underground bunkers 500 feet below the surface but it wouldn't hurt to have a plan. Preparation will prove just as valuable when facing naturally occurring disasters while lessening the strain on an already overburdened emergency response system. While the actual threat of an improvised WMD attack is low, before 9/11 nobody in America ever thought an attack of that magnitude could occur on our soil. Preparedness will be the key to survival when disaster does occur.

20
Terrorism And The Media

Instant media coverage of terroristic events have an immediate impact on all those who view them. Suicide bombings and the more recent mass shootings are not indicators of a potential future threat by themselves but could be considered a potential catalyst for future acts of terrorism. These acts tend to inspire others with a variety of motivations. Although media coverage of horrific events have been broadcasted to the masses before, it was never possible for the news to travel instantaneously around the globe while influencing so many people. Most that are influenced by these acts will express sorrow or even anger at the pain that has been caused. I am more concerned with the next Stephen Pera or Dr. Bruce Ivins who see these events unfold and decide to voice their outrage through an act of terrorism that only an extremist could conceive.

The pace with which information travels is quicker and more widely distributed now than ever before in history and will only get faster. Anyone with access to the internet can now become an "informed" commentator on worldwide events, regardless of their credentials or personal motives, and further influence others to extremist beliefs. Information technology has experienced a dramatic evolution in the last decade with the average American developing an affinity, and some say dependence, on instant communications. Compared to past decades, we are exposed to far more information from multiple mediums from advertising and programming, to social media and smartphones. This technology is primarily used to maintain instant access to friends and family but has also experienced a shift toward its use to organize for collective action. Social networks have become a more instant source of information and are increasingly trusted among users, despite a lack of source verification.

From the anarchists of the late 19th century to the terror events instigated specifically for the broadcast media of the 20th and 21st century terror has increasingly become tailored for mass-market consumption. The kidnapping and murder of Israeli athletes at the 1972 Munich Olympic Games, the high-profile aircraft hijackings that came to define air travel of the 70's and 80's, and culminating with the September 11 attacks of 2001, terror has reached a frenzy point that could not be accomplished without the use of instant media. From Twitter, Facebook, live Internet news footage from any number of news outlets or the so-called "iReporters" that enable anyone with a cell phone to live-stream any event to the world instantly and in high-definition, terror is now a spectator event.

This instant access not only allows viewers to be casual observers, but also surrogate victims in the sense that they are now a witness to the violence. Worldwide coverage now ensures that the terrorist will now have the largest possibility viewing audience, extending far beyond the immediate area of the attack. Most of us remember where we were during the 9/11 attacks simply because of the profound affect that it had on so many of us. Much of the world watched as United Airlines Flight 175 struck the South Tower of the World Trade Center and for a moment we were united in our shared outrage and fear at such a despicable act. But this level of anxiety would have never have been achieved if we had only heard about it by word of mouth after the fact as this sequence of events affected so many people who watched it unfold in real time.

Much of this is theater from the perspective of the terrorist. The sense of great fear and impending danger that is caused by such spectacular attacks is greater than the horror caused by naturally occurring disasters. For example, in 2008 the cyclone Nargis struck the Republic of Myanmar (Burma) killing over 138,000 people, far more than the almost 3,000 killed on 9/11. But how many have ever heard of the cyclone Nargis? The attacks of 9/11 went on to change the landscape of civilization, redefining the way that we view foreign cultures and religions. The media contributes to this anxiety by amplifying the shock felt by all who witness these attacks. Multimedia allows each of us to experience these events as they unfold in front of us, unscripted and unrated, and we witness these attacks living vicariously through the eyes of the camera lens. Adding to the terror is bad reporting and misunderstanding that is further spun as it is picked up by adjacent news agencies and recycled as "factual" information for the audience. There were several conflicting and incorrect reports on 9/11 that the White House had been struck by another hijacked plane, that a car bomb had been detonated outside of the State Department, and that a fifth airliner was on a suicide mission to another unknown location, all increasing fear and uncertainty as emergency services personnel were rerouted in an effort render assistance.

The established news outlets are not only to blame for their role in contributing to the effectiveness of these attacks. The Internet has been, in many ways, more effective medium at spreading panic. From false rumors that another subway bombing was to occur in the wake of the 2005 London bombings to buzz that Al-Qaeda was already in league with Mexican drug cartels and had smuggled biological agents across our southern border, a significant amount of anxiety can be spread through the Internet rumor mill. The operators of websites that profit off of the number of unique visitors to their site have a financial incentive to publish ridiculously hyped stories that users will view in an attempt to gather information in an effort to be more prepared for the next crisis. False predictions by so-called experts and recycled email chain letters still continue to generate excitement even though they have circled the globe several times and have proven incorrect at every turn. Doctored footage, Photoshopped images, and even fictitious Nostradamus predictions have contributed to the uncertainty by those who revel in seeing their version of a story circulate the Internet tides. Social media has forever changed the landscape of mass communications where any blogger or individual with access to social media can communicate using the same mediums as a legitimate authority.

Even a well-intentioned government message can contribute to the fear, as was the case when the Department of Homeland Security unveiled its color-coded terror threat indicator in 2002. For a time, the color indicating the current terror threat status was briefed at every press conference and news report, sparking a false sense of dread or security as it fluctuated between orange and amber causing many to believe the wild Internet claims that another attack was imminent. Without a clearly defined protocol to justify the color code, the security assessment was never upgraded to blue or green indicating a generally secure environment. Warnings such as these, somewhat justifiably, create public awareness but also stir undue public concern that is out of proportion to the actual threat. While there are several good reasons for such a warning system from keeping the populace informed to better preparedness to pre-empting an attack in the face of little factual intelligence there are just as many less dignified reasons for such a system. The system can be used for political gain when bureaucrats point to improvements as justification to increase spending on the pet project of their choice or as agencies adjust the threat level in order to deflect blame in the event that an attack that they did not see coming were to occur.

Consider the well meaning warnings post-9/11 of another attack, possibly involving biological or chemical warfare as an endless parade of "experts" were trumpeted before the television cameras to give their increasingly fantastic opinions of how the next wave of attacks would be conducted. From aerosol sprayers designed to kill the crop supplies to shooting sprees at crowded shopping malls during the holiday season, each of these tales kept the viewers glued to their seats in the hopes that a shred of information might be the one to save their life. Predictions that chemical or biological attack was forthcoming caused a run on plastic sheeting and duct tape at hardware stores. When these attacks never materialized the public began to display an apathetic aversion to the warnings in a manner similar to the old tale of the child who cried wolf. This weariness led the Department of Homeland Security to retire the color-coded warning system in April of 2011.

These warnings are capable of magnifying the terror without any action having been taken and are used by terrorist organizations to influence our behaviors and fears while we are at our most vulnerable. From a resource standpoint, they are cost-effective, causing us to expend already overstretched assets to chase down leads that lead to nowhere while the terrorist profits off of the additional exposure without having to go through the difficulty of conducting an actual attack. Terrorist organizations get the most bang for their buck by making empty threats that are rebroadcast by the media, spun and altered by Internet sources, reacted to by world governments, and felt by the populace.

It cannot be underestimated, the importance of keeping terrorism in perspective. The value of terrorism to the perpetrator is that they have a psychological impact on the population that outweighs the physical destruction caused by an attack. Terrorists, use the emotion of fear against the populace in order to magnify their own capabilities. When the populace responds with fear to a terror attack it allows the instigator a maximum amount of return on his initial investment. In order to deflate some of the hyperbole associated with terrorism it is necessary to peel back the layers and remove some of the shadowy mystique associated with it. By first recognizing that terror as actors on a scale, both large and small, have commonly employed it as a weapon throughout history and that it will continue to be present as long as it holds an added value to its practitioner. Violence, and the fear of it, will continue to influence behavior, as is our nature. Once that is accepted, and combined with the knowledge that perpetrators of such activity are humans, and fallible, and follow a somewhat predictable cycle when planning and conducting their attacks, their inscrutability tends to fade. Terror attacks will undoubtedly, cause pain and suffering, but the targeted population can reduce the hold that terrorists have over their behaviors by keeping their acts in perspective.

There is a difference between the act of terrorism and the threat of terrorism. It is evident in the way that terror groups claim credit for failed attacks and consistently provide warnings of attacks that fail to materialize. The terrorist loses much of his power if the populace is able to view the threat of terror from its proper perspective. The threat of terror will continue to be used by a variety of groups around the world for its actual effectiveness and perceived value. It has already proven its worth many times over by its ability to influence the actions of individuals and governments with the expenditure of comparatively few means. By recognizing that terrorism is a permanent part of our world like crime or disease, one can take precautions to defend against this possibility and prevent oneself from becoming a victim. Those that are moved by these events as witnessed through the use of multimedia are victims as well, and should also take precaution.

The use of real-time data analysis to take advantage of social media characteristics to gather and assess information is but one way to put this medium to work for good. However, there are some current technological and privacy obstacles to overcome with regards to crowd-sourcing risk assessments. This information must be first identified as a threat and then collated in a format that is usable by law enforcement and the public simultaneously. Our own spirit and ability to persist in the face of such horror is what determines the effectiveness of the methods of terrorism. By recognizing the difference between the threat and the actual event we can disallow the terrorist the ability to influence us from afar and deny him the victory that he seeks.

21
A Virtual Battleground

Computer technology has experienced a quantum growth in capability in the last fifteen years that have changed the once open architecture into something capable of as much wrong as right. Each new convenience intended to streamline operations and increase connectivity also opens new pathways to be exploited by those with the requisite skill and intent. A number of risks are now elevated in the field of cyber security as the capabilities and financial resources of nations are increasingly under the control of individuals and automated systems. Viruses carry with them the potential for catastrophic consequences as our world grows more intertwined. This electronic battlefield is rife with ambiguity as attackers are able to conceal their points of origin and even intent until the damage has been done. Strategies are fluid and adaptable, much more so than in the physical world and just because a tactic works once it is unlikely that it will work again as defensive countermeasures are quickly devised and instituted. Attacks take place nearly instantaneously as data packets are streamed through fiber-optic cables across the globe. This front has no tangible lines or safe zones as these threats go beyond established national boundaries, existing in an unregulated, apocalyptic panorama. Policies of deterrence and lines of attack applicable to the physical battlefield do not correlate exactly in cyberspace. But, one doesn't have to be on a battlefield, or even a member of the military, to become a casualty in this new evolution of the terror medium.

I have recently come to think of the computer as the next weapon of mass destruction. With the proper motivation, creative imagination, a susceptible target and the right program an adversary is capable of causing damage that is out of proportion to their available resources. What we have come to associate with conventional warfare, tanks, artillery, and bomber aircraft are slowly being augmented-or even replaced- by code that no physical armor can shield against. The cyber realm brings together the most advanced aspects of human knowledge, experience, information, and the intentional implementation of signals into computers and communication systems. With the modification of Infantry tactics from wars past, technologically advanced countries employ their own Internet versions of deception, denial, and attack but through a new format. The tactics of the cyber criminal range from the relatively annoying such as the capabilities of the 'hacktivist' to the physically damaging- think Stuxnet. The new deception involves the use of IP spoofing techniques to impersonate another system or network address to gain information about a person, place, or institution. In wars gone by enemy troops were denied terrain through the use of artillery, now the tactic is "denial of service" and primarily clogs network entryways with repeated requests for use. Logic bombs and trapdoors litter the cyber landscape as nations and collectives prepare potential targets for later disruption. The strategic attacks of large air battles and bombings could be equivocated to cyber attacks intended to corrupt code through the use of malicious viruses. It is safe to say that most conventional conflicts of the future will be augmented in some way by these forms of attack.

Defensive measures too, have their modern updates for this unconventional cyber era only with a wider range of factors. Radar, used to detect aircraft has its own counterpart- intrusion detection systems observe network activity, log records and unusual data patterns. Responses to this perceived threat are then routed to a central workstation, or command post, for further action. The reinforced walls that form protective barriers around military forward operating bases are replicated by firewalls in cyberspace that prevent unwanted traffic from entering your perimeter. Finally, there are your soldiers, who are your last line of defense. They must be fit, well armed, and ready to act with reflexive instinct to defend their post- this may be replicated by one or a number of analysts who are the final guardians of your digital fortress. However, in an interview with Wired magazine a former Director of the USAF Cyber Task Force, Lani Kass, remarked "If you're defending in cyber, you're already too late."[70]

The most sophisticated cyber capabilities, those with the potential to weaken our economic and military leads, currently belong to nation-states but this domain is no longer exclusive and currently being siphoned off by individuals computer hacking collectives. Ranging from irritating to highly disruptive, computer hacking is the most widespread variety of cyber intrusion and allows anyone with the necessary skill set to steal state secrets, heist the intellectual property of private business, and affect vulnerabilities within the national infrastructure and defense mechanism. These non-state actors have a wide range of intentions, from those who just seek the challenge of outwitting cyber security measures to those who want to manipulate the Internet to intimidate or cause harm for ideological reasons or purely personal gain.

Private citizens are most at risk from cyber criminals acting for personal profit or gain and many of us have already come into contact with these elements through social engineering or phishing scams that populate our email inboxes from time to time. The current generation of hacker is a dynamic and vibrant adversary who demands relentless vigilance and variation. Their success is made possible because the vast majority of users are not familiar with the threat and do not take their own cyber security seriously, essentially they do not lock their own system back doors. As long as our nation and private citizenry relies upon computer systems to manage the complex affairs of our country and the comparatively simple affairs of our individual lives then there will be risk.

In 1999, practically the stone-age compared to today's technology, both private citizens, corporations, and government were equally susceptible to viruses and malware as illustrated by the "Melissa" virus- named for a Miami stripper. "Melissa" was initially promoted through XXX rated sites and I'm sure that most of us are aware by now that pornographic solicitation over the Internet is one of the most heavily promoted (and financially profitable) uses for the Net. A recent Forbes Magazine article interviewed the authors of "A Billion Wicked Thoughts" who have conducted their own independent research on the subject. They estimated that in 2010 about 13 percent of Internet searches were for adult-related content and claimed that there were 260 million porn pages out there.[71] Mind you, this was before .XXX domain names became available. Bottom line: sex gets people's attention and is an especially effective tactic when incorporated with phishing scams. David Smith, a computer programmer initiated the macro-virus by posting an infected document, that he had created, to an alt.sex newsgroup using a stolen America On Line account.

This is basically how "Melissa" worked: The target would receive an email message from a sender with a subject line reading "Important Message from [the name of sender]', and a body message of "Here is that document you asked for…don't show anyone else ;-)". Attached to the email is a seemingly harmless item titled "List.DOC". Are you curious yet? These days many of us would never venture any further down the rabbit hole but this virus made it's first appearance in March of 1999, before computer security awareness was such a prolific issue, and caused the Microsoft Corporation, Intel, and several government entities to shut down incoming email servers as they became inundated with a virtual tide of overwhelming traffic.[72] The virus was able to spread quickly and cause a stampede of email traffic by disabling some security features in Word 97 and Word 2000 and gaining access to the users Microsoft Outlook address book. Once there, it would copy the top 50 addresses from the users folder, recreates the original Word document (complete with virus) and sends the message once again to these accounts using the victim's address as the sender. Word documents on many computers would then be corrupted with seemingly random insertions of the following quote, taken from Bart Simpson, "twenty-two, plus triple-word-score, plus fifty points for using all my letters. Game's over. I'm outta here." While the virus did not destroy files it was able to cause an estimated $100 million to $400 million dollars in cleanup costs, depending upon who you ask. David Smith pleaded guilty to one federal count of computer fraud and abuse and received a $5,000 fine and served a 20-month jail sentence for his effort. In his plea to the judge at his sentencing, he was almost apologetic; acknowledging that he was responsible for the entirety of the damage caused and revealed that he was not aware that it could spread so far or so fast. This represents the danger of hackers that don't realize the destructive power of their home computer. We've come a ways since then, but not too far.

The most celebrated 'hacktivist' collectives include LulzSec, Anonymous and others and are known for acts of online activism that appear to be conducted mainly to demonstrate member proficiency, collect and releasing unsecured data, as well as simple online graffiti designed to deface the websites of embarrassed targets. In fact, some members have claimed that their hacks are Constitutionally protected free speech likening them to the Occupy protests and deserving of First Amendment protections.[73] By an extremely small margin, there is some validity to this statement. Hactivism acts that result in the visual alteration of websites in a manner similar to graffiti probably should not be classified as cyber-terrorism. A nuisance, yes but website alterations for the purposes of a political or cultural statement may probably fall closer to the realm of vandalism. Attacks have been mainly focused on high profile government and law enforcement agencies and include the removal of a CIA website and hacking an FBI conference call as Bureau members wargamed exactly how to take down the two groups. While group members have either been arrested or gone into a self-imposed exile from their online activities they may never be far away as evidenced by the groups' unofficial slogan, "We are Anonymous. We are Legion. We do not forgive. We do not forget. Expect us."

If one were to gently peel back the curtain in order to eavesdrop on the motivations and tactics of hacker collectives you would see that they often seek the support of other, like-minded individuals in their private forums. Like any group with common interests hackers have constructed their own chat rooms to share ideas, tactics, coordinate, and devise strategy. Several thousand of these forums have popped up worldwide with many boasting thousands of participants. Hackers have developed their own communities through these forums where they are free to debate philosophy, popular media, and politics as well as share tactics. As the complexity to properly execute a hack attack has risen, so too has the need to enlist allies to execute complex attacks. Hacking has become a team sport requiring a broad array of expertise in the employment of these techniques. The vast majority of communications are devoted to introducing novice hackers to the practice by sharing tutorials and programs targeting websites and online forums. But, there are some "guns for hire" ads for anyone lacking the skill but seeking to engage in illicit online activity. 19 percent of forum discussions incorporated the topic of distributed denial of service attacks, SQL injection, and spam attacks, which experienced a 157 percent growth in discussion interest since 2007.[74] Interest in mobile hacking, particularly the iPhone, has developed a strong following for those seeking to build a reputation within these networks.

Social engineering, the practice of misleading a target to accomplish goals that may not be in his own best interest, is a trend that is gaining momentum through a practice known as "e-whoring." Entire packages of online content can be exchanged on these sites that include racy pictures, videos, personal messages that can be used to broker a first contact with a subject while pretending that the hacker is the woman featured in the material. This tactic allows the hacker to wait in adult chat rooms while pretending to be the woman featured in the pictures and videos while soliciting new customers. Programs that can be modified to worm their way in to a subject's computer are embedded within this information waiting to be activated. Once contact has been initiated between the two the hacker has opened a virtual doorway into the customers online life and increasing opportunities for economic or identity theft. Kevin Mitnick, one of the most prolific hackers of the 20th century captured the broader concepts of social engineering in his book, "The Art of Deception." To summarize his viewpoint, the computer is just a tool- what is really being hacked is the mind of the person at the other end.

There has been an upside to the many breaches in cyber security- recognition of the potential threat has led to increased cooperation among international law enforcement. This recognition of a threat that has left no nation untouched has revealed new weaknesses and led to the development of new security measures through collaboration with legitimate security and former hackers who have turned against their former comrades for a variety of reasons. Pacemakers can now be commanded to administer fatal, 800-volt shocks to someone over the Internet as was demonstrated in one such display. In fact, firmware already exists that can infect multiple such medical devices and spread as the physical distance between users is closed to within a few meters- just like a biological virus. Barnaby Jack, a security specialist with consultant firm IOActive identified this flaw as medical companies are now trending toward wireless devices and has remarked, "We are potentially looking at a worm with the ability to commit mass murder."[75]

Our technological assets are exposed because of a widening breach between network theory and application. The openly fluid and expanded nature of the Internet makes it ideally suited to nameless criminal activity. Mobile malware designed to infect cellphones and tablets is on the rise as criminals realize that these devices are capable of performing many of the functions and likely to contain as much sensitive personal and financial data as home computers. Android devices are particularly prized by online criminals as the operating system allows users to download applications from sources other than Google, including suspect unofficial services. [76] The complexity of systems is growing at a phenomenal rate as new improvements increase interconnectivity in an attempt to streamline processes while creating new pathways to be exploited within the growing web.

Java, considered to be the most widely used software on the planet due to its compatibility with Windows, Linux, and the Apple OS X operating systems, has also been compromised prompting a call to temporarily stop using the application from industry insiders. Malicious software has enabled some users of the system to commit identity theft as well as subordinate infected computers as part of a botnet. In 2012, the Java software was involved in almost half of all cyber attacks because of software vulnerabilities followed by the Adobe Reader program, which was used in 28 percent of occurrences and Microsoft Windows/Internet Explorer used in 3 percent of attacks.[77] Concerns over the misuse of the software have been so great that the chief of DHS's Computer Emergency Readiness Team has issued a warning calling for it to be disabled until a patch can be found, a rare move by a federal agency. Keep in mind that there is an excellent chance that Java script, in one form or another, is present on your home computer.

Estimates in damage from cyber attacks range from three billion to hundreds of billions of dollars each year. General Keith Alexander, director of the National Security Agency and U.S. Cyber Command, has said that cyber attacks are responsible for "the greatest transfer of wealth in history", citing Symantec Corporation and McAfee Inc., which have measured the theft of intellectual property to American companies at $250 billion and the world upwards of $1 trillion each year.[78] These figures insinuate that such attacks may be more effective when activated against the less effectively defended civilian infrastructure or business conglomerates in an effort to generate the financial and political pressure that terrorism relies upon. Pressure to yield or alter national policies could come from the ground swell or corporate entities if attacks were to be disproportionately levied against civilian targets. While the theft of intellectual property and personal data is a great economic issue, the unauthorized access to a network is cause for much more practical concern. Data corruption and disruption of a systems normalized routine can have adverse effects on operation leading to public safety concerns when introduced into the infrastructure. Data corruption occurs when functioning algorithms are altered to perform in an illicit manner, most often resulting in a deficiency within the system architecture. A system disruption is the result of a corruption that causes normal structural operation to cease, become bogged down, or impede the normal functioning of other systems.

One high profile example of a system disruption due to malware is the Stuxnet virus deployed in Iran in 2010. Though full disclosure by the Iranian government about the specific setbacks caused by the virus is opaque at best it has been surmised that Stuxnet was most likely used to manipulate equipment contained within highly classified nuclear centrifuge facilities at a uranium enrichment plant in an attempt to hinder Iranian nuclear aspirations.[79] Such an attack could be used in the future to target computer assisted industrial control systems that regulate infrastructural components. Terrorist groups or criminal organizations determined to assail critical communications; transportation, road or rail networks would focus on supervisory control and data acquisition systems susceptible to manipulation. Although it is not believed that any organization without state-sponsorship is capable of developing an updated Stuxnet equivalent the proliferation of this worm began soon after its escape from what is believed to be the intended target. The baseline code or the worm has been available online for years as it was dissected and reposted by fascinated tech aficionado's. As of September 2010, the Symantec Security Response organization had identified over 40,000 infected WAN IP addresses and 100,000 infected hosts worldwide.[80]

Of concern to the managers and security staff charged with the operation of regional infrastructure assets is the vulnerability of these elements to disruption by malware in a similar attack. These facilities rely heavily on computer networks to observe and manage industrial processes such as electricity generation, chemical production, water allocation, and transportation. In 2012, the U.S. energy sector was the target of almost 40 percent of cyber assaults on the infrastructure according to one DHS report.[81] Energy, transportation, and water purification are all key resources that impact our daily lives. The Department of Homeland Security has identified 18 separate infrastructure sectors that benefit the public by providing these services yet are at risk to sabotage by acts of terror or criminal activity.[82] Due to the increasingly interconnected nature of these systems they are all susceptible to acts of cyber terrorism designed to degrade or halt the operations of these essential utilities. The Stuxnet virus, while rumored to be focused on a specific target, escaped precisely because it was written to search for and manipulate vulnerabilities in software commonly used to manage infrastructure facilities around the world. Any attack targeting critical infrastructure is essential if used as a precursor to a conventional military attack and would create a perception among the civilian population of any country that a terror group was far more sophisticated an wide reaching if it were able to turn out the lights in every home in a portion of the country.

While the U.S. is better prepared to defend itself from cyber attack than many other countries there is almost a false sense of security that many of our citizens have developed due to the strength of our military. Note, I do not mean to imply that the U.S. is best prepared to defend against cyber attack, only that it is positioned technologically and financially to defend itself better than some others. Having said that, federal and business leaders needs to recognize the many potential inroads that make our Internet connected technologies so vulnerable and focus those technological and financial assets toward cyber security efforts through guidance and legislation. Unfortunately, just as 9/11 forced our hand and led to the dramatic realignment of our law enforcement and intelligence services, it may take the cyber equivalent of such an attack to force federal and civilian agencies to shore up the gaps in digital security. A 2009 Inspector General report conducted by the DHS warned that, "a disruption in control system operations may result in the loss of productivity and life, and have a negative impact on the economy and national security".[83]

The enormity of the 2003 power failure that affected the U.S. highlighted some of the vulnerabilities in our most complex systems to natural disasters or sabotage. This blackout affected almost 10 million people in Ontario and 45 million throughout the Northeastern U.S for two days while parts of Canada experienced rolling blackouts for two weeks. In January 2003, the Microsoft worm known as "Slammer", the fastest growing virus in history was able to infiltrate a computer network at an Ohio nuclear power plant, shutting down safety monitoring equipment for almost five hours. It infected approximately 75,000 hosts and is responsible for network outages, airline cancellations, and ATM failures. There are certain fail-safes built into our national infrastructure designed to mitigate the effects of a catastrophic damage. For example, the power grid is sectioned regionally, mitigating the chance of a catastrophic outage. While the national power grid is healthy enough to withstand most fluctuations it is still vulnerable to disturbances at regional and local substations responsible for transmission and normalization maintenance.

This grid is essential to quality of life, the national economy, and basic security measures yet it remains at risk to natural disaster, sabotage (physical and cyber) as well as human error. The North American power grid is the most prevalent and complicated in the world, covering 211,000 miles while supplying power to everyone in the U.S., Canada, and parts of Mexico.[84] The U.S. economy is estimated to lose between $75 billion to $180 billion dollars annually due to power outages.[85] Some of the critical elements of these systems were instituted in the 1960's, long before the advent of the Internet or the use of telecommunication networks to coordinate system operations. Automated telecommunications networks, to which most substations have upgraded due to increased network complexity, should have mandatory security safeguards built in as part of the design architecture, yet not all of these stations are equipped with standardized network security. Many of the older control systems were integrated directly into the Internet without security firewalls to protect against intrusion, relying on human technicians to detect anomalies and counter any system assault. Factors such as an increased number of system access points, the use of subcontractors with remote access to repair and manage components and a reliance on standard IT platforms such as Microsoft Windows have all contributed to a declining security situation. As the number of attacks, coupled with increased sophistication of network hacking increases, the reliance of human awareness and capabilities is being pushed to the wayside in favor of a computerized defense. But, even this opens up potential conduits into the larger system as they must be network integrated, another weakness, in order to be effective. Analyses of these systems that were conducted to prepare for the potential Y2K computer crisis identified many of these system entry points and have thus provided a blueprint for security improvements to begin.[86]

The power industry finds itself in an unenviable position, responsible for providing a steady flow of power in response to demand, while also held accountable for defending itself against attack. The system analysts and technicians can represent a networks' most glaring strength and weakness. While these operators have proven to be more adaptable to changing conditions within a technical environment they are also susceptible to inattentiveness, human error, or outside influence. The screening of employees for technical competence and potential subversive inducements should be incorporated into assessments of network operations.

Recommendations to shore up vulnerabilities within the infrastructure range from the conventional- beefing up physical security and structural integrity to mitigate risks from natural disasters to encrypting the software within the utilities systems. "Red Team" exercises, in which friendly computer analysts stage mock-assaults on computer networks in order to identify vulnerabilities revealed the potential for a system outsider to gain unauthorized access and assume control. For the sake of simplicity of operation a centralized control system is easier to operate yet exposed to becoming the focal point of attack conversely, regionalized control systems can be efficient while maintaining a higher and more consistent rate of customer service. But it is highly likely that a terror group or independent hacker collective would attempt to exploit a single system therefore, smaller, localized transmission systems have much less to lose if they fail. Better yet, a large system that is able to "raise the drawbridge" in the event of a system failure and isolating itself while temporarily shifting responsibility to local substations until the issue is resolved. Fortunately, several programs are available, and relatively simple to implement, in order to raise security awareness among the industry and supporting companies.

It is presently a challenge for experts in the field to identify the source of these attacks. They can be initiated from anywhere, including Internet cafes, any active Wi-Fi connection, or "zombie" computers subordinated through a botnet. The machinery used to initiate such an attack is inexpensive and, to a degree, disposable- allowing a hacker mobility as he is not tied to logistical anchors. These types of operations are not capable of directly harming individuals, and with the exception of a few notable viruses, usually do not damage equipment. A cyber terror attack would be most effective if used to supplement a physical attack rather than as the sole strategy. I think that it is important to remember that at the current level of technology that has been demonstrated thus far cyber attacks are most effective when used to augment a conventional attack including guns, explosives, etc. Given the somewhat unpredictable nature of cyber attacks due to network complexity, success is more likely to facilitate an operation rather than result in a specific outcome as a standalone attack. Because defenses are quickly shored up after each successful cyber attack certain techniques should be employed only sparingly and are not suited for protracted operations. The priorities for affected infrastructure cyber security management should be to determine if the attack is meant to supplement a physical attack in order to take advantage of damaged systems while making it appear that all operations are proceeding as normal while recovering.

A group known as the Izz ad-Din al Qassam Cyber Fighters has claimed credit for a relentless crusade targeting the websites of several Western financial institutions in retribution for an inflammatory Youtube film trailer that purported to ridicule the life of the Prophet Mohammed. Capitol One, J.P. Morgan Chase and Bank of America have all been targeted by a modified version of distributed denial of service (DDoS) attacks with threats to hit more in the future.[87] This technique employs an advanced version of a botnet by taking over entire Web servers as opposed to enlisting thousands of individual machines. The use of servers in lieu of individual computers indicates an evolution in technique and refined sophistication of a tactic that is likely to be replicated. While these instances of attacks were used to target banks the tactic could just as easily be configured to target other institutions.

Even the term "cyber-terrorism" is something of a misnomer as it implies that the activities of cyber-criminals, hacker/cracker collectives, or nations operating in the cyber-realm are interchangeable or related. Depending upon the viewpoint of the target of malicious cyber-activity one may claim that they have been the victim of cyber-terrorism but to date politically motivated terrorists have not employed the Internet to support attacks. Recruitment-yes. Funding-yes. Spreading ideology and communications-yes. But actually conducting an attack that is in whole or partially supported through the Internet-not yet. Thus far, Internet communication has allowed extremist groups to more easily share methods and technical data that supports their operations while eliminating the need for travel and reducing opportunities to come into contact with international customs and law enforcement officials. Lone wolf extremists, those that have been mentioned previously, now access information and ideas without ever having to physically contact anyone while preparing for their role. This communication medium is likely to result in an increase in lone wolf attacks as information becomes easier to come by. Difficulties in the acquisition of weapons, explosives or WMD components as well as the anonymity that it provides will lead to an increased use of the Internet to supplement conventional operations.

The spectrum of capabilities that compose the realm of cyber-security continues to evolve leaving much still to be accomplished. In order to begin to rectify the situation, programs and hardware must be developed with security in mind as a necessary subcomponent. The days of developing new hardware in the hopes that a security "patch" will be developed and installed at a later date are behind us. Systems, and the personnel who maintain them, should be employed only after verification of compatibility and resistance to corruption have been verified. Finally, internationally recognized standards of Internet security could be adopted, perhaps in a manner similar to international trade standards. The penalty for noncompliance? No security standard, no connectivity. In the past, security flaws in commonly used Web applications often led to individual or limited impact. Now there is a potential for regional, and in the future global impact, as one consequence of the integration of terrorism and computing. There are serious technological hurdles to overcome in order to enable a safe system that is able to remain connected globally while providing a consistent resource. The very systems that manage the increasingly connected and complex web of networked computers are the greatest vulnerability, if only for their inability to process information as adaptively as their human counterparts. The constantly evolving, and ingenious, nature of both technology and human shrewdness to bypass security obstacles-cyber and physical- will present a formidable enigma for security specialists in the decades to come.

22

Those Who Cannot Remember The Past…

In spite of all that America has been through in the last decade there are those who still question the need for a large, bureaucratic organization such as the Department of Homeland Security. This really isn't anything new as it seems the federal government has had to defend itself vigorously following the realignment of every new homeland defense and security apparatus since World War II. But it seems to be important to remind the public that these changes are only an attempt to streamline the efforts of multiple levels and departments of government. There seems to a fear at some local and state levels that whenever such a realignment occurs that the federal government is siphoning off some of the power and authority from the lower tiers. But this restructuring has already occurred several times in our nations history, usually following a national crisis and in response to the public cries for a stronger, better organization. One of the first such restructurings occurred following WWII with the establishment of the National Security Act as America, victorious after WWII began to accept its place as a world leader.

The signing of the National Security Act of 1947 into law by President Truman indicated an acceptance of America's role as a superpower and principal on the world stage. The isolationist mentality that had characterized America's previous stance on international affairs was outdated given the United States involvement in two world wars and emergence as a recognized guiding force in international affairs. With the emergence of the Soviet Union as a military and political rival following World War II, the United States could not afford to passively observe as their standing in the world body was eclipsed by what was perceived as a potential threat. This Act established a unified military command structure and planted the seeds for an intelligence and response apparatus that would grow into what we know as the Department of Homeland Security today. This first attempt at streamlining was intended to improve the foreign policy decision-making process with the creation of the National Security Council, the Central Intelligence Agency and the unification of the War Department and the Department of the Navy under the Department of Defense. The new framework was far from perfect and has undergone many evolutions in the half-century since it was signed but it could be argued that this Act represented the first acknowledgment by the United States of its role and policy of internationalism which has shaped the course of world events since World War II. This mentality lives on today and is present in all aspects of our foreign political relations, business dealings, and military campaigns which can, in some way, trace their origin to a desire for the democratic values upheld by the United States.

The 9/11 Commission report established a new foundational policy for America after the terrorist attacks and traced some of this new policy back to the National Security Act by stating that it was created, "largely as a result of lobbying from the Pentagon for a forum where the military could object if they thought the State Department was setting national objectives that the United States did not have the wherewithal to pursue". Since its inception under President Truman, the Council's function has been to advise and assist the President on national security and foreign policies. In recent years, the NSC became a critical component following several terrorist acts on the homeland.

Following the bombing of the World Trade Center in 1993, former President Bill Clinton ordered his National Security Council to coordinate the response. After Al Qaeda's terrorist acts in the latter half of the 1990's, Presidential directives reinforced the authority of the National Security Council to coordinate domestic as well as foreign counterterrorism efforts, through the interagency Counterterrorism Security Group. The NSC was critical in the evaluation of events and realignment of agency structures following the 9/11 attacks. Shortly thereafter, it was determined that there was not enough security to better manage the nation. As a result, the Homeland Security Council was created to parallel the NSC.

The purpose of the Act was to enforce a much-needed change and, about 65 years later, another change was needed to accommodate the growing threat to the nation. This included the addition of the Department of Homeland Security (DHS), who would have better oversight over intelligence and security matters, and report to the NSC. How well are they are doing? That could be argued in either direction and would require further discussion. What is most beneficial about our current government alignment is that we are our own harshest critics. Because of our open way of discussion as a nation there almost seems to be no topic that is off-limits or opinion that is too taboo to voice. Our media is among the most vocal in the world and with the emergence of social-media as a popular method of communication we are exceedingly prone to look inward for the source of our problems.

The signing of the National Security Act of 1947 was a formal recognition of our shortcomings and desire for improvement. Most recently we have witnessed this acknowledgement by the world body following the results of the 2012 U.S. Presidential election. In the hours following, tangible movement by NATO members began to occur regarding the conflict in Syria while Israeli President Benjamin Netanyahu and Palestinian leadership allowed peace talks to stall as they awaited election results. Similar trends occurred in political, military, and economic realms as much of the world waited to see who would represent the United States for the next four years. Much of this can be attributed to our ability as a nation to seek change through actions such as the signing into law of policies meant to improve our communication between our political, military, and intelligence spheres.

Before the National Security Act of 1947, the armed forces were the sole authority on national security and homeland defense. The international threats of our present show us that national security is more important than ever. The war on terrorism is an everlasting fight that sometimes spills out in our own backyard as we learned on 9/11. The agencies that were essentially developed from the National Security Act of 1947 are now working harder than ever to keep the fight overseas.

For all of the criticism of our intelligence services inability to predict 9/11, the intelligence failure really shouldn't be too surprising given the agency structure that was established during the Cold War in order to protect the individual freedoms of American citizens. When President Truman formed the Central Intelligence Agency as a result of the National Security Act of 1947 there was a concern that this organization's reach would extend to the average citizen creating a "Gestapo-like organization".[88] By establishing directives that prevented the CIA from investigating domestic activity and by allowing the FBI to have jurisdiction over law enforcement and domestic activity he created a separation of the powers meant to keep America safe. This division was largely successful in preventing the infringement of personal freedoms during the Cold War but has left the United States vulnerable in the modern era of terrorism. These divisions do not extend to the CIA and FBI but also to many federal agencies that in an era of more predictable hostility, such as the Cold War, were never designed or reasonably expected to cooperate with one another. For example, at its inception who could have ever expected the need for the Postal Service to communicate with the Bureau of Alcohol, Tobacco, and Firearms or the Department of Agriculture with the FBI? Or the need for any of these seemingly omniscient agencies to seek out the average citizen to help identify transnational terrorists?

The FBI established much of the framework for all American investigative services linked to today's Homeland Security Division. Just after winning the war here at home with the Mob and big gangsters of organized crime, the FBI found itself in the middle of an intelligence war with Germany and Japan. President Roosevelt was becoming increasingly worried that Germany and Japan were forming an alliance with a mission to overturn democracy wherever it stood while plotting numerous criminal activities to assist with this mission. Early in 1934, the president ordered the FBI to find out if American Nazi groups were involved with any foreign agents of any kind. Later In 1936, the President ordered the FBI to gather any intelligence of possible threats to national security imposed by extreme fascist and communist groups. Prior to the war, the FBI was responsible for uncovering more than 50 German and Japanese spies operating in the United States. Later after forming its Special Intelligence Service, the FBI was responsible for identifying over 800 Axis spies, 250 propaganda agents, and 200 agents smuggling strategic war materials all by 1946.

President Truman introduced the idea of containment in 1947 in order to contain the spread of Communism by helping embattled countries along its frontiers and borders. The extensive, and sometimes illegal, counterintelligence work conducted by the FBI during this era resulted in the capture of relatively few Soviet spies and undermined the Bureau's credibility as a law enforcement organization due to their tactics. From a counterintelligence perspective, much of the information gathered was unusable because it had either been illegally obtained or did not violate federal espionage statutes. The Special Intelligence Service was disbanded after the war, and the President Truman's newly formed CIA took the place of the Office of Strategic Services (OSS), and was asked to take over the operation and expand American intelligence activities worldwide.

Under the Truman Doctrine, the United States went to war in Korea and eventually President Eisenhower extended it to the Middle East. President Kennedy and Johnson used this same doctrine as justification for the war in Vietnam. Later still, the Reagan administration came into office declaring that one of its focal points of foreign policy would be a war on terror. The Reagan Doctrine, however was a rollback strategy from Truman's plan, under which the United States gave aid to anti-Communist rebels fighting Soviet states on the periphery of empire in Nicaragua, Angola, and Afghanistan. All of these events led by different presidential administrations shaped the framework leading to the current Homeland Security doctrine and development of the agency itself.

❖   ❖   ❖

Several events from the Cold War era stand out in that they highlight deficiencies within interagency cooperation structure or response system that, through many evolutions and 9/11, eventually led us down the road to the Department of Homeland Security in its current form.

The Three Mile Island incident (1979) in which a partial nuclear meltdown resulted in the accidental release of small doses of radioactive gases, is one example of the need for an organization such as the DHS. While the actual damage has been determined to be negligible in the years since the accident, review of the incident identified deficiencies in communications, emergency response training, civil defense management, and federal regulations. Subsequent investigation identified a sense of false security that was prevalent at many levels of the response framework that allowed so many redundant systems to fail. Not just the technological fail-safes within the plant but the emergency protocols for nearby civilians and political authorities responsible for maintaining civil order. In the years since the incident, and many lessons learned during that period, an emphasis has been placed on an increased interagency cooperation and improvements to existing radiological response plans culminating in the development of the National Response Plan in cooperation with the Department of Homeland Security.

The infamous hooded Unabomber (1978-1996), Theodore Kaczynski, began a reign of terror in the late 70's with the use of the U.S. Postal system as a guided method of delivery for several improvised explosive devices responsible for killing three and maiming over 20 Americans, some of them random targets. While thousands of potential leads were investigated over the years in order to determine the identity of the Unabomber by a joint task force including representatives of the ATF and U.S. Postal Service under the lead of the FBI, the case would not be broken open without the assistance of the public. In 1995 the Unabomber sent the FBI his "manifesto" which was published publicly in the hopes that this essay would revitalize the stalled investigation and generate new leads. This communication with the public worked, resulting in the identification and arrest of Ted Kaczynski and highlighting a need for stronger interagency cooperation and a more thorough examination of open source communications with the public, a basic tenet of disaster prevention and response acknowledged throughout DHS today.

The Tylenol poisonings (1982) were an act of terrorism that occurred on American soil and was successful because of the limited communications among local and federal, medical and investigative authorities. This act resulted in seven deaths across the country and nearly crippled one of the most successful producers of over-the-counter painkillers. This event can be said to form the catalyst for a discussion on crisis communications between the public, media, large corporations, and the emergency response framework. If such an event were to occur today the public and emergency response would be much different. Warnings would be spread instantaneously through social media and the National Poison Data System could provide near real-time surveillance to assist medical and investigative authorities in connecting the dots. Although there is no direct correlation between the Tylenol poisonings and the DHS in its current form, it was the fear of a repeat of such an incident coupled with concerns over political terrorism that led to the passage of the Pandemic and All-Hazards Preparedness Act of 2008 with the intention of improving situational awareness in public health emergencies.

The fears over bovine spongiform encephalopathy, or Mad Cow disease (1986), caused concern within not only the agricultural food industry and consumers but also investigative agencies over the potential for an intentional contamination of America's food supply by a biological agent. Positive identification of two vectors with the disease occurred in the United Kingdom in 1986. This raised alarm within the consumer food industry over beef importation agreements between the United States and other countries, especially the differing inspection and regulation standards depending upon the country of origin. Much of the onus of prevention of the spread of contaminants, intentional or unintentional, has now fallen upon the U.S. Customs and Border Protection agriculture specialists to determine if food imports meet U.S. entry requirements at ports of entry. In effect, they are the last line of defense before such items are allowed dissemination throughout the U.S.

The decade prior to 9/11, arguably the defining moment and wake-up call for the United States intelligence and law enforcement bodies, brought with it several events that also provided an impetus to restructure this network for 21st century threats. In 1993 an international group of terrorists attempted to topple the World Trade Center using a vehicle laden with about 1,200 pounds of explosives. The blast left a crater 200 feet wide and killed six while injuring over 1,000 people. This event is significant not only for the fact that it was a terrorist strike on American soil but it was also the first attempt by an organization to bring down the WTC, chosen for it's symbolic rather than strategic value. Although this method of attack was unsuccessful in bringing down the Tower it was the same method chosen by Timothy McVeigh in his bombing of the Murrah Federal Building just two years later. The WTC bombing was one of the first instances of terrorism that had no state sponsor but instead united individuals from several countries, all with a common hatred of their perception of American capitalism and its proportional influence on international affairs. This hatred was no longer limited to achieving political objectives by restrained influence, as had been the hallmark of previous acts of terrorism. In fact, Ramzi Yousef, the mastermind of the attack, later said that he had hoped to kill as many as 250,000 people. This brand of terrorism called for a unity of effort between intelligence assets at the national and local level as well cooperation between federal and local law enforcement agencies.

International terrorism has also impacted the development of the Department of Homeland Security. There have been many instances of foreign terrorism but perhaps none more frightening or wrought with terrifying implications should it be employed on American soil than the employment of a liquefied version of Sarin gas in the Tokyo subway system in 1995. In an effort to increase its effectiveness, the chemical was released at five locations simultaneously in an act that may be indicative of future terrorism trends. By releasing the agent in several locations the odds of success were significantly improved while increasing the affected area and numbers of casualties. This attack was carried out in an effort to overwhelm the law enforcement, municipal transit, and medical response systems of Tokyo in a tactic that is known as "swarming" and likely to be repeated in future attacks. The actions of the Aum Shinrikyo cult clearly identified the need to prepare the civilian population for chemical and biological terrorism, as this capability was no longer relegated to military use. In response to this attack, FEMA adopted Terrorism Incident Annex G to the Federal Response Framework in 1997.

9/11 is forever etched into the memories of people worldwide. In the most dramatic and deadly terrorist attack on record, the 19 terrorists belonging to al-Qaeda delivered four coordinated suicide attacks on the United States in New York City and Washington D.C. Almost one week later on September 18th, letters containing deadly biological spores of anthrax where mailed to several news and political offices killing five and infecting 17 others. Although these two terrorist events have never proven to be related, the threat and reality of international and domestic terrorism was never more real nor was the need to drastically improve the U.S. National policy of deterrence and response to terrorism and other national disasters.

The United States Department of Homeland Security, in its current form, was established November 25, 2002 by the Homeland Security Act of 2002 in response to the September 11 terrorist attacks. The DHS has five core missions that are the basis of its homeland security strategy: The prevention of terrorism, border security, the enforcement of immigration law, cyber security, and disaster preparedness. The driving concepts of security, resilience, customs and exchange provide a foundation for the Department over-arching objectives. This vision is more specifically defined in the Quadrennial Homeland Security Review report to Congress, which prioritizes goals and mission areas in accordance with the Department mandate.

Historical acts of terrorism, not only confined to the United States, have emphasized the need for interagency cooperation and a functional intelligence structure in order to anticipate and respond to threats to the United States. In creating this new department, President Bush intended to consolidate more than twenty-two organizations related to homeland security into a single cabinet agency. The stated purpose of the DHS is to prepare for, prevent, and respond to domestic emergencies including acts of terrorism, man-made and natural disasters. The creation of this agency constitutes the most significant government reorganization in the United States since the Cold War and the National Security Act of 1947. The DHS is organizationally sub-divided into four distinct divisions: Border and Transportation Security, Emergency Preparedness and Response, Chemical, Biological, Radiological and Nuclear (CBRN) Countermeasures, and Information Analysis and Infrastructure Protection.

The Border and Transportation Security division assumed responsibility for operational assets of the Coast Guard, Customs Service, Immigration and Naturalization Service and Border Control, and the Animal and Plant inspection service of the Department of Agriculture, and the Transportation Security Agency. This restructuring resulted in a singular department having responsibility of all aspects of border management and control including the issuing of visas where working with a central information sharing database.

The Emergency Preparedness and Response division has FEMA as its core agency for managing and coordinating the federal government response to natural disasters and administer the grant programs for first responders. The agency also manages in coordination with the Department of Energy the Nuclear Emergency Search Team and the National Pharmaceutical Stockpile in coordination with the Health and Human Services Department. Lastly, the division is responsible for implementing the National

Response Framework (NRF), which ensures effective communication is maintained and appropriate equipment is deployable and available during an emergency.

The Chemical, Biological, Radiological and Nuclear Countermeasures division, as the name implies, is responsible for preparing for and responding to CBRN acts of terrorism and manages efforts to develop diagnostics, vaccines, antibodies, antidotes, and various other countermeasures.

The Information Analysis and Infrastructure Protection Department consolidates and analysis multisource intelligence information related to homeland security and distributes threat executive and operational threat briefings, issue timely warning, and assess critical infrastructure vulnerabilities including food and water systems, energy systems including nuclear, electrical, gas, oil and dams, agriculture and health systems, and all modes of transportation systems, chemical and defense systems, postal and shipping entities. The department works closely with state and local governments, federal and private groups to ensure steps are taken to reduce the vulnerabilities of high-risk targets.

If the attacks of September 11th demanded a reaction, the Homeland Security Act of 2002 was certainly the response. This act was a drastic governmental reorganization second only to the National Security Act of 1947. It created the Department of Homeland Security and tasked it with the responsibility of maintaining "homeland security", a somewhat generic and all-encompassing term that has led to some confusion as to the extent of their mandate. President Bush stated that the mission of the department would be to "prevent terrorist attacks within the United States, reduce America's vulnerability to terrorism while minimizing the damage and enabling recovery from attacks that do occur."

It could be said that in light of the risks faced today, many in the world would yearn for the days of the Cold War. The measured use political or economic pressure to accomplish an objective holds an almost nostalgic feeling for those who lived through that era. Images of thousands of Soviet troops, tanks, and missiles on Parade through Red Square in Moscow almost seem quaint when compared to the end result of terrorist acts that have dominated the news media in the first decade of the 21st century. In this first decade Americans have witnessed attacks on their soil that have used their own transportation and infrastructure against them, biological agents delivered through the postal system, and the apparent targeting of civilians by an enemy that is, at times, faceless and accepting of innocents as collateral damage. The Department of Homeland Security represents the modernization of the Cold War application of intelligence and law enforcement in an attempt to rectify the mistakes of the past. Since its inception, this organization has sought to balance the parallel goals of the prevention of terrorism while maintaining civil liberties, the safeguarding of the national infrastructure and commerce while continuing to evolve the most effective aspects of interagency and international cooperation.

The sense of national pride and security that Americans felt about having been able to defend it's own soil was shattered on 9/11 and the ensuing volatility of public reaction shaped a prevalent attitude that allowed for extreme changes to policy. 9/11 was an almost Darwinian moment for America as it forced an immediate and capricious evolution in almost every aspect of the national defense, economy, politics, and culture. The people supported aggressive changes to legislation and the bureaucratic process in an effort to regain the lost sense of security and collective solidity. It is said that extraordinary times call for extraordinary measures and the USA PATRIOT Act could only be passed at a time when the perceived threat was so great that the need for a sense of security would take precedence over civil liberties. The USA PATRIOT Act is perhaps the best known, and startling, example of extreme policy change that would have been unthinkable prior to 9/11 yet is responsible for spurring the forward progression of homeland security and defense strategy. It is possible that at no other time in the nation's history had public perception grown so out of synch with government views as to the necessary limitations of this Act than in the two years following it's implementation when the Department of Justice praised it as vitally necessary to preserve America's system of ordered liberty for future generations. This institutional change has been the subject of a much less-divisive discussion between the public and the government, often cited as the catalyst for a greater level of engagement between the city, county, state, and federal government.

Previous incarnations of America's intelligence and security apparatus could be characterized by their compartmentalized and hierarchal structure. No single bureaucracy was able to quickly or easily share information with another in an effort designed so as not to infringe upon the rights of the American citizen while protecting against external, conventional threats. Since 9/11, the Cold War notions of threats to the United States have changed in the psyche of the American people. That event, the defining moment in the national conscious, elevated terrorism to a new and terrible status where thousands could perish as the result of one attack. Whereas before 9/11, this sort of power that was held only by national governments was now in the hands of madmen with extremist ideologies. The scale of this disaster was so profound that seemingly overnight the institutions and legislation that before had provided for the security of the homeland were reconsidered, shuffled, and streamlined toward the common mantra- never again. The birth of the Department of Homeland Security and the passage of the PATRIOT Act are but two polarizing examples of attempts to evolve the functionality, effectiveness, and interagency cooperation among the security apparatus. The American population witnessed visible changes to the security landscape in the form of an increased security presence in public places, heightened security measures at transportation hubs, and an overall awareness that acts of terrorism are no longer relegated to occurrences on foreign soil or the evening news, they can happen in our own backyard.

Throughout this ongoing evolutionary process one must define measurable markers of success. Issues of discretion prevent our national security structure from publicly, or even privately, hailing the successes of our government in preventing terrorism making it somewhat difficult to accurately ascertain if the changes wrought have achieved their purpose. Chief Justice of the United States, William Rehnquist, has remarked that, "In any civilized society the most important task is achieving a proper balance between freedom and order".[89] This could be held as one measurable area of success in that the confidence that the citizens have in their government to protect them while also protecting their civil liberties can be measured through public opinion. Has the general disquiet regarding the lost sense of security since 9/11 dissipated? Is the public opinion that for all of the changes to legislation and revamping of the system resulted in an improved security structure for the United States? Americans are split on this issue as indicated by a recent survey which found that 59% of the public credit the U.S. government with changes to security policies making it more difficult for terrorists to attack.[90]

Although America's national security framework continues to undergo a metamorphosis in an effort to stay ahead of threats to the homeland not all products of a bygone era in defense should be discarded. The international allies and intelligence partnership cultivated during the Cold War are still relevant during the current conflict. It has been argued that the shift from the prioritization of national security to the recognition of the importance of international security considerations and the humanitarian implications of intra-state conflicts was an evolution that was already in progress on 9/11 and this global strategy serves to protect U.S. interests. Countries, such as the members of the North Atlantic Treaty Organization, that have proven themselves staunch allies throughout that era are still critical to the United States due to their geographical locations and shared interest in world stability. Perhaps the American people can best answer the question as to the direction future evolutions of Homeland Security should take. When asked to summarize the most important step that law enforcement and counter terrorism officials could take to protect the country from terrorism the composite answer, in layman's terms, was "More people to protect the country, increased profiling, better intelligence, and improved border security".[91]

While the aforementioned events helped shape the mission of the Department of Homeland Security, they certainly didn't solidify it. Despite the fact that the original mission of the department appeared clearly defined by President Bush, it continues to evolve to this day. One obvious, and large, expansion of the department is oversight of natural and other man-made disasters. By overseeing the Federal Emergency Management Agency, the Department of Homeland Security has taken on the responsibility for much more than terrorist activity. The DHS has expanded into many other departments and areas, which may be why upwards of 38% of professionals in the field, have mixed or undefined views regarding the mission of the department. It is this ambiguity, this vagueness, which requires specificity in order to shore up the loopholes and cracks in our defense that will be exploited by terrorist organizations in the future.

Homeland security is a broad term with key elements that define the strategy towards its accomplishment. The defense of the nation and economic security contribute toward the overall security of the nation and must be decisively fixed and coupled with strategic security concerns. Key concepts such as security, resilience, and customs & exchange were all identified as part of the broader strategy under the 2012 Quadrennial Homeland Security Review, which includes the more specific mission guidance of terrorism prevention, border security, and cyberspace security among others. This strategy has specified functional requirements that have measurable targets of effectiveness that seek to remove some of the barriers of communication that were in place during the Cold War and encourage agency interoperability.

The Department of Homeland Security and the many agencies that it oversees continue to undergo its evolutionary process. The previous analogy to Darwinism and our intelligence failures as a forcing function toward improvement are perhaps my most controversial statement on the subject of our Nation's national security strategy. This is not intended to sow the seeds of conflict or point the crooked finger of criticism toward any singular entity but rather facilitate discussion. As Americans, we all have a responsibility to the security of the nation from natural and man-made threats. Transparency in government, given necessary security considerations, and the recognition that we can all benefit from a humbling discussion on our domestic security and preparedness framework is the torch that will illuminate the path forward.

References

1   Bush, G. W. (2006, July). You Will Make History. *Vital Speeches of the Day, 72*(18/19), 530-534.

2   Howard, R. (2006). Homeland Security and the New Terrorism. In *Homeland Security and Terrorism: Readings and Interpretations* (pp. 4-4).

3   Henslin, J. M. (2010). Sociology: A down-to-earth approach. (10th ed.) Boston: Allyn & Bacon.

4   Fox News. 2012. Click, print, shoot: Guns made on 3D printers. Retrieved from www.foxnews.com/tech/2012/12/21/click-print-shoot-guns-made-on-3-d-printers-not-as-far-fetched-as-you-might-think.

5   Department of Homeland Security. 2012. *Department of Homeland Security Strategic Plan Fiscal Years 2012-2016. www.dhs.gov/xlibrary/assets/dhs-strategic-plan-fy-2012-2016.*

6   DHS. 2013. Fusion Centers and Joint Terrorism Task Forces. Retrieved from www.dhs.gov/fusion-centers-and-joint-terrorism-task-forces.

7   Raymond, Kelly W. 2012. *Active Shooter, Recommendations and Analysis for Risk Mitigation*. New York City Police Department.

8   Andrew Berwick, 2083–A European Declaration of Independence, London, 2011, p. 844.

9   *START, press release, "Background Information: Far-Right Attacks on U.S. Law Enforcement," April 2009, http://www.start.umd.edu/start/media/Far-Right_Attacks_on_US_Law_Enforcement_PressRelease.pdf. The scholars who developed the information in the press release defined "far-right ideology" as "principles such as fierce nationalism, anti-globalization, suspicions of centralized Federal authority, support for conspiracy theories, and reverence for individual liberties (including gun ownership."*

10   FBI. 2012. *Reports and Publications*. www.fbi.gov/stats-services/publications/terrorism-2002-2005.

11   Chermak, Steven M. and Joshua D. Freilich. 2009. *Database of Extremist Crime, 1990-2009*. National Consortium for the Study of Terrorism and Responses to Terrorism: University of Maryland Press.

12   Bjelopera, Jerome p. 2012. *The Domestic Terrorist Threat: Background and Issues for Congress.* Congressional Research Service. www.fas.org/sgp/crs/terror/R42536.

13   Anti-Defamation League, *Guidebook,* p. 16. Lane died in 2007 while serving 190 years in prison for his involvement with a terrorist group named the Order. See "Founder of Terrorist Group Dies in Prison," *Terre Haute Tribune-Star,* May 29, 2007, http://tribstar.com/local/x1155692948/Founder-of-terrorist-group-dies-in-prison. Among other writings, Lane also drafted an influential racist ideological tract titled *The 88 Precepts.*

14   Fredrick J. Simonelli, "The Neo-Nazi Movement," Southern Poverty Law Center, http://www.splcenter.org/get- informed/intelligence-files/ideology/neo-nazi/the-neo-nazi-movement. See also: Charles S. Clark, "An American Nazi's Rise and Fall," *American History,* vol. 40, no. 6 (February 2006), pp. 60-66; Simonelli, "The American Nazi Party," *Historian,* vol. 57, no. 3 (Spring 1995), pp. 553-566. A follower assassinated Rockwell in 1967. For information on Christian Identity, see Kevin Borgeson and Robin Valeri, *Terrorism in America* (Sudbury, MA: Jones and Bartlett, 2009), pp. 47-72; Martin Durham, "Christian Identity and the Politics of Religion," *Totalitarian Movements and Political Religions,* vol. 9, no. 1 (March 2008), pp. 79-91; Tanya Telfair Sharpe, "The Identity Christian Movement: Ideology of Domestic Terrorism," *Journal of Black Studies,* vol. 30, no. 4 (March 2000), pp. 604- 623; Anti-Defamation League, "Christian Identity," http://www.adl.org/learn/ext_us/Christian_Identity.asp?xpicked= 4&item=Christian_ID.

15   Federal Bureau of Investigation, *White Supremacist Extremist Violence Possibly Decreases But Racist Skinheads Remain the Most Violent,* January 28, 2010. Hereafter: Federal Bureau of Investigation, *White Supremacist Extremist Violence.*

16   Federal Bureau of Investigation. 2011. *White Supremacist Extremist Violence,* p. 4.

17   Southern Poverty Law Center. 2011. Active U.S. Hate Groups. www.splcenter.org/get-informed/hate-map.

18   Somashekhar, Sandhya and Carol D. Leonnig. 2012. *'Lone Wolf' domestic terrorism threats are hard to track*. The Washington Post.

19   Department of Homeland Security. 2009. *Rightwing Extremism: Current Economic and Political Climate Fueling Resurgence in Radicalization and Recruitment*. www.fas.org/irp/eprint/rightwing.pdf.

20   Department of Homeland Security. 2009. *Rightwing Extremism: Current Economic and Political Climate Fueling Resurgence in Radicalization and Recruitment*. www.fas.org/irp/eprint/rightwing.pdf.

21   New America Foundation. 2011. *The Homegrown Threat*. www.homegrown.newamerica.net/.

22   Anti-Defamation League (ADL). 2003. Extremist Pleads Guilty to Possessing Chemical Weapons. www.adl.org/learn/news/extremist_chemical.asp.

23   Singh, Simran J. and Prabjhot Singh. 2012. *How Hate Gets Counted*. The New York Times. www.nytimes.com/2012/08/24/opinion/do-american-sikhs-count.html?_r=0.

24   Potok, Mark. 2000. *The Year in Hate*. The National Forum 80: 50.

25   Dolan, Eric W. 2011. ACLU's Mike German: Domestic surveillance no longer based on probable cause. www.rawstory.com/rawreplay/2011/09/aclus-mike-german-domestic-surveillance-no-longer-based-on-probable-cause/.

26   Wasem, R. E., Lake, J., Seghetti, L., Monke, J., & Vina, S. (2004). *Border Security: Inspections Practices, Policies, and Issues* (RL32399). Washington, DC: U.S. Government Printing Office.

27   Alliance To Combat Transnational Threats (2011, February). *Fact Sheet: Alliance to Combat Transnational Threats-Arizona/Sonora Corridor*. Retrieved from http://cbp.gov/xp/cgov/newsroom/fact_sheets/border/arizona_factsheet.xml

28   Maurer, D. C. (2010). Quadrennial Homeland Security Review: 2010 Reports Addressed Many Required Elements, but Budget Planning Not Yet Completed. *GAO Reports,* , 1-40.

29   C-span.org (2011, February 4). U.S., Canadian Leaders Set to Announce New Border Security Agreement. Retrieved April 22, 2011, from http://www.c-span.org/Events/US-Canadian-Leaders-Set-to-Announce-New-Border-Security-Agreement/107374

30   National Commission On Terrorist Attacks Upon The United States (2004). *The 9/11 Commission Report.* New York: W.W Norton & Company.

31   Department Of Justice (2010). *Department of Justice Observes Anniversary of Amber Alert Program.* Retrieved from http://www.ojp.usdoj.gov/newsroom/pressreleases/2010/OJJDP10039.htm

32   Moon, B. (2010). *Travelers react to TSA's full-body scans and pat-downs.* Retrieved from http://marketplace.publicradio.org/display/web/2010/11/15/pm-travelers-react-to-tsas-fullbody-scans-and-pat-downs/

33   Potter, Mark. 2012. Faced with gun-toting drug smugglers, Arizona ranchers demand security at the border. www.dailynightly.nbcnews.com/ news/2012/12/26/16047580-faced-with-gun-totin-drug-smugglers-arizona-ranchers-demand-security-at-the-border/.

34   Zirulnick, A. (2011, May 18). *Al Qaeda reportedly taps Saif al-Adel as successor, potentially signaling a rift.* Retrieved from http://www.csmonitor.com/World/terrorism-security/2011/0518/Al-Qaeda-reportedly-Saif-al-Adel-as-successor-potentially-signaling-a-rift.

35   Lister, Tim and Paul Cruickshank. 2013. 'Mr. Marlboro': The veteran jihadist behind the attack in Algeria. CNN. Retreived from www.cnn.com/2013/01/17/wrold/meast/algeria-who-is-belmoktar/index.html.

36
The Washington Post (2011, June 16). *Bin-Laden Deputy Named Al-Qaeda Leader.* Retrieved from http://www.washingtontimes.com/news/2011/jun/16/bin-laden-deputy-al-zawahri-named-al-qaeda-leader/.

37   Fox _News (2011, June 17). *Suspect in Custody After Police Find 'Suspi-cious' Backpack at Arlington National Cemetery.* Retrieved from http://www.foxnews.com/us/2011/06/17/suspicious-vehicle-shuts-down-several-major-roads-near-pentagon/

38   Reuters (2011, June 6). *Pakistani Taliban vow revenge attacks on US targets.* Retrieved from http://www.dawn.com/2011/06/pakistani-tal-iban-vow-revenge-attacks-on-us-targets.html

39   International Herald Tribune (2011, June 6). *Kashmiri planned reprisal attacks for Osama's death.* Retrieved from http://tribune.com.pk/sto-ry/183308/kashmiri-planned-reprisal-attacks-for-osama-death/

40   Inter-services Public Relations, Pakistan (2011, June). *Press release; 139th Corps Commanders Conference.* Retrieved from http://ispr.gov.pk/front/main.asp?o=t-press_release&id=1763#pr_link1763

41   CNN. 2011. *Al-Zawahiri appointed al Qaeda's new leader, jihadist web-sites say.* Retrieved from http://www.cnn/2011/WORLD/meast/06/16/al.qaeda.new.leader/index.html?hpt=hp_t2

42   Lindell, M. K., Perry, R. W., & Prater, C. S. (2006). Introduction to Emer-gency Management. In *Fundamentals of Emergency Management* (pp. 7-9).

43   McEntire, David. (2004). The Status Emergency Management Theory: Issue, Barriers, and Recommendations for Improved Scholarship. Re-trieved from https://online.apus.edu/educator/student/getfile.cgi?m k1275*3022644*mpos=3&spos=0&slt=79yGAX6svuRE6*edmg502a0 01win09*Weektwo*DavidMcEntireStatusEmergencyManagementThe ory.pdf

44   Goltz, James, 1984. Are the News Media Responsible for the Disas-ter Myths? A Content Analysis of Emergency Response Imagery. Re-trieved from http://training.fema.gov/EMIWeb/downloads/IJEMS/ARTICLES/ARE%20THE%20NEWS%20MEDIA%20RESPONSIBLE%20 FOR%20THE%20DISASTER%20MYTHSA%20CO.pdf

45   Quarantelli, E.L., 1987. Disaster Studies: An Analysis of Social Historical Factors Affecting the Development of Research in the Area. Retrieved from http://training.fema.gov/EMIWeb/downloads/IJEMS/ARTICLES/ DISASTER%20STUDIES%20AN%20ANALYSIS%20OF%20THE%20SO- CIAL%20HISTORICAL%20FACTOR.pdf

46   Hoffman, Susanna; Oliver-Smith,Anthony. 1999, Angry Earth Disaster in Anthropological Perspective. New York. 1-72
Quarantelli, E.L., 1993. Converting Disaster Scholarship into Effective Disaster Planning and Managing: Possibilities and Limitations. Retrieved from http://training.fema.gov/EMIWeb/downloads/IJEMS/ARTICLES/ CONVERTING%20DISASTER%20SCHOLARSHIP%20INTO%20EFFEC- TIVE%20DISASTER%20PLA.pdf

47   Bankoff, G. (2003, August). Vulnerability as a Measure of Change in Society. International Journal of Mass Emergencies and Disasters, 21(2), 5-30. Retrieved from https://online.apus.edu/educator/temp/ mk1275/edmg502a001win09/Weektwelve/VulnerablityasaMeasure- ofChangeinSocietyBankoff.pdf

48   Shelton, R.E., 1984. Emergencies and Rationality The Case of Three Mile Island. Retrieved from http://training.fema.gov/EMIWeb/down- loads/IJEMS/ARTICLES/Emergencies%20and%20Rationality%20 The%20Case%20of%20Three%20Mile%20Islan%20R%20E.pdf

49   Hazards and Vulnerability Research Institute (HVRI) (2010). *Social Vulnerability Index for the United States 2006-10*. Retrieved from http://we- bra.cas.sc.edu/hvri/products/sovi.aspx

50   National Oceanic and Atmospheric Administration (NOAA) (2012). *Spatial Trends in Coastal Socioeconomics*. Retrieved from http://www. coastalsocioeconomics.noaa.gov

51   NOAA Coastal Services Center (2012). *Coastal County Snapshots*. Retrieved from http://www.csc.noaa.gov/digitalcoast/tools/snapshots/

52   First World War (2011, August). *Weapons of War- Poison Gas*. Retrieved February 11, 2012, from http://www.firstworldwar.com/weaponry/ gas.html.

53   Health And Safety Executive (HSE) (2006, May). *Union Carbide India Ltd, Bhopal, India. 3rd December 1984.* Retrieved from http://www.hse. gov.uk/comah/sragtech/caseuncarbide84.html.

54   Kratovac, Katarina. 2007. Iraq chlorine attacks raise new concerns. Associated Press. Retrieved from usatoday30.usatoday.com/news/ world/iraq/2007-02-22-chlorine-iraq_x.htm.

55   Tucker, J. B. (2000). Toxic terror: assessing terrorist use of chemical and biological weapons. Cambridge, Mass.: MIT Press.

56   Garcia, A.F., Rand, D., Rinard Jr., J.H.; (2011) HIS Jane's CBRN Response Handbook 4th Edition; HIS Global Limited, UK

57   Seto, Y. (2001). *The Sarin Gas Attack in Japan and the Related Forensic Investigation.* Retrieved from http://www.opcw.org/news/article/the-sarin-gas-attack-in-japan-and-the-related-forensic-investigation/.

58   Department of Homeland Security (2005, April). *National Planning Scenarios: Executive Summaries.* Retrieved from http://cees.tamiu.edu/ covertheborder/TOOLS/NationalPlanningSen.pdf

59   Salama, Sharon S., and Lydia Hansell. 2005. Does Intent Equal Capability? Nonproliferation Review 12, No. 3.

60   Tucker, J.B. (Ed). (2000) Toxic Terror: Assessing Terrorist Use of Chemical and Biological Weapons.

61   Garcia, Antonio F., Dan Rand, John H. Rinard Jr. IHS Jane's CBRN Response Handbook. 2011. IHS Global Limited.

62   AMPC Meat & Livestock Cooperative. 1996. www.biotracer.org/assets/PDF-documents/Wuest-**Salmonella**.pdf.

63   Salama, Sammy. 2006. *Manual for Producing Chemical Weapon to Be Used in New York Subway Plot Available on Al-Qaeda Websites Since late 2005.* James Martin Center for Nonproliferation Studies. http://cns. miis.edu/other/salama_060720.htm.

64   United States Department of Labor. 2012. Occupational Safety & Health Administration. www.osha.gov/SLTC/bioterrorism/index.html.

65   Rubinson, Lewis, Jennifer B. Nuzzo, Daniel S. Talmor, Tara O'Toole, Bradley R. Kramer, Thomas V. Inglesby. 2005. Augmentation of Hospital Critical Care Capacity after Bioterrorist Attacks or Epidemics. *Critical Care Medicine.* 33: 2393-2403.

66   Federal Bureau of Investigation. 2008. *FBI 100: The Unabomber.* http://www.fbi.gov/news/stories/2008/april/unabomber_042408.

67   United States General Accounting Office (2003). *Bioterrorism: A Threat to Agriculture and the Food Supply* (GAO-04-259T). Washington, DC: U.S. Government Printing Office.

68   U.S. Food and Drug Administration (2002, July). *Public Health Security and Bioterrorism Preparedness and Response Act of 2002 (PL107-188).* Retrieved from http://www.fda.gov/food/fooddefense/bioterrorism/ucm111086.htm.

69   Tucker, J.B. (Ed). (2000) Toxic Terror: Assessing Terrorist Use of Chemical and Biological Weapons.

70   Wired. 2007. Air Force Readying for Cyber Strikes. Retrieved from www.wired.com/dangerroom/2007/10/also-nsa-target/.

71   Ruvolo, Julie. 2011. "How Much of the Internet is Actually for Porn." Forbes Online Edition. Retrieved from www.forbes.com/sites/julieruvolo/2011/09/07/how-much-of-the-internet-is-actually-for-porn/.

72   SearchSecurity. 2012. "Melissa Virus." Retrieved from www.searchsecurity.techtarget.com/definition/Melissa-virus.

73   *Schwartz, Mathew J. 2012. Anonymous Says DDoS Attacks Like Free Speech. Information Week. Retrieved from www.informationweek.com/security/government/anonymous-says-DDoS-attacks-like-free-speech/.*

74   Imperva. 2011. Hacker Intelligence Trend Report #5. Hacker Intelligence Initiative. Retrieved from http://www.imperva.com.

75   Kirk, Jeremy. 2012. Pacemaker hack can deliver deadly 830-volt jolt. Computer World. Retrieved from www.computer world.com/s/article/9232477/Pacemaker_hack_can_deliver_deadly_830_volt_jolt.

76   Watchguard. 2013. WatchGuard's 2013 Security Predictions. Retrieved from www.watchguard.com/docs/.../wg_2013_security_predictions. pdf.

77   *Finkle, Jim. 2013. US warns on Java software as concerns escalate. NBC News. Retrieved from www.nbcnews.com/technology/technolog/us-warns-java-software-security-concerns-escalate-.*

78   *Maass, Peter and Megha Rajagopalan. 2012. Does Cybercrime Really Cost $1 Trillion? www.propublica.org/article/does-cybercrime-really-cost-1-trillion.*

79   *Albright, David and Andrea Stricker. 2010. Stuxnet Worm Targets Automated Systems for Frequency Converters: Are Iranian Centrifuges the Target? Institute for Science and International Security.*

80   *Falliere, Nicholas, Liam O Murchu and Eric Chien. 2010. W32.Stuxnet Dossier. Symantec Security Response.Retreived from www.wired.com/images.../Symantec-Stuxnet-Update-Feb-2011.*

81   Colman,Zack. 40 percent of cyberattacks targeted energy sector. *The Hill.com,* January 14, 2013, http://thehill.com/blogs/e2-wire/e2-wire/277045-dhs-energy-sector-target-of-40-percent-of-cyber-attacks.

82   *DHS website, Critical Infrastructure and Key Resources, http://www.dhs. gov/files/programs/ gc_1189168948944.shtm, last accessed January 8, 2013.*

83   *DHS. 2009. Challenges Remain in DHS' Efforts to Security Control Systems. Department of Homeland Security, Office of Inspector General.*

84   *Department of Energy. 2002. Vulnerability Assessment Methodology; Electric Power Infrastructure. Retrieved from http://www.esisac.com/publicdocs/assessment_methods/VA.*

85   *Amin, Massoud and Phillip F. Schewe. 2007. Preventing Blackouts. Scientific American. Retrieved from www.Sciam.com.*

86   *The Energy Library.2012. North American Electricity Grid. Retrieved from www.theenergylibrary.com/node/647.*

87   *Samson, Adam. 2012. Cyber Warriors Deal Blow to Bank Websites by Adapting Common Strategy.* www.foxbusiness.com/industries/2012/10/10/cyberwarriors-deal-blow-to-bank-websites-by-adapting-common-stategy//.

88   Treverton, Gregory F. 2002. *Dissect the Divisions.* Rand Corporation. http://www.rand.org/commentary/2002/06/09/BS.html.

89   Rehnquist, William H. 2000. *All the Laws but One: Civil Liberties in Wartime.* Vintage Press.

90   Cote, Eric, Cara Klein, and Kim Wallace. 2011. *A Changed Nation: An In-depth Look at Changed American Attitudes, toward Terrorism, Personal Freedoms, and Security a Decade after 9/11.* 9/11 Opinion Survey.

91   Cote, Eric, Cara Klein, and Kim Wallace. 2011. *A Changed Nation: An In-depth Look at Changed American Attitudes, toward Terrorism, Personal Freedoms, and Security a Decade after 9/11.* 9/11 Opinion Survey.